LOANS & GRANTS FROM UNCLE SAM

Am I Eligible and for How Much?

SEVENTEENTH EDITION
ANNA LEIDER

OCTAMERON
ASSOCIATES

Address editorial correspondence to:

Octameron Associates
PO Box 2748
Alexandria, VA 22301
703/836-5480 (voice)
703/836-5650 (fax)

octameron@aol.com (e-mail)
www.octameron.com

ISBN 1-57509-134-8

PRINTED IN THE UNITED STATES OF AMERICA

CONTENTS

．．．．．．．．．．．．．．．．．．．

CHAPTER 1

■ ■

APPLYING FOR
FEDERAL STUDENT AID

*Leider's Law: Any reduction in the funding of governmental social
programs will lead to an increase in the complexity of administering the
remaining dollars. From this it follows that the number of program
administrators will increase in inverse proportion to the number of
program beneficiaries.*

The Purpose of This Guide

Right now, federal student aid programs are managed so that Uncle Sam
holds all the cards. The purpose of this guide is to deal you a hand with at
least one ace, so you can play more effectively; maybe even win the first
round. Our primary goal is to help you overcome the program's biggest flaw:
its disastrous timing. We want you to be able to assess your eligibility for
federal aid when you start choosing colleges.

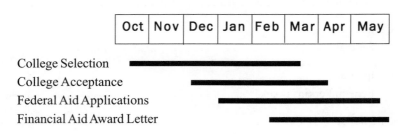

Oct	Nov	Dec	Jan	Feb	Mar	Apr	May

College Selection
College Acceptance
Federal Aid Applications
Financial Aid Award Letter

As you can see from the chart above, you may not learn whether you're
eligible for aid until after you've picked and been accepted by the college(s)
of your choice. Should you learn that Uncle won't help, or will help with
fewer dollars than expected, your carefully laid plans may no longer possible. You may have to start over, and with little time to spare. We don't want
this to happen.

But even this chart is theoretical. In fact, you may not know the composition of your aid package until much later. And even then, mid-year rescission
bills can shrink the grant you'd already been promised while mid-year rule
"clarifications" can make you suddenly ineligible for federal funds altogether. Even if the rules don't change, Uncle Sam can be so late
getting information to aid administrators, they aren't sure which end is up.

Eligibility for Federal Student Aid

You can receive federal student aid if:

1. You are a US citizen or national; a US permanent resident; or an eligible non-citizen (e.g., a refugee or a person granted asylum).
2. You are enrolled in an "eligible" program at an "eligible" school. Students working toward associate, bachelor or graduate degrees need not worry much about what makes a program "eligible." Students looking at correspondence schools or proprietary schools should inquire about the school's status before sending off tuition deposits.
3. You have certified that you are not in default on any federal student loans (unless you've made satisfactory repayment arrangements), nor have you borrowed in excess of the allowable limits. This statement appears on the aid application.
4. You are registered with Selective Service (males age 18 through 25).
5. You promise that all money received will be used for educational expenses at XYZ college. This statement appears on the aid application.
6. You have a HS diploma or its equivalent, or have met other basic standards as established by your state (and approved by Uncle Sam). Home-schooled students without the equivalent of a high school diploma are eligible for federal student aid if they have completed a secondary school education in a state-recognized home school setting.
7. You are making satisfactory progress in your course of study.
8. You have a valid Social Security Number.
9. You show you have need (to qualify for any need-based program).

Special Eligibility Situations

Study Abroad. You are eligible for aid if the program is approved for credit by your school (assuming you are attending an "eligible" school). Furthermore, there must be a contractual agreement between the home institution and the international school.

Distance Education. You can receive federal aid if the course is part of an accredited program.

Jail. Students incarcerated in federal or state institutions are not eligible for federal student loans or Pell grants; they may, however, receive Supplemental Educational Opportunity Grants and Federal Work-Study. Students incarcerated in local institutions are not eligible for federal student loans, however they may receive Pells, SEOGs, and Work-Study.

Demonstrating Need

Demonstrating need for federal student aid begins with a formula applied to the information you submit on your aid application. The formula has numerous elements, some of which change annually.

Visualize the formula as a long row of machines that pound, grind, stretch and squeeze. Your financial information is fed to these machines. After it has been pounded, ground, stretched and squeezed, it emerges as your **Expected Family Contribution (EFC)**. You can use the appendices to estimate your family's EFC.

If your EFC is less than your college's cost of attendance, you are eligible for federal need-based aid (Perkins and Stafford Loans, Work-Study and Supplemental Educational Opportunity Grants). If your EFC is less than about $5,200, you'll be eligible for a Pell Grant as well.

Dependent vs. Independent Student

The financial aid process classifies students by dependency status:

Dependent students are at least partially dependent on their parents for support. The income and assets of both student and parent are used to determine the amount a family must contribute to college costs.

Independent students are not dependent on their parents for support. Only their own income and assets (and those of any spouse) are evaluated to determine contribution to college costs. Establishing independence usually gives you an advantage: By not having to include parental income and assets, your expected contribution will most likely be lower and that will result in more student aid.

To be considered independent under federal regulations, a student must meet one of the following conditions:

1. Be 24 years of age by December 31 of the award year (for example, December 31, 2010 for the 2010/2011 award year).

2. Be a graduate or professional student.

3. Be married or separated on the date he or she files the aid application (engagements and upcoming divorces do not affect status).

4. Have children who receive more than half of their support from you.

5. Have legal dependents (other than children or a spouse) who live with you and receive more than half of their support from you.

6. Be an orphan, ward of the court, or in foster care (at any time after turning 13 years of age.)

7. Be an emancipated minor, or in legal guardianship (as determined by a court); or an unaccompanied youth who is homeless, or at risk for homelessness.

8. Be a veteran of the U.S. Armed Forces; or be serving on active duty in the U.S. Armed Forces (for purposes other than training).

9. Be judged independent by the financial aid administrator based on documented unusual circumstances.

A Very, Very Important Point

OK, you say. I am eligible to apply. But why should I? I'll never qualify for federal aid. My family makes too much money. We own prime real estate near Guffey, Colorado. So why bother with the paperwork? There are three answers to this question.

One—A lot of government employees and contractors make their living processing forms. If applications came only from people who qualify for awards, their work load would be cut in half. There would be a drastic increase in lay-offs and unemployment. Do you want to be responsible for increasing our nation's unemployment figures?

Two—Colleges expect you to apply. They don't know this book exists. They assume the only way you can figure out if you qualify is to run through the application drill. As they see it, Uncle Sam offers an unlimited amount of federal aid, and they want to make absolutely certain you bring your share of that money to Frugal U. In fact, most colleges feel so strongly about this, they won't consider you for other aid unless you can prove you applied for federal aid and were turned down, or you have need beyond that covered by federal aid.

Three—Your state expects you to apply. It, too, feels strongly about this and may not consider you eligible for state programs unless you've applied for federal aid.

We know our first answer did not inspire you to apply. But our last two answers should—if you want to receive any aid at all.

A Tip For the Men

Have you registered for Selective Service? It is a prerequisite for qualifying for federal student aid and Congress has announced, in a loud, clear fashion, that federal aid will be denied to young men age 18 to 25 who are not registered.

You can register via the FAFSA (see below), or online at **www.sss.gov**. If you want to confirm your registration, or your exemption status, you can reach Selective Service at 847/688-6888.

Applying for Federal Student Aid

You apply for federal student aid using a **FAFSA** (Free Application for Federal Student Aid). A central processor matches your application information against several national databases to verify your eligibility for aid. For example, it checks your Selective Service status, your Social Security number, your citizenship status, and your financial aid history (to make sure you're not in default on any student loans). The processor also checks your data for inconsistencies and contradictions.

Next, the processor evaluates your finances, calculates your "Expected Family Contribution" (EFC) and incorporates your EFC into an eligibility document called a Student Aid Report (SAR). Finally, the processor sends you a copy of your SAR and transmits your data to all the schools you designate on your FAFSA, your state higher education agency and the state higher education agencies of all the schools you list on your FAFSA.

You may use the appendices to get a close estimate of your EFC.

Paper FAFSAs

In the fall, students may call the Federal Student Aid Information Center, (800/4-FED-AID) and request up to three paper copies of the FAFSA. (Forms will no longer be supplied to high school guidance offices.) *Uncle Sam also prints the application in Spanish.* You fill out the FAFSA as soon after January 1 as possible and snail mail it to the address listed on the form. You pay no fee.

The 2010/2011 FAFSA will be blue and purple, and include new questions to gather information about any student earnings from work under a cooperative education program.

FAFSA on the Web (www.fafsa.gov)

Students may also use FAFSA on the Web (www.fafsa.gov) in either English or Spanish to file an electronic FAFSA directly with the central processor. Uncle continues to enhance his online application and reports that nearly all forms are now filed electronically.

FAFSA on the Web includes worksheets, online help, detailed instructions and an EFC Estimator, however, families won't see their estimated EFC until *AFTER* they submit their form. FAFSA on the Web also includes internal edits that help prevent errors and reduce rejections. Finally, parents with multiple students in college can transfer their parental data to additional FAFSA applications with the click of a mouse.

At the FAFSA web site, families can print a pre-application worksheet to collect data and make it easier (and faster) to complete your FAFSA online.

Paper FAFSAs take four weeks to process; electronic FAFSAs take only one. *If possible, save time and file electronically.* Don't view this as a chance to procrastinate. Consider it a two-week head start on your equally-needy, but technophobic classmates. Save often (in case you get bumped off-line), and in your eagerness, don't click "SEND" until you've checked your answers carefully!

Also, don't be confused by www.FAFSA.com. This enterprising financial aid consultant nabbed a prime domain name, but charges families to complete the forms. If you want to pay for their services, that's fine. But you can do it yourself for free. Your choice.

Personal Identification Numbers (www.pin.ed.gov)

If you want to file your FAFSA online, apply now for a "Personal Identification Number" (PIN) which will act as your electronic signature. (No need to wait until January 1.) Otherwise, you have to print and snail mail the FAFSA signature page, thus losing out on some benefits of electronic filing.

Not only does your PIN verify your identity when completing a FAFSA, you can use it later to track the status of your application, make online corrections, or even to review your entire financial aid history. You request PINs directly from the Department of Education (www.pin.ed.gov).

If your parents must sign the FAFSA, they need to have their own (separate) PIN.

Fafsa4Caster (www.fafsa4caster.ed.gov)

A good way to get a head start on the process is to use Fafsa4Caster. Prior to January 1, families can use this tool to receive an early estimate of their eligibility for federal student aid. Even better, when you start work on your FAFSA, much of the data you entered using Fafsa4Caster will be transferred to the real form.

Renewal FAFSAs

You must re-apply for aid every year. If you filed a FAFSA in 2009/2010, you will receive a Renewal Reminder Notice in early January that provides instructions about how to reapply for aid using Renewal FAFSA on the Web. (Renewal FAFSAs must all be filed online.) Some of the fields will be "pre-populated" with data you provided last year, so unless there's a change in information, you can skip some of the questions.

The renewal reminder notice will be sent to the e-mail address you listed on your 2009/2010 FAFSA. If you did not include a valid e-mail address, or the e-mail is undeliverable, you will receive a paper reminder.

Applying for Collegiate Aid

The focus of this publication is on federal student aid, but we don't want you to miss out on the other large source of financial aid—money from your college. Over 60% of all four-year private colleges, and over one-quarter of all four-year public colleges, require a second aid application to determine eligibility for collegiate aid. Unfortunately, there is no single, standard form or formula. Some schools have developed their own application to gather additional knowledge about your family's finances. Others use the College Board's Financial Aid PROFILE. Some schools use both.

Financial Aid PROFILE

The basic PROFILE requires the same sort of data as the FAFSA, with a few extra questions about income, assets, expenses, and resources. But the College Board has accumulated nearly 200 additional questions that schools may ask. These questions pry into everything from the student's career objective, to whether the student has applied for outside scholarships, to whether the family has recently sold any income generating assets (and the purpose for which they were sold), to the year, make and model of all the family's motor vehicles. PROFILE can also include a business/farm supplement and collect information on the noncustodial parent.

PROFILE information should be in your guidance office this September. If you're applying to one of the 250+ PROFILE schools, you must register and complete the form online (profileonline.collegeboard.com)—it will be customized with each of your school's questions.

You'll also find extensive online help at profileonline.collegeboard.com.

Unfortunately, you have to pay a fee for all this fun; $25 to register (which includes one school report) then $16 for each additional school or program that is to receive your information. Students from low income families may receive a fee waiver for up to six reports.

Schools cannot require you to file PROFILE to be considered for federal student aid, but they can require it before awarding aid from their own resources. Lesson: Find out which schools require what forms to make sure you're considered for every aid source possible.

Also, you may file PROFILE well before January 1, which helps colleges get a head start on estimating financial aid packages. Check the filing deadlines carefully—registration for PROFILE may begin as early as October 1 with schools receiving results in early November.

When to Submit the FAFSA

Right after January 1, but not before. You'll need to have your income tax information close at hand. Certain items on your aid application and the income tax form will have to agree right down to the last decimal. Most importantly: your family's Adjusted Gross Income, the amount of federal income taxes paid, family size, and number of dependents. Up to 30% of all applications are checked against income tax return. Some schools ask every student for copies of the family's 1040—just to keep people honest.

These odds create quite a dilemma. The IRS says you don't have to file tax forms until April 15. Many people wait until the last minute claiming to work most efficiently under pressure. We think it's because they want to be filmed by a TV crew when they join the line outside the post office at 11:59pm on April 15th. Important: If you wait that long to do your income tax and student aid application, it won't matter if the numbers match. Even though the final FAFSA deadline for the 2010/2011 year is not until June 30, 2011, you will have missed the deadlines set by most colleges.

Our advice: Don't wait until April 15th—if you really are pressed for time, file for aid using estimated information. You will then be asked, later on, to provide copies of your signed tax forms for verification. If the numbers match, the estimate will survive. Otherwise, there will be a recalculation. Lesson: Even an estimate must be accurate.

A Good Use of the Winter Holiday

To make sure you're one of the early birds, start collecting the necessary financial records over the winter holidays. Print a copy of the FAFSA on the Web worksheet to help you gather the correct information (but please don't submit the worksheet in lieu of a FAFSA—it's not an official document).

Assembling Information for the Application

Start collecting the information you need to fill out the application form (as well as to do your income taxes) as soon as possible. You'll need to know:

- Taxable income for both parents and students, including wages, pensions, capital gains, rents, interest, dividends, annuities, unemployment compensation, alimony received and business income.
- Non-taxable income, including worker's compensation, housing and food allowances, child support payments received, untaxed pensions and IRA distributions, veteran's non-education benefits, tax-exempt interest income, and earned income credit.
- The value of cash, savings, and checking accounts (as of the day you plan to sign the application) for both parents and the student.
- The net worth of other investments: stocks, bonds, commodities, precious metals, trusts, and college savings plan. Again, this information should be as of the date you sign the application.
- The market value of real estate other than your home. Creative financing has artificially inflated the market value of much real estate. You may not want to use recent transaction prices as true guides, but go for a somewhat more conservative valuation.

Accuracy

In completing the form, be as accurate as you can. If you don't understand something, call Uncle Sam at 800-4-FED-AID, or ask a guidance counselor or financial aid administrator. Many colleges now have toll free numbers for exactly that purpose.

Once you complete the form, sign it. If you are a dependent student, at least one of your parents must sign as well. File online if possible. Otherwise, mail the paper FAFSA to the address on the form and nowhere else.

What Happens Next?

In due time (three weeks if you filed a paper application; one week for an online application) the people who own the computer that processes your form will prepare a document, called a **Student Aid Report** or SAR.

- If you recorded an e-mail address on your FAFSA (whether you used a paper form, or FAFSA on the Web), you will receive an e-mail with a link to an online SAR which you can access by providing your social security number, date of birth, and first two letters of your last name.
- If you didn't record an e-mail address, and you used a paper FAFSA, you will receive a paper SAR in the mail.
- If you didn't record an e-mail address, and you used FAFSA on the Web, you will receive a SAR Information Acknowledgment—it provides less detailed information than the SAR, and cannot be used to make corrections.

The Student Aid Report (SAR)

The first part of the SAR displays your Expected Family Contribution (upper right hand corner) and information about your eligibility status, verification requirements (see below) and instructions on how to correct any mistakes or assumptions made during processing.

The second part of the SAR displays the information upon which your EFC is based. The order of the data elements follows the same order as the FAFSA. If, based on reading this book, you thought your EFC should be $500 and now you learn that it's $5,000, you may want to check the information summary carefully to see if you or the computer got a decimal point in the wrong place.

If anything is incorrect under the "You Told Us" column, cross it out and enter the correct data in the "Corrected Items Only" column. For example, if you reported taxable income rather than AGI, now is the time to make that correction.

Also, if anything is missing, you must provide the missing data so your eligibility can be recalculated. After making corrections or supplying missing information, the student (and parents for dependent students) signs the form and returns it for reprocessing.

If you have a PIN, you can use FAFSA Corrections on the Web (www.fafsa.gov), to make all of these corrections online.

Note: You may not use this form to provide new information, i.e., you may not change the value of your assets to reflect a different worth than as of the date you filed your original application.

SAR Information Acknowledgment

If you complete the FAFSA online you will receive an SAR Information Acknowledgment. Like the SAR described above, this acknowledgment contains information on your eligibility status as well as a summary of the information used to calculate your EFC. Review this information carefully, and if you need to make corrections, you can do so (using your PIN) at Fafsa on the Web (www.fafsa.gov).

Verification

If your EFC has an asterisk next to it, you are a candidate for verification which means the financial aid administrator might need to substantiate the data you provided in your application before awarding you any aid. For more on verification, see Chapter 3.

"Eligible" and "Ineligible" Students

At the same time the processor sends you your SAR, it transmits to your school an equivalent document called an Institutional Student Information Record (ISIR). If the student is *eligible* for a Pell Grant, the school may use this ISIR to report that fact to Uncle's Pell Grant Disbursement System. That's how the school gets its money. If the student is *ineligible* for a Pell Grant, the school may start building an aid package using other resources.

"Rejected" Students

In addition to eligible and ineligible students, there are also "rejected" students whose eligibility cannot be calculated because the application contained too much inconsistent information. Examples: A blank or invalid date of birth (many students accidently put the current year), a missing name, an incorrect social security number, or illegible data. Part 2 of that student's SAR is called an "Information Request Form." If you follow its instructions for providing missing data and submit it for reprocessing, you can become an "eligible" or "ineligible" student.

Regardless of how students apply, they will receive a rejected paper SAR if a student or parent signature is missing.

Applying to More than Four Schools

If you apply online, you may ask to have your data sent to ten colleges. Unfortunately, the paper FAFSA only has space for you to list four colleges; if you are applying to more than four, here are some suggested strategies:

1. List the four schools with the earliest deadlines. If you start the process early, you have plenty of time to get your data to the others.
2. List your top four schools. If you're running short on time, make sure your preferred colleges get your information first.

3. List the four most expensive colleges. If you will need financial aid (beyond the unlimited amounts provided by Uncle Sam) to afford the school, make sure the pricey schools get your data before they run out of institutional aid.

4. List public colleges first, then private institutions—a reverse of the advice above. Most private colleges use PROFILE and/or their own financial questionnaire to get the same information, and they can use this information to begin estimating your eligibility for financial aid.

5. List in-state schools first (public and private), to increase your chances of receiving money from your home state.

Whichever rationale you choose, you can add additional schools once you receive your Student Aid Report (SAR).

Meanwhile, Back at the Financial Aid Office

Once the aid administrator knows your eligibility status he or she can start building your aid package—the combination of awards that makes up the difference between what college costs and what you can pay. If you are eligible for a Pell, it becomes the bottom layer of the package. If you are not eligible, the FAA must look somewhere else.

Questions—Problems

Useful Phone Contacts

For information about federal programs, call the Federal Student Aid Information Center, 800/4-FED-AID, from 8am to midnight, EST, seven days a week (TTY: 800/730-8913). Trained staff can help you:

- Complete the FAFSA
- Check on the status of your FAFSA
- Make corrections to your Student Aid Report (SAR)
- Request a duplicate SAR
- Explain Expected Contribution
- Answer questions about eligibility

You may also request Uncle's free book, *Funding Education Beyond High School*. (Blind and visually-impaired students may request audio highlights of the book on a compact disc.) The number is NOT to be used for financial counseling, to interpret policy, or to expedite application processing.

Questions about electronic applications: For technical help with electronic FAFSAs and electronic Renewal FAFSAs, call 800/801-0576.

Useful Web Contacts

The Federal Student Aid Home Page (studentaid.ed.gov) is a good starting place for gathering information. You can view the site in English or Spanish. It includes links to FAFSA on the Web and Federal School Codes. (You record your schools' codes on your FAFSA so Uncle knows where to send your need analysis results.) It also includes links to:

- *Completing the FAFSA* (studentaid.ed.gov/students/publications/completing_fafsa/index.html) which provides very detailed FAFSA instructions, in English or Spanish.

- *Funding Education Beyond High School: The Guide to Federal Student Aid* (studentaid.ed.gov/students/publications/student_guide/index.html) which answers all your basic questions about federal student aid, in English or Spanish. Blind and visually-impaired students can hear highlights at www.FederalStudentAid.ed.gov/audio.

Information for Financial Aid Professionals (IFAP) *Library* (www.ifap.ed.gov) is for people who work in the student aid field, or families with an interest in the nitty-gritty of student aid regulations, including all of Uncle's "Dear Colleague" letters and "Negotiated Rulemaking" sessions.

Students.Gov (www.students.gov) was designed to be a 24/7 "Student Gateway to the U.S. Government." Its collection of (commercial and governmental) sites helps students find a job (or internship), e-file taxes, plan vacations, register to vote, buy postage stamps, and plan and pay for a college education.

College.gov (www.college.gov) is a new site, still being developed by the Department of Education. It is intended to be the federal government's main source for information about planning, preparing and paying for college.

Using the USPS

If you decide to apply using paper forms and snail mail, protect yourself against postal loss. (1) Make copies of anything you plan to entrust to the mail. (2) Apply online whenever possible. Not only will your information get to its destination much faster, your data has less chance of being interpreted incorrectly by a mere mortal.

CHAPTER 2

■■■■■■■■■■■■■■■■■■■■■■

SPECIAL SITUATIONS AND
SPECIAL CONDITIONS

Special Situations

Once upon a time, Dad went off to work every morning and Mom stayed home to cook, clean, and take care of the kids. This kind of family is rapidly disappearing. Less than 15% of all households are what used to be called "normal." Here is how you handle "special" situations on financial aid application forms.

Divorce or Separation

If the applicant's parents divorce or separate before the student applies for aid, the student must report the income of the parent with whom he or she lived for the greater portion of the 12 months preceding the date of application.

If the student did not live with either parent, or spent an equal amount of time with each parent, the student must report the income information of the parent who provided the greater amount of financial support during the 12 months preceding the date of application.

"Financial support" includes cash, food, clothing, housing, medical or dental care, and contribution to college costs.

Remarriage

If the applicant's parent remarries before the application is filed, the student must report the stepparent's income and asset information. There are no exceptions to this rule. Prenuptial agreements or disclaimers of support from the stepparent are not acceptable.

Death

If a parent dies before the student applies for federal aid, the student should report only the income and assets of the living parent, even though the tax return shows both parents' incomes.

If both parents die, or the remaining parent dies before the student applies, the student is considered independent and uses the Independent Student worksheets to determine aid eligibility.

Job Loss

If you have recently lost your job, or received a lay-off notice, you might qualify as a "dislocated worker" and be eligible for the Simplified Needs Test (which excludes assets) or an Auto-Zero EFC. The FAFSA now captures these situations if they occur before you file (Question 83 on the paper FAFSA).

Parents Who Refuse to Provide Information

If you truly don't have access to parental resources, complete the FAFSA as best you can (e.g., without including parental data). You will be allowed to submit the form, but you will only be considered eligible for unsubsidized federal student loans. Solution? Let your colleges know about your situation, and what you've done on the FAFSA. Many students today come from non-traditional families and schools are becoming experts at wading through prickly situations to be as fair as possible. The school might decide to override your status and allow you to apply for aid as an "Independent Student."

Why is the system so strict about this? If students whose parents refused to provide information got lots of student aid, everyone's parents might start refusing to provide information.

There are, however, three situations in which your high school counselor or college financial aid administrator can sign in place of your parents.

1. Your parents reside outside the United States and can't be contacted by "normal" means.

2. You don't know where your parents are (and we don't mean they've been gone for a half-hour, and you want to send your form off at that particular moment).

3. Your parents are determined (by proper authority) to be physically or mentally incapable of signing the application.

Special Conditions

The above paragraphs cover special situations that exist before you submit the FAFSA. For events that occur after you submit the application (special conditions), you'll have to speak with the aid administrator.

"Professional Judgment"

Schools may use "professional judgment" to make three kinds of adjustments in determining your eligibility for federal student aid:

- *First*, they may change your student status from dependent to independent, provided you give them convincing reason.

- *Second*, they may re-calculate your Expected Family Contribution. Schools aren't allowed to change the Federal Methodology formula, or adjust your "bottom line" EFC directly, but they can modify the data elements used in the calculation, for example, lower the value of your assets, or use expected year income, rather than prior year. Of course, they may wait until Spring semester to adjust your award, so they can examine your 2009 tax return.

- *Third*, they may adjust the components of your cost of attendance figure. For example, if you have an unusually expensive commute, they may increase your transportation allowance.

A survey done by The College Board and the National Association of Student Financial Aid Administrators showed that "professional judgment" was generally based on a combination of written need analysis policies and the staff member's own judgment. Eleven percent of all reviewed cases resulted in a change in dependency status; thirty-seven percent resulted in a lower Expected Family Contribution, and ten percent resulted in a higher cost of attendance.

If you feel your family contribution is too high, or your cost of attendance too low, and you are able to prove your case (for example, you face one of the situations described below) please contact the financial aid administrator. If you aren't truly "needy," we hope you'll be content with using low interest loan money to pay the bills, thus preserving scarce grant money for families who are less well-off.

Be aware, some reviews lead to higher expected family contributions and lower costs of attendance. Lesson. Make sure your facts back up your case.

Special Conditions for Dependent Students

What counts as a special condition? There is no defined list of situations that qualify, but the following items should give you the idea. In general, "special condition" is synonymous with "unpleasant condition," or events relating to death, divorce, unemployment and natural disasters.

1. A parent or stepparent whose 2009 income from work must be reported became unemployed in 2010.

2. A parent or stepparent who received some form of nontaxable income or benefit in 2009 lost that income or benefit in 2010. Nontaxable income and benefits include: untaxed social security benefits, court-ordered child support payments, nontaxable retirement or disability payments, welfare benefits, and Aid to Families with Dependent Children.

3. A parent or stepparent whose 2009 income from work must be reported has been unable to pursue normal income-producing activities during 2010 because of a disability or a natural disaster (usual examples: floods, hurricanes, and earthquakes).

4. A parent or stepparent whose 2009 income must be reported dies after the student files a regular application.

5. Parents divorce or separate after the student files a regular application.

6. The student's last surviving parent dies after the student files an application. In that case, the student becomes an independent student.
7. The family has unreimbursed medical expenses that exceed 3½% of their adjusted gross income.
8. The student has younger siblings enrolled in private secondary schools.

Special Conditions for Independent Students

1. An applicant who worked full-time in 2009 is no longer employed full-time in 2010. This is intended to help the applicant who leaves work to return to school.
2. An applicant's spouse whose 2009 income from work must be reported became unemployed for at least ten weeks in 2010.
3. An applicant or applicant's spouse who received some form of nontaxable income or benefit in 2009 lost that income or benefit in 2010. Nontaxable income and benefits include: untaxed social security benefits, court-ordered child support payments, nontaxable retirement or disability payments, welfare benefits, and Aid to Families with Dependent Children.
4. An applicant or applicant's spouse whose 2009 income from work must be reported has been unable to pursue normal income-producing activities during 2010 because of a disability or a natural disaster (for example: floods, hurricanes and earthquakes).
5. An applicant divorces or separates after filing the original application.
6. The applicant's spouse whose 2009 income must be reported dies after the applicant files a regular application.
7. The applicant or applicant's spouse has unreimbursed medical expenses that exceed 3½% of the combined adjusted gross income.
8. The applicant has dependents enrolled in private secondary schools.

Other Considerations

Don't try to explain away high vacation expenses, or a sibling's five-star wedding, or the necessity of a newly remodeled kitchen. But do note legitimate "involuntary" expenses or unusual situations that might convince an aid administrator to re-evaluate your contribution. Here are some additional questions to ask yourself:

- Has your College Fund declined significantly in value since the date you filed your aid application?
- Is one of your parents about to retire? Do they have a skimpy retirement fund?
- Are your parents repaying their own student loans, or those of an older sibling?
- Are your parents helping an older sibling with graduate school?

- Do you have consumer debt resulting from past unemployment?
- Do you have high child care costs?
- Have you received notice that you will soon be laid off?
- Is your contribution from student income figure inflated because you took a year off to work?
- Is your contribution from student assets inflated because the family saved its money in the student's name? Did the parent put it there? Or did it come from some other source, like grandparents, aunts or uncles?
- Is your contribution from parental income figure inflated because of a one-time, unexpected bonus or capital gain? Is that money being double-counted as an asset, as well?
- Will you be attending camp (for example, in dance or tennis) or serving the community in lieu of taking a paying summer job?
- Did you pay more in state and local taxes than need analysis allowed?
- Are your parents paying nursing home costs for their own parents?
- Did the school exclude consideration of your Hope or Lifetime Learning tax credits?
- Do you have siblings attending expensive private colleges (who received less-than-generous aid packages)?
- Are your retirement assets all "out in the open," rather than hidden in a 401(k), IRA or Keogh?
- Do you live in a region with a high cost of living, like New York City or San Francisco?
- Is your new business eating up assets, rather than generating income?
- Are you an independent student who was required to report parental income and assets on the aid application?

CHAPTER 3

■ ■

VERIFICATION, OUCH!

Dear Student:

"Your aid application indicated you were married, but listed a household size of one. Your most recent income tax return listed you as single with two dependent children. Please explain all this and give us the correct information."

This fictional student is a candidate for verification. But your application does not have to be nearly this confused to require verification.

How Are Forms Selected for Verification?

When the processor receives your FAFSA, in addition to calculating EFC, it checks for inconsistencies and flags those with "questionable information," for example, a family that reports a very low income figure relative to the amount of taxes paid, a family that reports a very low income figure yet has no earned income credit, or a dependent student who reports his parents' marital status as "married" but household size as "two."

The processor also matches FAFSA information to other databases to catch students who have defaulted on loans, whose names don't correspond with their social security number, whose citizenship status is in question, or who should have, but didn't register for the draft.

Finally, the processor will let the aid administrators know which forms have been "edit-selected for verification" which is bureaucratese for "these forms smell rotten." A look at your EFC should tell you if you are one of the lucky ones to be verified. If it has an asterisk, you know you've won something. If it has a "C," you know it's the grand prize! The computer has identified an eligibility problem that must be resolved before any student aid may be awarded. The aid office will want to see all sorts of documentation (including a copy of your income tax return).

What Items Must the FAA Verify?

Verification is performed by the overworked aid administrator at the school you will attend. At a minimum, verification will include household size, number enrolled in college, adjusted gross income, US income taxes paid, and certain untaxed income and benefits (for example, social security benefits, child support received, payments to IRA/Keogh plans, interest on tax-free bonds, and earned income credit). But it can cover other areas, as well. It may require verification of a student's claim to being "independent." If the aid administrator doesn't want to stop here, verification can go further, to cover every item on the application, welfare benefits, housing allowances, business value, trust funds, investment property. You'll have to provide a copy of your final US Income Tax return as well as whatever additional documentation is requested.

If, after the checking, your household is as you claimed, and your numbers are within certain tolerance limits, there is no need to reprocess the form. If you are outside the limits, the FAA must recalculate your family contribution.

Tolerance Levels

If the total differences between your AGI, untaxed income and US income taxes paid as reported on your original FAFSA and as submitted for verification are $400 or less, the financial aid administrator need not recalculate your EFC. For example, if your actual AGI is $500 higher than you originally reported, and your taxes paid are $100 more than you originally reported, your net tolerance is $400 and the financial aid administrator need not take further action.

		On FAFSA	Verification
	AGI	$30,000	$30,500
+	Untaxed Income	0	0
−	Taxes Paid	$3,000	$3,100
		$27,000	$27,400

There is no tolerance at all for differences in non-dollar items like household size. If there's a discrepancy, the financial aid administrator must recalculate the family's expected contribution.

Completing Verification

Verification is a hassle for the applicant and for the aid administrator, but with up to 30% of all applications selected each year, odds are you will go through the process. So we say again: Be honest and accurate in filling out the forms. Make sure the FAFSA items that correspond to income tax items are identical. And, make sure you have back-up documentation for other statements you make, such as the status of your assets. Then, if the aid office requests the information, you can run it through a copy machine and send it off.

CHAPTER 4

■■■■■■■■■■■■■■■■■■■

MEET YOUR FRIENDLY PELL GRANT

What Is a Pell?

The Pell Grant used to be called the Basic Educational Opportunity Grant or BEOG. But in an eponymous mood (look this word up for an extra ten points on your SAT), Congress decided to rename the program in honor of the distinguished (retired) senator from Rhode Island, Claiborne Pell, who introduced, and won legislative approval for this form of assistance.

Pells, as they are now known, are a huge and broad-based program. About $28.6 billion will be dispensed to over 7.59 million students in 2010/2011 with an average award equal to $3,770. Most recipients come from families with incomes under $50,000. You should be aware, however, that the program is complex in design. It is subject to frequent rule changes. And, when all is said and done, your grant may be less than you had expected.

But don't be put off by such cynicism, the Pell Grant program does work. Money does materialize. And it can flow right into your pocket.

Who Are Pells For?

Pells are for undergraduates only. They represent the foundation of all financial aid packages presented to students whose ability to pay college bills falls short of college costs. You may receive a Pell for up to 18 semesters of undergraduate education. And, students who are accelerating completion of their degrees by enrolling year-round may receive up to two Pell awards in an academic year. On top of the Pell, students often receive additional aid—state grants, scholarships, work programs, and loans.

How Much Are Pells Worth?

For 2010/2011, the President budgeted for a Pell range of $555 to $5,550. The minimum Pell equals 10% of the maximum Pell funded for that year. Students who are eligible for a Pell that is between 5% and 10% of the maximum Pell shall receive the minimum (10%) Pell. Students eligible for less than 5% receive nothing.

How large a Pell will you get? It varies with your Expected Family Contribution (EFC) and your school's cost of attendance. Pells, when combined with your EFC, cannot exceed the cost of college.

- If your school costs more than the maximum Pell, your grant will approximate the maximum Pell minus your EFC. *Example*: If the cost of college is $15,000, and the maximum Pell is $5,550, an EFC of $1,000 translates into a $4,550 Pell.
  (Calculation: $5,550 − $1,000 = $4,545)
- If your school costs less than the maximum Pell, your grant will approximate that cost minus your EFC. *Example*: If the cost of college is $3,000, an EFC of $1,300 translates into a $1,700 Pell.
  (Calculation: $3,000 − $1,300 = $1,700)

We say "approximate" because aid administrators use payment schedules that show the exact amounts, rounded to the nearest $50 or $100.

Also, if the top award is $5,550, you should know that students who qualify for between $275 and $555 receive $555. Students who qualify for between $0 and $275 get nothing. Eligible students will be those with EFCs ranging from $0 to about $5,275. (Throughout this chapter, we have assumed a top award of $5,550, but with the FY2010 budget not yet settled (at press time), keep your eyes and ears open!)

Beginning with the 2011/2012 academic year, the maximum authorized Pell will be indexed to the CPI plus 1 percent, with an estimated maximum grant of $6,900 by 2019. But remember, there is a big difference between "authorized limits" and "funded limits"—each $100 increase in the maximum Pell costs the government at least $560 million, and probably more. A weak labor market usually leads to increasing numbers of Pell eligible students going to school, and a corresponding explosion of Pell costs.

Variables You Must Consider

In actuality, several variables influence the size of the award. These variables include award reductions if you are less than a full-time student, congressional actions that remove dollars from amounts already appropriated, and appropriations that are not large enough to fund all entitlements.

Add these variables up, and you will become a cynic at an age when you should still believe that good triumphs over evil and getting up early in the morning makes you healthy, wealthy, and wise.

Variable #1—When You Are Less Than a Full-Time Student

If you qualify for an award, the size of the award will correspond to the percentage of the load you take. If you are a part-time, half-time or three-quarter time student, you receive 25%, 50% or 75% of your award, respectively. Let's illustrate:

- **Bob L. Head** is a half-time student studying sports marketing. Her Family Contribution is $1,000. Assuming the maximum Pell Grant is $5,550, Bob qualifies for an award of 50% of $4,550 or $2,275.

- **Matilda Waltz** is a three-quarter-time student studying dance at Ozzie State. Her Family Contribution is $0 which qualifies her for the maximum grant. Matilda's award? 75% of $5,550 or $4,162.50
- **Bruce Driver** is a part-time student at United Pacific State. His Family Contribution is $4,950. Bruce's award? It is 25% of $600 or $150. Since this is less than the minimum grant, Bruce gets nothing. If his Family Contribution had been $0, he would have gotten 25% of $5,550 or $1,387.50. (Note: all part-time students receive about 25% of a full award, no matter how many courses they take.)

Variable #2—Taking Money Out of the Program

Year in and year out, politicians demonstrate their concern for the public by talk of "balancing the budget" or "cutting spending." To accomplish this, they can remove (or "rescind") money already appropriated. One year, for instance, they sliced $140 million off the Pell appropriation. Congress then had to reduce all awards already authorized by shaving each one by $50.

The good news is Congress doesn't always go after the Pell program. One year, they took billions out of the education budget, but salved their consciences by increasing the maximum Pell by $30.

Variable #3—Insufficient Appropriations

Legislators take a healthy guess at how many people will apply for aid, how many of those who apply will be eligible for Pells under whatever rules are in effect that day, and what the average-size grant will be. Based on that guess, legislators appropriate money for the program. If more students than expected apply and prove eligible, and the individual awards are to be larger than anticipated, the money in the program will not stretch. In some years, the shortfall has exceeded $1 billion.

When the Pell program has shortfalls Congress can (1) vote to appropriate more money; (2) trim the top award by a few hundred dollars, or (3) fiddle with the EFC formula so fewer (middle-income) students are eligible.

Where Can the Awards Be Used?

Pells can be used at any of the 7,000+ colleges, universities, vo-tech schools, or schools of nursing that take part in federal financial aid programs. All these schools must be accredited by an approved accrediting agency. Before enrolling at any school, a student should determine whether or not it is an accredited participant in Uncle Sam's aid programs.

Distance Education Courses

You may also be able to qualify for a Pell Grant if you are enrolled in a distance education course provided the program is accredited. For help in determining the legitimacy of an online degree program, check out the Council for Higher Education Accreditation, www.chea.org.

The subject of online courses continues to be studied more thoroughly by Congress—the government must figure out how to get money to legitimate students, yet prevent fraud. Uncle worries about virtual schools enrolling virtual students with real Pells. To be safe, limit your online study to e-courses from established institutions with bricks and mortar campuses.

Jail

You can even qualify for a Pell if you are incarcerated in a local jail (but not a state or federal correctional institution). Your cost of attendance figure is limited to tuition, fees and books—it does not include room or board because they are generously provided by the inmate's host institution.

> **Linda Lockenstock** is in a local jail for the unauthorized photocopying of this publication. She decides to study copyright law (full-time). Lockenstock qualifies for a maximum Pell of $5,550. Tuition at Ironfence U. is only $2,000. Since Pells, combined with your EFC can't exceed your cost of attendance, Lockenstock receives a $2,000 grant.

CHAPTER 5

■■■■■■■■■■■■■■■■■■■

LOANS, LOANS, LOANS, LOANS. . .

The Role of Uncle Sam

Here is the good news about Uncle Sam. He helps students get college loans below the current interest rate. In some cases, he will even pay the interest while the student is in school. He will guarantee loans against default. He will cancel loans if the borrower dies, becomes totally disabled, or goes into bankruptcy. And, he will permit loan deferment while the borrower does worthwhile things like giving smallpox vaccines to headhunters in New Guinea.

Now here is the bad news. Uncle will tamper with his programs. He will change interest rates when least expected. He will widen eligibilities one year and restrict access the next. He will invent new forms. He will write incomprehensible regulations and design procedures that are impossible to follow. Finally, he will hire more staff to administer what he has wrought, and pay for expensive studies to tell him what he did. In other words, Uncle Sam runs his financial aid programs as he does the rest of the country, with a lot of paper and even more red tape. He won't change, no matter how many Paperwork Reduction Acts are passed, so you must learn to appreciate the good, and get used to the frustration.

An Overview of Federal Student Loans

No two federal programs have the same features. Interest rates differ. Total amounts you can borrow vary. The type of borrower (e.g., graduate student, undergraduate student) may be specified. In addition, some programs are based on need, others are open to everyone. Some programs are heavily subsidized, others are not. And finally, some programs come with a grace period, while others require you to begin repayment immediately.

Program Acronyms

You may need an interpretation of some of the acronyms and abbreviations Uncle uses for his student loans:

- *FFEL*—Federal Family Education Loan, which consists of subsidized and unsubsidized Staffords and PLUS Loans. These loans are made by commercial lenders.

- *FDSL*—Federal Direct Student Loan, which consists of Direct subsidized and unsubsidized Staffords and Direct PLUS Loans. These loans are made by the federal government.
- *Stafford Loans*—formerly GSL or Guaranteed Student Loan
- *PLUS*—PLUS Loans, it's a long story. See Chapter 7.
- *Perkins Loans*—formerly NDSL or National Direct Student Loans
- *HPSL*—Health Professions Student Loan

How Much Loan Money Is Available?

Stafford and PLUS are entitlement programs—there is no funding limit. The amount borrowed depends entirely on how many eligible students and parents seek out loans. Currently, Uncle has well over $300 billion in outstanding in student loans. You may read newspaper headlines like "Student Loan Program to be Cut by $X Billion." This number does not refer to the amount available to be borrowed, but rather the amount that Uncle pays to subsidize interest rates or gives to schools to cover administrative costs. Cutting these allowances reduces incentives and makes it more difficult for private lenders and schools to cover their expenses. Although some might abandon the program, if more money is needed to provide loans to eligible students, then, Congress must appropriate more money—or change the laws.

The amount in "revolving loan funds" (such as the Perkins program) depends on how much is appropriated each year and how responsible students are about repaying their outstanding loans.

Staffords and PLUS loans account for almost $95 billion in annual loans. Perkins Loans run around $1 billion dollars (and could increase to $5 - $6 billion next year). And medical loans contribute about $400 million.

Keeping Records

Students should set up a file to keep track of their student aid transactions, including all documents concerning their education loans. Most importantly, students should keep:

- Copies of correspondence with the lender, school and guarantor.
- A copy of their loan application, Promissory Note and Loan Disclosure Statement.
- A record of any loan checks received.
- A copy of their repayment schedule.
- A copy of request for forbearance (if necessary) or deferment.
- A record of all payments made by the borrower.
- The name of a contact person at the lender's.
- Entrance and exit interview forms

Mental Preparation for Indebtedness

In Romans (Chapter XII, Verse 8) we are told, "Owe no man anything." That is good advice. But in biblical times, there were no $40,000 schools. The Methusela Institute of Geriatrics never charged more than half a silver shekel per lunar semester. That low rate kept students out of the hands of the money-changers.

But today it's nearly impossible to get an education without going into debt. In fact, the average undergraduate debt now exceeds $18,000. In a way, this debt becomes a rite of passage to adulthood. When you think about it, in a predominantly middle class society, indebtedness is not only a normal condition, it is a necessity—like air and water. Our economy depends on it. Without debt, businesses would have no money for capital, and families would be without shelter, transportation—or vacations.

Students, however, may still not be aware of the sustaining power of borrowing. Their view of the future excludes the use of somebody else's money. To hear a typical child tell it:

"I have gone to school every day for sixteen years. I have had to listen to teachers every day for sixteen years. I have had homework every day for sixteen years. I can't wait to graduate and land a good job. Then I'll get my own apartment and a sports car. In the winter, I will ski at Crested Butte. In the summer I will scuba dive in the Bahamas. I am counting the days."

We say to this child, "You are right about counting. But count money, not days." Here is why. Say the child hit the jackpot and found a $35,000 per year job following graduation. Take home pay: about $2,100 per month. Let's look at that child's dream budget:

Apartment rental, utilities (including cable and cell phone)	$ 950.00
Monthly payment, used car	$ 150.00
Insurance, maintenance, gas	$ 150.00
Food, Sundries	$ 350.00
Clothing	$ 150.00
Miscellaneous	$ 100.00
Vacation fund	$ 50.00
Music and Entertainment	$ 150.00
MONTHLY PAYMENT ON $20,000 STUDENT LOAN	$ 218.00
TOTAL	**$2,268.00**

Something will have to give. And it won't be the student loan. Make your own dream budget. And then begin to scale it down. That's what we mean by mental preparation.

Experts recommend that student loan repayments not exceed 8 percent of your adjusted gross annual salary—on a $35,000 income that would be $2,800 or $233/month. Unfortunately, 25% of borrowers have loans in excess of 15% of their annual income.

Fear of Loans

Some people may require little more than mental preparation to enter the spirit of indebtedness. "Monthly payments" may have been their first words—after all, their baby furniture was purchased on credit. Mortgage burning parties were a neighborhood ritual. And the winters in Aruba meant summers with the bank loan officer.

Studies confirm that many people are afraid of loans. They did not grow up with them. Instead, going into debt was something to be avoided at all costs. Debt meant the surrender of freedom, and the possibility of more serious consequences. The study found an unwillingness to take out Stafford Loans, even though the students were eligible. Common questions included, "What happens if I can't find a job after graduation?" "How can I pay back then?" And, "What will they do to me if I can't pay it back?"

The answer: Quit worrying. Federal student loans have features that make them less frightening. For example:

1. You don't make any payments on a student loan until at least six months after you have completed your studies. That gives you half a year to find a job and earn good money.

2. If for some reason things don't work out and you haven't found a job, you are still protected. You can ask the lender for "forbearance." Forbearance means permission to stop making payments temporarily because you have problems—unemployment, poor health—that interfere with earning money.

3. Inflation works in your favor. The dollar you borrow is worth a lot more than the dollar you pay back.

Never, Never Default

Loans must be repaid. You must never default on a student loan. Defaulting is morally wrong as well as legally wrong.

It is morally wrong because not repaying a loan from a revolving fund can deprive a future college student from access to low-cost aid. That future student might be your brother or sister, or it might be your son or daughter. It is morally wrong because defaulting provides ammunition to those who feel federal student aid should be reduced or cut. And, it is morally wrong because you have in effect stolen money that did not belong to you.

Of course, defaulting is also legally wrong and the defaulter can end up in court. Currently, student loan defaults cost us over $2 billion each year as we (the taxpayers) must compensate for people who unilaterally decide to convert their loan to a grant. Back in 1990, default rates averaged 22.4%, but thanks to Uncle's increasing vigilance (and, maybe, a few bookkeeping changes), they now average only 6.7% overall—11% at trade schools; 5.9% at public colleges; and 3.7% at private colleges.

And who are these defaulters? A University of Kentucky researcher describes them as having two personality traits—low anxiety levels and a high tolerance for complexity in their lives. Translation: People who aren't likely to care about collection efforts. But here is what they can expect:

- Defaulters may see up to 10% of their wages garnished, until their loans are repaid. That percentage may soon increase to 15%.

- Defaulters may meet collection agencies and attorneys. Their property may be seized. They may end up in court. Their names may be given to the Justice Department (which prosecutes nearly 1,000 cases/year).

- Defaulters will receive a letter from the IRS explaining they will not receive a tax refund unless they negotiate a plan to pay off what they owe. Note: if you are filing a joint return, and your spouse is the defaulter, neither of you will receive a refund. Some states have instituted this policy when it comes to state refunds.

- Defaulters will be reported to credit bureaus. They may encounter difficulties in obtaining housing, automobile or business loans. The default will remain on your record for seven years.

- Colleges may refuse to provide defaulters with transcripts. As many employers require proof of academic achievement, this could impact on employment.

At this time, Uncle Sam is not quite in the same league as the Canadian Mounties. He doesn't always get his man—or woman. But, he is learning fast. And, with the help of IRS computers, he soon will. If you are in default, and want to set up a repayment schedule, call the Department of Education's Debt Collection Customer Service hotline at 800/621-3115.

Getting Out of Default

If you should find yourself in default, contact your lender to arrange some sort of repayment plan. You may be able to regain your borrowing privileges if you make on-time payments for six months.

Gaining an Advantage

Some loan programs offer additional advantages and opportunities. Here is a smart-shopper sampler:

Staffords:

- Schools do not have to certify you for subsidized Staffords of less than $200. If you fall into this low-need category, think carefully about your family's financial situation, and if appropriate, discuss it with the financial aid administrator. Otherwise you'll have to make do with unsubsidized Stafford money.

- Repayment options can make your loan burden more manageable, but also more costly (due to longer repayment periods).

- Some lenders give extra bonuses (in the form of lower interest rates) to students who consistently make their payments on time, or who repay their loans automatically via electronic bank transfers.

- Some lenders may pay your origination fee and/or your guarantee fee.

- Middle-income families may deduct interest payments on their education loans.

Perkins Loans:

The availability of new loan money depends on the success of schools in collecting outstanding loan money. That success also influences the receipt of new loan capital. Obviously, Uncle is not going to fund a school that doesn't know how to collect. Thus, your selection of a college can influence how much low-cost student aid you might receive.

Deduction for Student Loan Interest

You may deduct up to $2,500 per year in interest paid on "qualified education loans." This definition includes federal student loans as well as commercial education loans, but not loans from people related to the taxpayer. The deduction will be phased out for single filers with incomes between $60,000 and $75,000 and joint filers with incomes between $120,000 and $150,000. Income levels will be indexed annually for inflation.

CHAPTER 6

■■■■■■■■■■■■■■■■■■■■

FEDERAL STAFFORD LOANS

Historical Perspective

Once upon a time, students had a hard time borrowing money. Bankers lend only against collateral—a house, savings, or tangible personal property. Students had no collateral and so they were unable to get loans.

Then Uncle Sam entered the picture. "Make the loans," he told the bankers, "and I will guarantee them. The United States is every student's collateral." It was a splendid idea. Uncle established a 7% interest rate on student loans—a figure that ran close to the prevailing interest rates. He also said he would pay the interest while the student was still in school. The program would cost the Treasury some money, but not too much.

This is not, however, a happily-ever-after story. Suddenly, interest rates took off to 12%, 15%, 18%, and 20% or more. This increased Uncle's costs from a few hundred million dollars per year to several billion for he had committed himself to (1) pay the interest on the loans while the student was enrolled and (2) pay the difference between 7% and the going interest rate during the repayment period. Critics of the program also pointed to all the savvy families who borrowed money at 7% while busily investing what should have been tuition money in Money Market accounts earning 17%. Uncle Sam tried to rein in what had fiscally become a runaway program.

In 1980, the interest rate was raised from 7% to 9%. In 1981, families were divided into two groups—those with incomes of $30,000 and under, and those with incomes of over $30,000. Eligibility requirements were established for each group and a loan origination fee was added.

Since that time, Uncle has eliminated the $30,000 threshold, and played with the interest rates and the fees—increasing them one year, decreasing them the next. In 1992, the rate was tied to the 91-day T-bill, and in 1993, the program was divided into two—subsidized loans for students with financial need, and unsubsidized loans for students without need. Students without need no longer receive interest subsidies while in school, or during the grace period before repayment.

Finally, in 2006, the interest rate was again changed, this time back to a fixed 6.8%, with a plan to reduce the rate to 3.4% over the next few years.

As you can see, the stability of the Stafford program corresponds directly to interest rates and the federal debt and deficit. If interest rates stay low and the national debt shrink, everyone will hail the program as Uncle's gift to students. If interest rates rise and the debt keeps growing, everyone will take steps to pass on part of the borrowing costs to students.

Parallel Universe

Another "innovation" was to create two parallel loan programs:

Federal Family Education Loans (FFEL) which consists of Subsidized Staffords, Unsubsidized Staffords and PLUS. These loans are made by commercial lenders; and

Federal Direct Student Loans (FDSL) which consists of Direct Subsidized Staffords, Direct Unsubsidized Staffords, and Direct PLUS. These loans are made by Uncle Sam.

Interest rates, loan limits, fees, deferments, cancellations, and forbearance terms are essentially the same. Repayment options vary slightly. The main difference, as far as the student is concerned, is who lends them the money.

So why are there two programs? For many years, there has been a disagreement between elected officials over who best can run the programs—private lenders or Uncle Sam (with help from private contractors).

With a new Administration, and the recent troubles in the banking industry, Direct Lending now has the upper hand. The House has passed legislation that would convert all new federal student loans (Stafford and PLUS) to the Direct Loan Program beginning July 1, 2010. At press time the Senate had not yet acted, but the Department of Education had contacted all affected colleges to suggest steps they could take to ease the transition. Just in case.

Stafford Loans: An Entitlement Program

The Stafford Loan is an entitlement program—there is no dollar ceiling set by Congress. Anybody and everybody who is eligible for a loan can get one. Currently, loan volume is running over $61 billion per year with over 14.5 million loans issued. By any informed guess, at least two million non-borrowers are eligible for subsidized loans (And, all non-borrowers qualify for at least a non-need based loan). So why don't they apply? Some may be following the wisdom of Shakespeare's Polonius, "Neither a borrower nor a lender be." But many more are just thoroughly confused by the constant changes in rules, eligibility requirements, and administrative details which have followed this program since its inception.

Program Summary

Federal Stafford Loans are low-interest loans to undergraduate and graduate students who are US citizens or resident aliens.

Students with financial need may receive a subsidized loan in which Uncle pays the interest while they are in school and during any deferments. *Students without financial need* may receive an unsubsidized loan in which interest accrues while they are in school and during any deferments. And finally, students may receive a combination of the two, the size of which depends on their student status and family income.

Loan Limits:

Dependent Undergraduates: Freshmen may borrow up to $3,500 per year. Sophomores may borrow $4,500 per year. Juniors, seniors and fifth-year undergrads may borrow $5,500 per year. If a student is borrowing under both the subsidized and unsubsidized program, these annual limits each increase by $2,000. For example, a freshman who receives a $1,500 subsidized Stafford may borrow an additional $4,000 under the unsubsidized program for a total of $5,500. The maximum undergraduate loan amount is $31,000 (of which no more than $23,000 can be subsidized).

Independent Undergraduates: Freshmen may borrow up to $3,500 per year. Sophomores may borrow $4,500 per year. Juniors, seniors and fifth-year undergrads may borrow $5,500 per year. If a student is borrowing under both the subsidized and unsubsidized program, these annual limits each increase by $6,000 for freshmen and sophomores and $7,000 for juniors, seniors and fifth-year undergraduates. The maximum an independent student may borrow during his or her undergraduate years is $57,500 (of which no more than $23,000 can be subsidized). Note: Dependent students whose parents have been turned down for a PLUS loan qualify for these higher limits as well.

Graduate Students may borrow up to $8,500 per year. If a student is borrowing under both the subsidized and unsubsidized program, this limit increases by $12,000 per year to a maximum of $138,500 (of which no more than $65,500 can be subsidized). This limit includes any money borrowed as an undergraduate.

Health Profession Students. Health Education Assistance Loans were discontinued. As a result, students in health-related fields may borrow increased amounts of unsubsidized Stafford money (up to $224,000).

Additional Limits. In no case may a Stafford Loan exceed the cost of attendance at your school minus any other financial aid you receive.

Prorated Loan Limits. Borrowing limits are prorated for programs of less than a full academic year, e.g., students attending the equivalent of one-third of an academic year are eligible for one-third of the maximum annual loan amount.

Interest Rate: The interest rate on subsidized loans is now fixed at 5.6% and will decrease to 4.5% for loans disbursed after July 1, 2010 and

3.4% for loans disbursed after July 1, 2011. The interest rate on unsubsidized loans is 6.8%.

Interest Subsidy. In the subsidized program, Uncle pays the interest while the student is enrolled and during the six-month grace period following completion of studies. In the unsubsidized program, students may forgo making payments, but interest continues to accrue. This interest is capitalized (added to the principal) only once—at the beginning of repayment.

Tip: If you have an unsubsidized loan, don't let the interest capitalize; instead, pay the interest while you're in school. The charges are minimal, and you'll save hundreds of dollars during repayment. Also, if your income is below the caps described in Chapter 10, you can deduct the interest payments from your AGI saving you tax dollars as well.

Grace Period. One grace period is permitted under the Stafford program—six months in length following completion of studies. There are no grace periods after subsequent deferments.

Who Makes Loans? Contact your college's financial aid office. All schools may be transitioning to Direct Lending, in which case your loan would go straight from Uncle Sam to your university. Currently, private lenders—Banks, Credit Unions, etc.—also make federal student loans.

Eligible Schools: Accredited colleges and universities, vo-tech and trade schools; and eligible foreign schools. Over 7,000 total.

Question. What do I do if I've taken out an unsubsidized Stafford and I still need more money to pay for college?

Answer: Have your parents take out a PLUS loan or ask your state guarantee agency (Chapter 11) if your state offers low interest loans. Check with your home state and the state in which your college is located.

Income Requirements

Families must demonstrate need to be eligible for a subsidized Stafford Loan. Families without need may receive an unsubsidized Stafford.

What is Need? It's the cost of your college minus your expected family contribution (EFC) minus any aid (e.g., private scholarships) you bring to the college. Family contribution, to refresh your memory, is determined by a federally-approved formula called the "Federal Methodology" (see the appendices for the calculation), and is based on information you provide when you fill out the Free Application for Federal Student Aid (FAFSA).

What is Remaining Need? It's your calculated need, minus the value of any Pell Grant you receive. Let's run through some examples:

1. **The Shishka Family.** One Shishka, Bob, is starting at a two-year college. Annual cost: $9,000. The family was judged capable of contributing $4,000 to college costs which means they would have qualified for an $1,550 Pell Grant ($5,550 - $4,000). Earlier, young Shishka won a $1,000 scholarship in a recipe contest for his barbecue sauce. What's this family's remaining need?

     $9,000 - ($4,000 + $1,550 + $1,000) = $2,450

2. **The Knight Family.** Two children. Lance and Lot. Lance, the chivalrous one, goes to Gallahad State. Annual cost: $20,000. He receives a $5,000 scholarship. Lot, the gallant one, goes to Round Table U. Annual Cost: $6,000. He earns a $800 educational bonus from the National Guard. The Knight family contribution was judged to be $4,000 for each child. What's this family's remaining need?

     For Lance: $20,000 - ($5,000 + $4,000) or $11,000.

     For Lot: $6,000 - ($5,000 + $800) or $200.

3. **Donnie Dodge** is a graduate student at a $35,000 school. He has a family contribution of $8,000 and receives a $15,000 scholarship through the Challenger Program. What's his remaining need?

     $35,000 - ($8,000 + $15,000) or $12,000.

Even though it is authorized, don't think your bank will let you have a $200 loan just because you have a need of $200. The cost of paper processing would make this highly unprofitable. In fact schools need not certify eligibility for loans under $200. Let's see how the students in our first two examples might have fared in their first year of college:

- Shishka Bob qualifies for an $2,450 subsidized Stafford and a $3,050 unsubsidized Stafford ($5,500 - $2,450) which he may use to help pay his $4,000 Expected Family Contribution.

- Lance Knight would be eligible for a $3,500 subsidized loan, and a $2,000 unsubsidized loan. His brother Lot would probably not be certified for a subsidized loan, but could borrow the full $5,500 under the unsubsidized Stafford.

Remember, these loan limits all increase after the freshman year!

- Now let's turn to Donnie Dodge. He has $12,000 in need, so, as a graduate student, he would be eligible for the maximum, $8,500 subsidized Stafford. How about the unsubsidized Stafford? This is a little trickier. His cost of attendance is $35,000. He received a $15,000 scholarship and a $8,500 subsidized loan, which leaves him eligible for a $11,500 unsubsidized loan ($35,000 - $15,000 - $8,500). The maximum unsubsidized loan is higher than this ($12,000), but a federal student loan may not exceed the cost of attendance minus financial aid received. Donnie may, however, use the unsubsidized loan to pay his EFC.

Will We Qualify for a Loan?

People always ask, "Will we qualify for a loan?" There is no easy answer. It depends on income, size of family, number of students in college at the same time, and the cost of attendance. The cost of attendance, remember, includes tuition, fees, room, board, books, transportation, and personal care expenses. It can even include the cost of a new computer. At our most expensive schools, this cost now exceeds $50,000.

Use the appendices to estimate your family contribution. Now, compare your family contribution to the cost of the college you plan to attend. If your family contribution is less than the cost of college, you have need and are eligible for a subsidized Stafford. If your family contribution is greater than the cost of college, you do not have need but are eligible for an unsubsidized Stafford, which has been discussed throughout this chapter.

Applying for Stafford Loans

The FAFSA doubles as a Stafford Loan application. It allows your school to determine the amount of subsidized and unsubsidized loans you are eligible to receive. Your school records this information on a "Master Promissory Note" (MPN). You fill in your name, address, date of birth, social security number, driver's license number, two personal references, and your preferred lender—the federal government (for Direct Loans) or a commercial institution (for FFEL). Finally, you sign the form and return it to your school.

If your school participates in Direct Lending, Uncle will use your MPN to wire money directly to your school account. Otherwise, your school returns the form to you, you give it to your preferred lender, and your lender uses it to wire money directly to your school account (your lender may choose to issue you a check, instead).

Important: Even though unsubsidized Staffords are not based on financial need, you must file a FAFSA to be eligible.

When Should You Apply?

As soon as possible after choosing which college you will attend. Most students wait too long to get the process underway, creating application traffic jams. Our suggestion: Start in late spring. You want to make certain your loan money is in place before the tuition bill comes due.

Finding Lenders

If all new loans are to be made under the government's Direct Lending Program (as proposed by the current Administration), you won't need to worry about finding a lender. The federal government will work with all accredited schools to originate federal student loans.

If commercial lenders stay in the program, and schools don't make the switch to Direct Lending, you should still have an easy time finding a lender, especially if you qualify for a big loan for a program of long duration at a traditional four year public or private university. It becomes more difficult if you qualify for only a small loan or seek a loan for a trade school or a program of short duration. If you have difficulties locating a lender, ask the college for a list of lenders in your area. Or, call your state guarantee agency.

You and the Lender

Under the Higher Education Act, the lender must disclose important information to you when the loan is made and when repayment begins:

- A statement (in big, bold print) that this is a loan that must be repaid.
- The lender's name, mailing address and phone number.
- A statement indicating that the lender may sell or transfer your loan.
- A loan repayment schedule, including the loan amount, the interest rate, length of the grace period, and when you must start repaying.
- The yearly and cumulative amounts that may be borrowed.
- An estimate of your total debt, the monthly payment due the lender, including the minimum annual payment required and the minimum and maximum repayment periods.
- A tally of special charges such as loan origination and insurance fees and information on how these are collected.
- An explanation of the effect of the loan on eligibility for other student assistance.
- An explanation of special options available to the borrower for loan consolidation or refinancing.
- A statement that you have the right to prepay without penalty.
- An explanation of forbearance and of all deferment and cancellation provisions, including a notice of the Department of Defense's repayment options (to encourage you to enlist in the military).
- A statement that loan information will be reported to a credit bureau.
- A definition of default and a lurid description of what happens to defaulters (you may augment this description by re-reading Virgil's observations on his descent into hell—see Dante's *Inferno*).

Entrance and Exit Counseling

Schools must provide entrance and exit counseling for their borrowers—often this is done on-line rather than in-person. Sessions should review:

- The terms and conditions of loan programs, including interest rates, fees, loan limits, repayment options, and repayment schedules.

- The obligation of loan repayment, including the consequences of delinquency and default.
- The provisions for forbearance, deferment, and cancellation.
- The lender's obligation to keep the student informed about changes in the loan's assignment, including name, address and phone number of the new lender and/or servicer.
- The student's obligation to keep the lender informed about changes in enrollment status, name, and address.

What happens if your school or your lender fails to provide you with these items of information? Can you sue for civil damages or refuse to abide by the terms of your loan? No, you can't, however, you can report the school or the lender to the Department of Education.

Deferments, Forbearance, and Cancellation

Deferments

Deferments are granted whenever a student is enrolled at least half-time. You need not borrow more money to qualify for this deferment, but you must be at a school that meets Stafford eligibility requirements. Deferments are also authorized for:

1. Up to 3 years if unemployed and eligible for unemployment benefits.
2. Up to 3 years if facing economic hardship (e.g., working full-time for minimum wage, or less).
3. Study in an approved graduate fellowship program or in a rehabilitation training program for the disabled.
4. Active-duty military (or National Guard) service during time of war, national emergency or other military operations.

Forbearance

If unanticipated problems affect your ability to repay the loan, and you do not qualify for deferment, lenders may grant forbearance—permitting (1) the temporary cessation of payments, (2) an extension of time for making payments, or (3) smaller payments than were scheduled.

Typical reasons for forbearance: unemployment, poor health, personal problems or underemployment (you automatically qualify if your student loans exceed 20% of your gross income). You must also be granted forbearance if you're participating in a community or military service program with loan repayment incentives, or you're in a medical or dental internship or residency program. Finally, you must be granted forbearance (for up to 60 days) while changing repayment plans or completing the paperwork for loan consolidation.

Interest on the loan continues to accumulate during forbearance.

Cancellation

We hope none of you qualify for cancellation, which is only for death, and permanent total disability.

Repayment

Repayment begins after the first grace period or immediately after subsequent deferments and lasts from 5 to 10 years.

The minimum annual payment is $600.

Table 1 illustrates the 10-year repayment load on subsidized Staffords incurred by a borrower at 5.6% (the current interest rate) and 3.4% (the interest rate which will be in effect beginning July 1, 2011). You can estimate your monthly payments for loan amounts other than those listed by dividing the total loan by 91.72 (for 5.6% loans) or 101.61 (for 3.4% loans).

Table 2 illustrates the 10-year repayment load on unsubsidized Staffords incurred by a borrower at 6.8%. You can estimate your monthly payments for loan amounts other than those listed by dividing the total loan by 86.90

If one portion of your loan comes from the subsidized Stafford program, and another portion from the unsubsidized program, you can combine numbers from Tables 1 and 2 for a rough estimate of your loan burden. Or you can use a calculator like that found on the Sallie Mae website under "repaying student loans" (www.salliemae.com).

Table 1: Repayment Schedule for Subsidized Stafford Loans		
Loan Amount	Monthly / Total Payment (5.6%)	Monthly / Total Payment (3.4%)
$10,000	$109.02 / $13,082.80	$98.42 / $11,810.13
$23,000	$250.75 / $30,090.26	$226.36 / $27,163.44
$65,500	$714.10 / $85,691.53	$644.64 / $77,356.60
$XX	91.72	101.61

After increasing the maximum (subsidized plus unsubsidized) loan amount to $138,500 (see next page), Congress realized it must do something to lessen the repayment burden. For example, all lenders must offer a choice of regular or graduated repayment plans. For an explanation of your payment options and repayment schedules under federal loan consolidation, see Chapter 11.

Prepayment: Loans can be prepaid without penalty.

Table 2: Repayment Schedule for Unsubsidized Stafford Loans	
Loan Amount	Monthly / Total Payment (6.8%)
$8,000	$92.06 / $11,047.93
$31,000	$356.75 / $42,809.83
$34,500	$397.03 / $47,634.11
$57,500	$661.71 / $79,405.53
$73,000	$840.09 / $100,810.19
$138,500	$1593.86 / $191,263.64
$XX	86.90

Repayment by Uncle Sam

You can have your loan repaid by Uncle Sam:

1. For service in Americorps. Up to $5,350/year of service for up to two years.

2. For service as an enlisted member of the National Guard or Reserve: $1,500 or 15% of loan, whichever is greater, per year of service to a maximum of $10,000 (up to $20,000 in selected skills).

3. For service in the Regular Army: $1,500 or 33 1/3% of the loan, whichever is greater, per year of service to a maximum of $65,000.

In addition, there is a growing recognition that high debt levels affect career choices—the higher your debt, the less likely you are to work in a non-profit or public service field. So now:

1. Up to $5,000 in loans may be forgiven for teaching for five consecutive years in a "shortage area." Shortage areas may refer to a grade-level, subject area or geographic region—the definition varies by state. For a listing, go to www.ed.gov/offices/OSFAP/Students/repayment/teachers/stcol.html. This amount may be increased to $17,500 for those working in low-income areas teaching math, science or special ed.

2. A portion may also be forgiven for working in areas of "National Need" (as defined by Uncle Sam), for example, early childhood educators, child-welfare workers and medical specialists. Some federal agencies also forgive loans for their employees; the exact terms are up to the individual agencies.

3. Up to $6,000 per year (to a maximum of $40,000) for working as a civil legal assistance attorney.

4. The government now offers a "Public Service Loan Forgiveness Program" to forgive the balance of your loans if you have been repaying them for 10 years while working in a public service job (for example, law enforcement, social work, public health, or public education).

CHAPTER 7

■■■■■■■■■■■■■■■■■■■■

Historical Perspective

Once upon a time, Congress authorized a parent loan program which the Department of Education decided to call PLUS loans—Parent Loans to Undergraduate Students. Congress soon expanded the parent loan program to include independent undergraduates and graduate students. In making this move, Congress renamed the program "Auxiliary Loan Program to Assist Students." Within 24 hours of the law's passage, wits had discovered the new program could be abbreviated ALAS, an acronym that gave cynics a great opportunity to practice their specialty.

The Department of Education was not amused. It decided to ignore the official name of the program (ignoring what Congress directs often seems to be a specialty of the Department of Education) and went back to the PLUS acronym, even though the acronym didn't really stand for anything.

Program Summary

Previously, the PLUS loan was limited to the parents (or legal guardians) of dependent, undergraduate students who are enrolled at least half-time. Now graduate students are once again eligible for PLUS loans, however, they must first file a FAFSA and apply for a Stafford loan.

Loan Limits: You may borrow an amount up to the school's total cost of attendance minus other aid received. PLUS loans are not based on financial need, so you may use them to cover your expected family contribution. Many lenders won't make PLUS loans of less than $500 because these smaller amounts are not worth the paperwork.

Example: Ray Joseph attends an $10,500 college. He receives a $3,500 Stafford Loan and a $3,000 soccer scholarship. Remaining cost: $10,500 - ($3,500 + $3000) or $4,000. Ray's parents may borrow up to $4,000.

If parents cannot pass a credit check, they may secure an endorser who can. A student whose parent is still unable to secure a loan may borrow amounts up to the Independent Student limits proscribed in the unsubsidized Stafford program.

Interest Rate. The interest rate for Direct PLUS loans is 7.9%. The interest rate for FFEL PLUS loans is 8.5% (if that program continues).

Grace Period. None. Interest begins accruing when the loan is issued.

Origination and Insurance Fees: Lenders deduct a 3% origination fee which they forward to Uncle Sam, and a 1% insurance fee which they forward to a loan guarantor (an agency that insures loans against default). If your loan comes from Uncle Sam (via Direct Lending) you pay a combined 4% instead. In vying for your business, some lenders may pay part (or all) of these fees.

Lenders: Financial institutions such as banks, S&Ls, credit unions, insurance companies, as well as Uncle Sam (via Direct PLUS).

Locating Lenders: If you have trouble finding a lender, contact the state guarantee agency (Chapter 11) in your home state, or the state where your school is located. The agency must designate a lender, or loan you the money itself.

What Lenders Must Tell You: The same disclosures as for a Stafford Loan (see Chapter 6).

Eligible Schools: Accredited colleges and universities; eligible vocational, technical, trade, business and foreign schools.

Borrower Certifications: Borrowers must sign a certificate that the loan money will be used solely for defraying the cost of attendance at the school the student is or will be attending. They must also agree to allow the lender to investigate their credit record.

Applying for PLUS Loans

To apply for a PLUS loan, you must complete a simple application and pass a credit check. Parents (unlike graduate students) do not have to file a FAFSA (unless of course, your school says otherwise). If your school participates in Direct Lending, the aid administrator can certify your eligibility for a PLUS and ask Uncle to wire money directly to your school account. Some lenders allow you to apply for PLUS loans online or by telephone. Simply answer a few credit-related questions and you'll learn within minutes if you're approved.

Repayment

Repayment begins 60 days after the final loan disbursement for the academic year and extends from 5 to 10 years. Parent and student borrowers have the option to defer payment until six months after the student ceases to be enrolled at least half-time, however, interest continues to accrue.

Tip: As with unsubsidized Stafford loans, don't let the interest capitalize; instead, pay the interest while you're in school. The charges are minimal, and you'll save hundreds of dollars during repayment. Also, if your income is below the caps described in Chapter 10, you can deduct the interest payments from your AGI saving you tax dollars as well.

Parents must be given the option of standard or graduated repayment; in some case, they may be given the choice of extended repayment plans, as well. (see Chapter 10)

Minimum Annual Repayment: $600.

Prepayment: Loans can be prepaid without penalty.

Deferments, Forbearance, and Cancellations

Under certain circumstances, loans can be deferred, postponed, canceled or considered for forbearance. Usually these circumstances are unpleasant things like death, permanent disability, or economic hardship.

Interest continues to accrue during forbearance and deferments.

Uncle will repay a portion of your parents' PLUS loan if you (the student) serve in the Army, Army Reserves, Army National Guard or Air National Guard (again, see Chapter 6). There are no other forgiveness features.

Table 3: 10-Year Repayment Schedule for PLUS Loans		
Loan Amount	120 Monthly Payments (7.9%)	120 Monthly Payments (8.5%)
$5,000	$60	$62
12,000	145	149
30,000	362	372
50,000	604	620
80,000	966	992
$ XXX	82.82	80.65

You can estimate your monthly payments for loan amounts other than those listed above by dividing the total loan by 82.82 (if you have a Direct PLUS, or 80.65 (if you have an FFEL PLUS).

CHAPTER 8

■■■■■■■■■■■■■■■■■■■

FEDERAL PERKINS LOANS

Program Summary

Federal Perkins Loans are awarded to students with demonstrated financial need. Funds for the program are allocated to schools by Uncle Sam. Schools select the recipients and specify the loan amounts. Money is available to both undergraduate and graduate students. The average award is around $1,875.

Loan Limits:

Undergraduate: $5,500 per year to a maximum of $27,500.

Graduate students: $8,000 per year to a maximum of $60,000 (less any Perkins money borrowed as an undergraduate).

Interest Rate:

5%. Student does not pay interest while in school, during deferments, or during grace periods.

Deferments:

Deferments are authorized for:

- Students pursuing at least a half-time course of study as determined by an eligible institution.
- Students pursuing a course of study pursuant to a graduate fellowship program or rehabilitation training program for disabled individuals (this deferment does not include medical internships or residencies).
- Students engaged in services which qualify them for loan forgiveness (see below).
- Active-duty military (or National Guard) service during time of war, national emergency or other military operations.
- Up to three years if unemployed, and eligible to receive unemployment benefits (e.g., actively searching for full-time employment).
- Up to three years if facing economic hardship (e.g., working full-time at less than minimum wage).

Question: How do I get approved for one of these deferments?

Answer: Contact the school's student loan officer *before* your first payment is due and complete the paperwork he or she sends you. Simple.

Loan Cancellation:

Loan cancellation is available to:

- Full-time teachers in pre-schools, elementary or secondary schools serving handicapped students or low-income families.
- Full-time special education teachers or professional providers of early intervention services to children with disabilities.
- Full-time law enforcement or correction officers.
- Full-time teachers of math, science, foreign languages, bilingual education, or any other subject in which the state educational agency determines a "shortage."
- Full-time nurses or medical technicians providing health care services.
- Full-time employees of child or family service agencies providing services to high-risk, low-income children and their families.

The cancellation rate for each of the above: 15% for each of the first two years; 20% for each of the third and fourth years; and 30% in the fifth year.

- People serving in the Armed Forces if they are stationed in "an area of hostilities." *Cancellation Rate*: 12.5% per year of service to a maximum of 50%.
- People serving as Peace Corps or ACTION volunteers. *Cancellation Rate*: 15% for each of the first two years of service; 20% for each of the third and fourth years to a maximum of 70%.
- Full-time staff member employed in a professional capacity as part of a Head Start program. *Cancellation Rate:* 15% per year of service.

You might also be eligible to have your loan canceled if you are a full-time faculty member at a Tribal College or University; full-time librarian at a low-income school; full-time speech pathologist (with a masters degree) working exclusively at a low income school; or a firefighter.

Forbearance: Institutions must grant students forbearance for up to three years under special circumstances, for example, if the borrower's student loan debt burden equals or exceeds 20% of his or her gross income. Interest continues to accrue.

Repayment by Uncle Sam:

- For service as an enlisted member of the Army National Guard or Reserve: $1,500 or 15% of the loan, whichever is greater, per year of service to a maximum of $10,000 (or $20,000 in selected skills).
- For service as an enlisted member in the Army: $1,500 or 33 1/3% of the loan, whichever is greater, to a maximum of $65,000.

Outright Cancellation: We hope no one qualifies for outright cancellation, which is available only for death and permanent, total disability.

Grace Periods: Nine months after the student drops below half-time and six months after every deferment (except hardship deferments).

Repayment: Begins nine months after completing studies and extends over ten years (not including deferments and grace periods). Borrowers may now repay their loans using electronic bank transfers.

Minimum Annual Repayment: $480/year.

On the Horizon. The Administration wants to greatly expand the Perkiins Program so that 2.5 million students would share $5.77 billion. To help fund this increase, it would eliminate the in-school interest subsidy.

Table 4: Repayment Schedule for Perkins Loans

Loan Amount	Monthly Payment	Number of Months	Total Interest	Total Payment
$5,500	58.34	120	1500.18	7,000.18
8,000	84.85	120	2,182.38	10,182.38
16,000	169.70	120	4,364.75	20,364.75
22,000	233.34	120	6,001.44	28,001.44
27,500	291.68	120	7,501.63	35,001.63
60,000	636.39	120	16,367.28	76,367.28

You can estimate your monthly payments for loan amounts other than those listed above by dividing the total loan by 94.28.

Finding Perkins Money

Perkins Loans are a tremendous deal. But Perkins money is not evenly distributed. Most of it is allocated to four-year colleges (public and private). And even within this group, some have plenty of Perkins money and some may not have enough to put together one loan. Why this disparity? Loan collection practices. Colleges which are too lax about collecting past loans have no new funds to distribute. Colleges that go after their borrowers, however, have plenty of money being returned to the revolving fund and Uncle Sam rewards their diligence by adding extra shots of new capital.

Uncle adds up to $300 million in new capital each year, otherwise schools must make due with the $1 billion "revolving fund" (money paid back by borrowers each year).

Our advice: Ask schools about their Perkins default rate. A high rate means no low-interest money, and possibly a school full of people who are so selfish they cheat future students out of loan money. A low rate points to more generous loans, a more conscientious group of students, and more efficient administrators.

CHAPTER 9

■ ■

LOANS AND GRANTS
FOR MEDICAL TRAINING

Bureau of Health Professions

The federal government spends lots of money—almost a half billion dollars per year—to educate future doctors, nurses, and other health professions. Most of this money is given directly to the schools; schools then select the recipients.

One bit of advice: You will gain an advantage over fellow applicants if you indicate a willingness to practice in a "shortage area." Don't worry about what a shortage area is. Its definition and location will change several times between the time you apply and the time you graduate. What's important to know is that "shortage areas" are a big thing at the Department of Health & Human Services. It has "primary medical care shortage areas," "dental manpower shortage areas," "rural dental shortage areas," "vision care shortage areas," "podiatry shortage areas," "pharmacy shortage areas," "psychiatric shortage areas," even "veterinary care shortage areas."

The nursing shortage is especially acute, which is why there are expanded grants and loan repayment options for nursing education.

For more information on Uncle's individual-based health care programs, visit the Bureau of Health Professions at bhpr.hrsa.gov/dsa. For example:

Health Professions Student Loans (HPSL)

Long-term, low-interest, need-based loans. Must practice in primary care. Apply through school.

Primary Care Loans (PCL)

Students in allopathic or osteopathic medicine may borrow up to the cost of attendance. Interest equals 5% and begins to accrue following a one-year grace period after you cease to be a full-time student. Deferment options of up to four years. Must practice in primary health care until the loan is repaid. Apply through school, bhpr.hrsa.gov/dsa/pcl.htm.

Nursing Student Loans

When money is available, these need-based loans go to half- and full-time students pursuing study at schools of professional nursing. Apply through your school's financial aid office.

Nursing Scholarship Program

Tuition, fees and monthly stipend of c. $1,300. Priority goes to those with a "zero" EFC (from the FAFSA), very competitive. Must practice for at least 2 years at a health care facility with a critical shortage of nurses. By late June, 877/464-4772, bhpr.hrsa.gov/nursing/scholarship.

Nursing Education Loan Repayment Program (NELRP)

Helps nurses repay educational loans in exchange for service in eligible facilities located in areas experiencing a shortage of nurses. For two years of service, the NELRP will pay 60% of the participant's loan balance; for a third year of service, NELRP will pay an additional 25% of the loan balance. By early-March. Nurse Education Loan Repayment Program, 877/464-4772, bhpr.hrsa.gov/nursing/loanrepay.htm.

Scholarships and Loans for Disadvantaged Students (SDS and LDS Programs)

Scholarships and low-interest loans for full-time, financially needy students from disadvantaged backgrounds who are enrolled in health professional and nursing programs. Apply through school.

Exceptional Financial Need Scholarships

All tuition plus stipend. Good for one year only. At year's end, participants have priority for a NHSC Scholarship (see below). Must practice in general dentistry or primary care medicine for five years after residency. Apply through school.

National Institutes of Health

Medical researchers at NIH can qualify for up to $35,000 in loan forgiveness, and an extra amount to cover federal and state income taxes that result from these repayments, 866/849-4047, lrp.info.nih.gov.

National Health Service Corps

The National Health Service Corps is a $145 million program operated by the Health Resources and Services Administration (HRSA). It recruits and places primary care specialists (physicians, nurses, dentists, dental hygienists and physician assistants) throughout medically underserved communities in the U.S. Eligible students may receive a full tuition (plus stipend) scholarships or participate in a loan repayment program. For more information, contact: National Health Service Corps, nhsc.bhpr.hrsa.gov.

National Health Service Corps Scholarship Program

The NHSC will pay tuition, fees, books and supplies, plus stipend (c. $1,100 per month) for up to four years. This very-competitive program is open to US citizens enrolled in a fully-accredited medical school, dental school, family nurse practitioner program, nurse midwifery program or physician assistant program. For each year of support, you owe one year of full-time clinical practice in high-priority health professions shortage areas. Minimum 2 year obligation. If you fail to comply with the terms of your contract, the penalty equals three times the cost of your scholarship, plus interest. The scholarship is tax exempt; the stipend remains taxable. NHSC Scholarship Program, 800/638-0824, nhsc.bhpr.hrsa.gov.

National Health Service Corps Loan Repayment Program

In exchange for providing primary care in federally-designated health profession shortage areas, the program will repay up to $50,000 in education loans for a minimum 2-year commitment. The program is open to primary care physicians (family medicine, OB/gyn, internal medicine, pediatrics, general psychiatry), mental health care clinicians (psychiatrists, psychologists, family counselors and clinical social workers), nurse practitioners, midwives, dentists, dental hygienists and physician assistants. By late March. NHSC Loan Repayment Program, 800/638-0824, nhsc.bhpr.hrsa.gov.

Faculty Loan Repayment Program

Helps eligible health-professions faculty from disadvantaged backgrounds repay their student loans. Up to $20,000 per year in exchange for a two-year service commitment, bhpr.hrsa.gov/dsa/flrp.

State-Based Programs

Many states have loan repayment programs (some of which are funded by the National Health Service Corps, nhsc.bhpr.hrsa.gov). For a listing, check out the financial aid section of the American Medical Colleges web site, www.aamc.org/students/financing/start.htm.

Military Medical and Nursing Programs

Armed Forces Health Professional Programs

Health Professions Scholarships for medical, dental, veterinary, psychiatric nurse practitioner, optometry and psychology students. Tuition, fees and $1,992 monthly stipend (adjusted each July). Additional sign-on bonus for certain medical and dental students of up to $20,000. Service obligation of one year for each year you receive the scholarship.

Health Professional Loan Repayment Program (HPLRP). Depending on branch of service, up to $40,000 per year in educational loans for officers serving up to four years on active duty in designated specialties

Financial Assistance Program. Residency training for graduate physicians, endodontists, periodontists, orthodontists and oral surgeons. $45,000 per year for up to four years plus $1,992 monthly stipend (adjusted each July). Service obligation.

Each branch of the service has its own point of contact:
- **Army:** Medical Department, 800/USA-ARMY, www.goarmy.com/amedd/index.jsp.
- **Navy:** Medical Command, 301/319-4118, www.navy.com/healthcareopportunities.
- **Air Force:** Dir. of Health Professionals, 800/443-4690, www.airforce.com/opportunities/healthcare/education.

ROTC Nurse Program (Army, Navy, Air Force)

Students at approved nursing schools affiliated with an Army, Navy, or Air Force ROTC unit. 2, 3, 4 year scholarships; tuition, textbooks, and fees, plus a monthly stipend. Service obligation.
- **Army,** Army ROTC, www.goarmy.com/rotc/nurse_program.jsp.
- **Navy,** 800/NAV-ROTC, www.nrotc.navy.mil.
- **Air Force,** HQ AFROTC, 866/423-7682, www.afrotc.com.

Navy-Specific Programs

For more information on the following programs, contact the Navy Medical Command, 301/319-4118, www.navy.com/healthcareopportunities.

1. *Navy Health Services Collegiate Program.* Up to $240,000 to finish graduate school in the form of a monthly salary and housing allowance.
2. *Navy Nurse Candidate Program.* $10,000 upfront plus $1,000 per month for 24 months for nursing school.

Army-Specific Programs

HQ, US Army Recruiting Command, Health Services Division, 1307 Third Avenue, Fort Knox, KY 40121, 800/USA-ARMY, www.goarmy.com/amedd/index.jsp

1. *Specialized Training Assistance Program (STRAP).* Monthly stipend for students and residents in designated specialties including nursing (specialties are identified every two years). $1,992+/month (adjusted each July). Recipients serve one year in the Reserve component of the Army Medical Department for every six months (or less) they receive the stipend.
2. *Health Professional Loan Repayment Program (HPLRP).* Army will repay up to $50,000 in educational loans for officers serving in designated specialties in the Reserves—$20,000 in each of the first two years, and $10,000 in the third year.
3. *Health Professions Special Pay.* Annual bonus to health care professionals in designated specialties (specialties are identified every two years) who join the Army Reserve. Bonuses vary from $5,000 to $10,000 per year for up to 3 years. Also, Active Duty bonuses from $6,000 to $14,000 per year, depending on the specialty.

4. *Army Nurse Candidate Program.* Bonus money for undergraduates pursuing nursing degrees: $5,000 when entering the program, another $5,000 at graduation, plus $1,000 per month during enrollment.

Uniformed Services University of the Health Sciences

Fully-accredited federal school of medicine and graduate school of nursing. Request catalogue, from Admissions Office, 4301 Jones Bridge Rd., Bethesda, MD 20814; 800/772-1743, www.usuhs.mil.

F. Edward Hebert School of Medicine. This tuition-free institution's main emphasis is on training medical officers for the Army, Navy and Air Force. While enrolled, students serve on active duty as Reserve commissioned officers in grade O-1 with full pay and allowances. Civilian and uniformed services personnel are eligible for admission. Seven year service obligation, exclusive of internship, residency or other service obligations.

Graduate School of Nursing. Offers degrees in Nurse Anesthesia, Psychiatric Mental Health Nurse Practitioner, Family Nurse Practitioner and Perioperative Clinical Nurse Specialist as well as a Ph.D. in Nursing Science.

Commissioned Officer Student Training & Extern Program Work Program (COSTEP)

For graduate awards, students must complete one year of medical, dental, veterinary school. For undergrad awards, students must complete two years in a dietary, nursing, pharmacy, dental hygiene, medical laboratory technology, therapy, sanitary science, medical records, engineering, physician's assistant, or computer science field. Student must return to studies following completion of COSTEP assignment. Serve as an extern in various divisions of the US Department of Health and Human Services during school breaks of 31-120 days duration. Ensign's pay during work phases, about $2,500 per month. COSTEP, 800/279-1605, www.usphs.gov/student.

Office of Minority Health Resource Center.

A central resource for minorities interested in the health professions. The Resource Center does not offer scholarships, but its trained information specialists will be glad to help you search its database of funding opportunities—via the Web, www.omhrc.gov or phone, 800/444-6472.

CHAPTER 10

■■■■■■■■■■■■■■■■■■■■■■■

IT'S PAYBACK TIME

*The plans outlined in this chapter will give you a general overview of
your loan repayment options. Exact details vary depending on the nature
of your debt. Besides, by the time you begin repayment, all of these choices
will probably be obsolete! For current information, contact the institution
that gave you your loan.*

Alternate Loan Repayment Options

Borrowers who face larger payments than they can initially handle under
regular repayment, may want to use an alternate plan, either Extended
Repayment, Graduated Repayment, or an Income-Based Repayment.
Borrowers may also consolidate their loans and take advantage of extended
repayment plans.

Table 5: Repayment Options for a $23,000 Subsidized Stafford Loan		
	Stafford Loan	**Consolidation Loan**
Standard Repayment **Total Payments**	$255, 120 months **$30,642**	$164.78, 240 months **$39,547**
Graduated Repayment	$115, 24 months $302, 96 months	$115 initial payment increasing to $263 final payment (after 20 years)
Total Payments	**$31,776**	**$43,281**

By letting you take longer for repayment, Uncle is not reducing your debt,
just the size of your payments (anywhere from 6-35%, depending on the size
of your loan). Without these options, your first paycheck, your second
paycheck, even your one hundred and twentieth paycheck could be
consumed by taxes, bus fare, burgers and student loan payments. With
longer repayment plans, paychecks can go toward an occasional candlelight

dinner at Chez Froggy or a spring trip to the Amalfi coast. But please note, under all of these plans, your monthly payments will be smaller but the total amount you repay much greater than under standard (10-year) repayment.

Uncle currently runs two parallel sets of repayment plans, one under Federal Family Education Loan (FFEL), the other under Federal Direct Student Loan (FDSL). FFEL is likely to be phased out. For more information, check with Uncle Sam or the institution that gave you your loan.

To help you decide which repayment plan is best for you, try using *FinAid's* online loan calculators: www.finaid.org/calculators.

- If the student is repaying Stafford loans only, the interest rate is 5.6% for subsidized amounts, and 6.8% for unsubsidized amounts.
- If the family is repaying PLUS only, the interest rate is either 7.9% (FDSL) or 8.5% (FFEL).
- If the student is repaying a consolidated loan, the interest rate equals the weighted average of all the consolidated loans rounded up to the nearest 1/8% with an 8.25% cap.

Table 5 shows the options for repaying a $23,000 subsidized Stafford. No matter what the interest rate (we've used 6%), total payments are lowest under standard repayment.

Standard Repayment

Unless borrowers make other arrangements, they must repay their loans in equal installments, spread over ten years. We included sample repayment charts in previous chapters.

Graduated Repayment

Borrowers must repay the loan within ten years, however, payments start small when income is low, and increase over time, while income also rises. Students sometimes have the option of making interest-only payments for the first few years.

Extended Repayment

Students with debts over $30,000 may extend repayment for up to 25 years and choose between a fixed or graduated repayment schedule.

Income-Based Repayment

All students may now take advantage of a new, income-based repayment. In this plan, a student's monthly loan payment will be limited to 15% of his or her discretionary income, defined as 15% of the amount by which the student's adjusted gross income exceeds 150% of the poverty line, divided by 12. Got it? The government will forgive any remaining balance after 25 years of repayment.

Borrowers who are using one of the other repayment plans may switch to this one. PLUS loans made to parents are not eligible for income-based repayment.

For more information, visit IBRInfo.org.

Table 6: Sample Maximum Payments under IBR				
	Family Size			
Income	1	2	3	4
$10,000	$0	$0	$0	$0
$20,000	$47	$0	$0	$0
$30,000	$172	$102	$32	$0
$40,000	$297	$227	$157	$87
$50,000	$442	$352	$282	$212

Loan Consolidation

Loan consolidation is another option, especially for students with multiple loans who are trying to simplify repayment. You may consolidate all federal loans—Stafford, Perkins, PLUS, Nursing, Loans for Disadvantaged Students and Health Profession Student Loans—and take advantage of the repayment plans just described. Married couples may no longer consolidate their individual loans into a joint loan.

For more on FFEL Consolidation, contact your current lender. For more on Direct Consolidation, visit www.loanconsolidation.ed.gov.

Sample Repayment Periods:
- 10 years for loans under $7,500;
- 12 years for loans between $7,500 and $9,999;
- 15 years for loans between $10,000 and $19,999;
- 20 years for loans between $20,000 and $39,999;
- 25 years for loans between $40,000 and $59,999; and
- 30 years for those lucky students with more than $60,000 to repay.

Interest Rate. The interest rate equals the weighted average of all your loans rounded up to the nearest 1/8% with an 8.25% cap. It is fixed at this rate for the life of the loan.

Interest Subsidies. If your consolidation loan contains subsidized loan money, you might retain the interest subsidy benefit on that portion of your consolidated loan during deferments.

Deferment: Deferment periods are not included in the number of years allowed for repayment. Also, *if you choose to consolidate a Perkins or Stafford loan, you could lose out on their deferment and forgiveness options, so read the rules carefully before your sign up..* Deferment is allowed:

1. While in school at least half-time;
2. While pursuing a graduate fellowship program or rehabilitation training program for persons with disabilities;
3. Up to three years for unemployment or economic hardship; and
4. Up to three years for active-duty military service.

Loan Forgiveness: Consolidation loans are eligible for the Public Service Loan Forgiveness program described in Chapter 6.

Loan Serialization

Students with multiple loans of the same type but from different lenders may be able to "collapse" or "serialize" their loans to create a single monthly payment. Technically, the loans remain separate, but now you're writing just one check a month without going through the hassle of consolidation (and possibly losing out on the borrower bonuses described below). Check with your lenders to see if they offer you this option.

Deduction for Student Loan Interest

You may deduct up to $2,500 per year in interest paid on "qualified education loans." This definition includes commercial education loans, but not loans from people related to the taxpayer. The deduction will be phased out for single filers with incomes between $60,000 and $75,000 and joint filers with incomes between $120,000 and $150,000. Income levels will be indexed annually for inflation.

Plan Now, Save Later

If the FFEL program survives, you should know that private lenders frequently reward students who repay their loans faithfully. They may give you one year, interest-free. They may lower your interest rate by 1% after receiving 48 on-time payments. They may lower your interest rate an additional .25% if you repay using automatic (electronic) monthly bank transfers. Or, they may lower your interest rate simply for having more than $7,500 in loans.

A student with $10,000 in Stafford loans could save as much as $1,193.

Tip: To benefit from these opportunities, set up overdraft protection on your checking account so you're sure not to miss an automatic payment due to "insufficient funds."

Before you take out a loan, be sure your lender offers these types of bonuses; otherwise, keep looking. Even consolidated loans qualify for reduced rates and bonuses. And don't simply rely on your college's list of "preferred lenders." The school's recommendations may be based on which bank offers the best service or easiest application, but not necessarily the best bargain, especially over the 10-30 year life of the loan.

Best Bets

Check with Discover Student Loans (www.discoverstudentloans.com) and SallieMae (www.salliemae.com). Here are two others:

- CitiBank CitiAssist, 800/967-2400, www.studentloan.com
- PNC Bank, www.eduloans.pncbank.com

Loan Locator

Most banks sell their loans, which means you may get your loan from one institution, but repay it to another. Of course, you are supposed to be notified of this switcheroo, however, if you lose track of your lender, try finding it via the National Student Loan Data System, www.nslds.ed.gov/nslds_SA.

CHAPTER 11

■■■■■■■■■■■■■■■■■■■■■

LOCATING LENDERS

A Directory of Guaranty Agencies

Many states are getting out of the loan business and letting larger guarantors take their place. For links, go to:

wdcrobcolp01.ed.gov/Programs/EROD/org_list.cfm.

Alabama
see Kentucky

Alaska
See Washington

Arizona
See USA Funds

Arkansas
800-622-3446
Student Loan Foundation
10 Turtle Creek Lane
Little Rock, AR 72202

California
877-ED-FUND
EDFUND
PO Box 419045
Rancho Cordova, CA 95741

Colorado
800-727-9834
College Assist
999 18th Street, #425
Denver, CO 80202

Connecticut
800-237-9721
CT Student Loan Foundation
525 Brook Street
Rocky Hill, CT 06067

Delaware
See Pennsylvania

District of Columbia
See ASA

Florida
800-366-3475
Student Financial Assistance
1940 N Monroe St., #70
Tallahassee, FL 32303

Georgia
800-505-4732
GA Student Finance Comm..
2082 East Exchange Place, #220
Tucker, GA 30084

Hawaii
See USA Funds

Idaho
See Washington

Illinois
800-899-4722
Student Assistance Commission
1755 Lake Cook Road
Deerfield, IL 60015

Indiana
See USA Funds

Iowa
800-383-4222
Iowa Student Aid Commission
200 10th Street, 4th floor
Des Moines, IA 50309

Kansas
See USA Funds

Kentucky
800-928-8926
Higher Ed. Assistance Authority
PO Box 798
Frankfort, KY 40602

Louisiana
800-259-5626
Student Financial Assistance
PO Box 91202
Baton Rouge, LA 70821

Maine
800-228-3734
Finance Authority of Maine
PO Box 949
Augusta, ME 04332

Maryland
See USA Funds

Massachusetts
See ASA

Michigan
800-642-5626
MI Guaranty Agency
PO Box 30047
Lansing, MI 48909

Minnesota
See Wisconsin

Mississippi
See USA Funds

Missouri
800-473-6757
Dept. of Higher Ed.
3515 Amazonas Drive
Jefferson City, MO 65109

Montana
800-537-7508
Student Loan Program
PO Box 203101
Helena, MT 59620

Nebraska
800-735-8778
NE Student Loan Program
PO Box 82507
Lincoln, NE 68501

Nevada
See USA Funds

New Hampshire
800-525-2577
Higher Ed. Assistance
Found.
4 Barrell Court
Concord, NH 03302

New Jersey
800-792-8670
Higher Ed. Assistance Authority
PO Box 540
Trenton, NJ 08625

New Mexico
800-279-3070
Student Loan Guarantee Corp.
7400 Tiburon
Albuquerque, NM 87190

New York
888-697-4372
Higher Ed. Services Comm.
99 Washington Avenue
Albany, NY 12255

North Carolina
800-700-1775
Education Assistance Authority
PO Box 14103
RTP, NC 27709

North Dakota
800-472-2166
Student Loans of ND
c/o Bank of ND
1200 Memorial Highway
Bismark, ND 58506

Ohio
See Wisconsin

Oklahoma
800-442-8642
Student Loan Program
P.O. Box 3000
Oklahoma City, OK 73101

Oregon
888-323-3262
State Scholarship Commission
1500 Valley River Drive #190
Eugene, OR 97401

Pennsylvania
800-692-7392
American Education Services/
   PHEAA
1200 North Seventh Street
Harrisburg, PA 17102

Rhode Island
800-922-9855
Higher Ed. Assistance Auth.
560 Jefferson Boulevard
Warwick, RI 02886

South Carolina
800-347-2752
Student Loan Corp.
PO Box 21487
Interstate Center, #210
Columbia, SC 29221

South Dakota
800-592-1802
Ed. Assistance Corporation
115-1st Avenue, SW
Aberdeen, SD 57401

Tennessee
800-342-1663
Student Assistance Corporation
404 James Robertson Parkway
Parkway Towers, Suite 1510
Nashville, TN 37243

Texas
800-845-6267
Guaranteed Student Loan Corp.
Box 83100
Round Rock, TX 78683

Utah
800-418-8757
Higher Ed. Assistance Auth.
60 South 400 West
Salt Lake City, UT 84101

Vermont
800-642-3177
Student Assistance Corporation
10 East Allen Street
Box 2000
Winooski, VT 05404

Virginia
888-775-3262
Education Credit Mgmt. Corp.
7325 Beaufant Springs Dr., #200
Richmond, VA 23225

Washington
800-562-3001
NW Education Loan Assoc.
190 Queen Anne North, #300
Seattle, WA 98109

West Virginia
See Pennsylvania

Wisconsin
800-236-5900
Great Lakes Higher Ed. Corp.
2401 International Lane
Madison, WI 53704

Wyoming
See USA Funds

America Samoa
See USA Funds

Guam
See USA Funds

Marshall Islands
See USA Funds

Federated States of Micronesia
See USA Funds

Commonwealth of the Northern Mariana Islands
See USA Funds

Republic of Palau,
See USA Funds

Puerto Rico
See Wisconsin

Virgin Islands
See Wisconsin

USA Funds
866-329-7673
P.O. Box 6028
Indianapolis, IN 46206

American Student Assistance
(ASA)
617-728-4200
800-999-9080
100 Cambridge Street
Boston, MA 02114

CHAPTER 12

■■■■■■■■■■■■■■■■■■■■■

WAIT, THERE'S MORE
(ADDITIONAL SOURCES OF
FEDERAL STUDENT AID}

Campus-Based Aid Programs

Uncle funds several additional programs—Supplemental Educational Opportunity Grants, Work-Study, ACG/SMART Grants and TEACH grants—that are campus-based. This means Uncle provides money for the programs, but gives it to the colleges to dispense in accordance with federal guidelines. Most of the money goes to full- and half-time students, however, a small sum will go to part-time students.

Supplemental Educational Opportunity Grants (SEOG)

Uncle will give the colleges $757 million for SEOGs next year. Colleges must match 25% of this money with funds of their own.

Size of awards. From $100 to $4,000 per year of undergraduate study.

Eligibility. Over 1.25 million undergraduates receive average grants of $762; priority goes to those receiving Pells.

Criteria for Selection. Need and fund availability. Be smart. Apply early.

Work-Study

Uncle will give colleges over $1 billion for work-study next year. Colleges are supposed to match some of this money with funds of their own.

Eligibility. Undergraduate and graduate students. Over 780,000 students receive an average of $1,500 each.

Criteria for Selection. Need and fund availability. Be smart. Apply early.

Program Description. On- and off-campus employment. Salary must at least equal minimum wage. You cannot earn more than your award stipulates. Thus, if you receive a $1,000 award, your employment lasts until you earn $1,000 and then it terminates for that academic year.

Schools are encouraged to use some of this money to fund community service jobs, including projects that will prepare communities to cope with emergencies and natural disasters. Employment may not involve political or religious activity nor may students be used to replace regular employees.

Academic Competitiveness Grants and SMART Grants

The federal budget for 2010 includes $1.386 billion for these two new grant programs. States and colleges will be responsible for helping to identify eligible students—as many as 996,000 students could qualify.

Academic Competitiveness Grants award up to $750 to first-year Pell-eligible students and $1,300 to second-year Pell-eligible students provided these students maintain at least a 3.0 GPA and complete a "rigorous second-ary-school program of study" that prepares them for college, e.g., 4 years of English, 3 years of math, 3 years of lab science (biology, chemistry, physics), 3 years of social science, and one year of a foreign language.

National Science and Mathematics Access to Retain Talent (SMART) Grants award up to $4,000 per year to Pell-eligible students in their third and fourth years of college. The average award is $3,176. To receive SMART funds, students must major in math, science, computer science or certain foreign languages (those deemed critical to national security) and they must maintain a 3.0 GPA in that major. If the school doesn't offer science majors, students must take courses that are equivalent to those of a science major.

TEACH Grants

Teacher Education Assistance for College and Higher Education (TEACH) Grants will award up to $4,000 per year (to a maximum of $16,000 for under-graduates and $8,000 for graduate students) to students completing the coursework necessary to begin a career in teaching.

You begin the process of applying for a TEACH Grant by indicating your interest in teaching when you complete the FAFSA. Like the other campus-based programs, the federal government gives money to the colleges to dispense. Next year, $75 million will be awarded to 25,000 recipients, for an average award of 3,000.

Recipients must agree to serve as a full-time teacher for at least four years in a high-need school within eight years of completing their course of study. Furthermore, they must teach Math, Science, Foreign Language, Special Ed, or some other subject deemed "high need" by the federal, state or local government. Students who do not fulfill their obligation must repay their TEACH Grant with interest as though it was an unsubsidized Stafford.

AmeriCorps (AmeriCorps.gov)

Participants receive a minimum wage stipend plus an annual education award for each year of full-time service (for up to two years). They may use the credit at any college or graduate school, or to pay down outstanding student loans. Furthermore, the money does not affect eligibility for other federal student aid. Previously the credit was $4,725 per year. In 2009, it increases to $5,350 per year and will be tied in value to the maximum Pell.

Currently, about 50,000 students serve in 450 different programs with Uncle providing most of the funding, but states and nonprofits doing the hiring. Prime projects are those that address unmet needs in education (assisting teachers in Head Start), the environment (recycling or conservation projects), human services (building housing for the homeless) or public safety (leading drug education seminars).

The new Edward M. Kennedy Serve America Act reauthorizes and expands national service programs, increasing the number of AmeriCorps positions to 250,000 by 2017 and introducing two new programs. In both of these new programs, recipients must use their awards within ten years.

1. **Summer of Service.** $500 education awards for 6-12th graders who perform 100 hours of service. ($750 for economically-disadvantaged students). Students may earn two of these awards.

2. **Silver Scholar.** $1,000 education awards for volunteers age 55 and older who perform 350 hours of service. Silver Scholar awards may be transferred to a child or grandchild.

While AmeriCorps is small in scope, its real importance has been to focus attention on our county's extensive network of service programs. With AmeriCorps adding new structure, and a solid core of workers, these programs have become a magnet for corporate money as well as for volunteers with only an hour to spare. The funded projects have brought huge economic benefits to the communities in which they operate as well as a heightened sense of personal and social responsibility for the AmeriCorps participants.

Interested students should apply directly to a funded program (for a list, visit www.AmeriCorps.gov, 800/94-ACORPS).

What Else Is New?

The Higher Education Act (which establishes the main federal student aid programs) expires every five years. In between reauthorizations, Congress passes a variety of smaller pieces of legislation. The most recent proposal is called the "Student Aid and Fiscal Responsibility Act." At press time it had been passed by the House, and given good reviews by the Administration, but not yet considered by the Senate.

Student Aid and Fiscal Responsibility Act
Pell Grants
- Increase the maximum Pell Grant from $5,350 to $5,550.
- Beginning in 2011, tie future increases in the Pell Grant to increases in the CPI (plus 1%)

Stafford/PLUS Loans
- Eliminate subsidized Stafford loans to graduate and professional students.

- Beginning July 1, 2010, end the Federal Family Education Loan Program, and convert all federal student loans (Stafford and PLUS) to the Direct Loan Program.
- Beginning July 1, 2012, tie interest rates to the 91-day Treasury Bill plus 2.3%, not to exceed 6.8%.

Free Application for Federal Student Aid (FAFSA)

- Simplify the FAFSA by allowing families to transfer income information (electronically) from their tax returns

Needs Analysis

- Beginning July 1, 2011, families with assets of more than $150,000 would not be eligible for need-based federal grants and loans; they would be eligible for work-study.
- The asset cap would increase each year, based on changes to the Consumer Price Index.

Highlights from The Higher Education Opportunity Act of 2008

After five years of deliberation, the new 1,158-page "Higher Education Opportunity Act" was approved overwhelmingly by the House and Senate, and promptly signed into law by President Bush. Here are some highlights:

Pell Grants and ACG/SMART Grants

- Increase the minimum Pell from $400 to 10% of the maximum grant.
- Enable low-income students to receive Pell Grants year-round.

Stafford/PLUS/Perkins Loans

- Increase Perkins loan limits for undergraduates from $4,000 to $5,500 and for graduate students from $6,000 to $8,000. Increase aggregate loans limits for undergraduates from $20,000 to $27,500 and for graduate students from $40,000 to $60,000.
- Allow service members to defer payments, interest-free, on Federal Direct Loans while they are on active duty.
- Expand federal loan forgiveness for students who become prosecutors, public defenders, teachers, and other public-service professions.

Free Application for Federal Student Aid

- Simplify the FAFSA and introduce EZ-Fafsa for low-income students.
- Phase out the paper FAFSA.

College Costs

- Provide in-state tuition for members of the Armed Forces and their dependents who have lived in a state for more than 30 days.
- Require colleges with the greatest cost increases to submit reports to the Secretary of Education explaining why their costs have risen, and what steps they are taking to hold costs down.

APPENDIX

■■■■■■■■■■■■■■■■

DETERMINING ELIGIBILITY
ENHANCING ELIGIBILITY
RETAINING ELIGIBILITY

Student Assets

Student assets are assessed at a higher rate than parental assets (20% versus 5.6%). If a family can choose between leaving junior's assets in junior's own bank account or maintaining them in the parents' account, opt for the parental account. For example, the Lay family has an Expected Family Contribution of $10,000. State U. Costs $11,000, making them eligible for $1,000 in need-based aid (most likely, a subsidized loan). Daughter Frieda keeps $3,500 in a bank account, in her name. That sum, all by itself, chips in $700 of the family's EFC. If the Lays closed out Frieda's account (with her approval, of course) and added the money to the family account, the EFC would drop to $9,496 ($9,500 with rounding). The family is now eligible for $1,500 in need-based aid.

Of course, the family could also use Frieda's $3,500 to buy her a new laptop computer, printer, and other essential back-to-school gadgets. Then, the EFC drops to $9,300.

Student Income

Fifty percent of a student's after-tax income (over $4,500) counts towards student aid eligibility. If possible, students might spend less time flipping burgers and more time doing interesting volunteer work. Reducing their student's income from $5,500 to $4,500 can lower EFC by $500.

Retaining Your Eligibility

Students must make "satisfactory academic progress" to continue receiving federal aid. Usually this means at least a "C" average or academic standing consistent with the school's requirements for graduation. Some students lose eligibility because they didn't realize the academic pace in college is faster than in high school. They overloaded themselves with courses and flunked them all. Don't let this happen to you. If you are not sure of your ability to handle college-level work, test the water before plunging in. You'll be a lot happier, and a lot richer.

■■■■■■■■■■■■■■■■■

Dependent Students
(2010/2011 Academic Year)

Parent's Contribution from Income

1. Parents' Adjusted Gross Income .... $_____
2. Parents' Tax-exempt Interest Income .... $_____
3. Veteran's Non-educational Benefits .... $_____
4. Parents' Other Untaxed Income and Benefits.
   This may include child support received, untaxed portions of pensions and
   IRA distributions, workers' compensation, disability payments, housing,
   food and living allowances for military, clergy or others .... $_____
5. Deductible IRA, Keogh, SEP, 403 (b), 401(k) pymnts made by parents ... $_____
6. **Total Income.** Add Lines 1 through 5 .... $_____
7. US Income Taxes paid .... $_____
8. State Income Taxes paid .... $_____
9. Social Security/Medicare Taxes paid .... $_____
10. Child Support paid by you for another child .... $_____
11. Hope credit and/or Lifetime Learning credit, AmeriCorps awards, taxable
    earnings from Federal Work-Study (or other need-based work program)
    and other student financial aid that may have been included in Line 6. .... $_____
12. Income Protection Allowance from Table A .... $_____
13. Employment Expense Allowance. If both parents work, enter 35% of
    the lower income or $3,500, whichever is less. If your family has a
    single head of household, enter 35% of that income or $3,500, whichever
    is less. Otherwise, enter $0 .... $_____
14. **Total Allowances.** Add Lines 7 through 13 .... $_____
15. **Parents' Available Income.** Line 6 minus Line 14. If negative, subtract
    from Line 30 .... $_____

Parents Contribution from Assets[1]

16. Cash, savings and checking accounts .... $_____
17. Net Worth of real estate (excluding primary residence), investments, stocks,
    CDs, bonds, trusts, commodities, precious metals, college savings plans . $_____
18. Business and/or Commercial Farm Net Worth (excluding family farms
    and family-controlled small businesses) from Table B .... $_____
19. **Total Assets.** Add Lines 16 through 18 .... $_____
20. Asset Protection Allowance. From Table C .... $_____
21. Discretionary Net Worth. Line 19 minus Line 20 .... $_____
22. **CONTRIBUTION FROM ASSETS.** Multiply Line 21 by 12%.
    If negative, enter $0 .... $_____

Parental Contribution

23. Adjusted Available Income. Add Lines 15 and 22 .... $_____
24. **PARENT CONTRIBUTION.** From Table D. If negative, enter 0. .... $_____
25. Number in College Adjustment. Divide Line 24 by the number in college at
    least half-time (excluding parents). Quotient is the contribution/student .. $_____

Student's Contribution from Income

26. Student's Adjusted Gross Income .... $_____
27. Student's Tax-exempt Interest Income .... $_____
28. Student's Other Untaxed income and benefits. See Line 4.
    Also include any cash support paid on your behalf which was not
    reported elsewhere .... $_____
29. Deductible IRA payments made by student .... $_____
30. Total Income. Add lines 26 through 29 .... $_____
31. US Income Taxes paid .... $_____
32. State Income Taxes paid .... $_____
33. Social Security/Medicare Taxes paid .... $_____
34. AmeriCorps awards, student financial aid that may have been included
    in Line 30, taxable earnings from Federal Work-Study or other
    need-based work programs .... $_____
35. Income Protection Allowance. Enter $4,500 .... $_____
36. Total Allowances. Add Lines 31 through 35 .... $_____
37. Students Available Income. Line 30 minus Line 36 .... $_____
38. **STUDENT'S CONTRIBUTION FROM INCOME**
    Multiply Line 37 by 50%. If negative, enter $0 .... $_____

Student's Contribution from Assets[1]

39. Add net worth of all of student's assets—cash, savings, trusts,
    investments, real estate .... $_____
40. **STUDENT'S CONTRIBUTION FROM ASSETS**
    Take 20% of Line 39 .... $_____

Family Contribution

41. If one student is in college, add lines 24, 38, and 40. .... $_____
42. If two or more students are in college at the same time,
    add for each, Lines 25, 38, and 40. .... $_____

Notes to Appendices

[1] Contribution from student and parent assets will equal $0 if Parents' AGI (Line 1) is
    less than $50,000 and the parents are eligible to file a 1040A, 1040 EZ, or no tax
    return at all.

[2] Contribution from assets will equal $0 if student (and spouse) AGI (Line 1) is less
    than $50,000 and the student (and spouse) are eligible to file a 1040A or 1040EZ
    or no tax return at all.

■■■■■■■■■■■■■■■■■■■■■■■■■■■■■■■■■■

INDEPENDENT STUDENTS WITH DEPENDENTS (2010/2011 ACADEMIC YEAR)

Contribution from Income (Student's and Spouse's)

1. Student's (and Spouse's) Adjusted Gross Income .... $_____
2. Student's (and Spouse's) Tax-exempt Interest Income .... $_____
3. Student's (and Spouse's) Veteran's Non-educational Benefits .... $_____
4. Student's (and Spouse's) Other Untaxed Income and Benefits.
    This may include child support received,untaxed portions of pensions and
    IRA distributions, workers' compensation, disability payments, housing,
    food and living allowances for military, clergy or others .... $_____
5. Deductible IRA, KEOGH, 403 (b) and 401(k) payments made by
    student (and spouse) .... $_____
6. **Total Income.** Add Lines 1 through 5 .... $_____
7. US Income Taxes paid .... $_____
8. State Income Taxes paid .... $_____
9. Social Security/Medicare Taxes paid .... $_____
10. Child Support paid by you for another child .... $_____
11. Hope credit, Lifetime Learning credit, AmeriCorps awards, taxable
    earnings from Federal Work-Study (or other need-based work program)
    and other student financial aid that may have been included in Line 6. .... $_____
12. Income Protection Allowance from Table A .... $_____
13. Employment Expense Allowance. If both student and spouse work, enter
    35% of the lower income or $3,500, whichever is less. If student qualifies
    as a single head of household, enter 35% of that income or $3,500,
    whichever is less. Otherwise, enter $0 .... $_____
14. **Total Allowances.** Add Lines 7 through 13 .... $_____
15. **Student's (and Spouse's) Available Income.** Line 6 minus Line 14 .... $_____

Contribution from Assets (Student's and Spouse's)[2]

16. Cash, savings and checking accounts .... $_____
17. Net Worth of real estate (excluding primary residence), investments, stocks,
    bonds, trusts, commodities, precious metals, college savings plans .... $_____
18. Business and/or Commercial Farm Net Worth (excluding family farms
    and family-controlled small businesses) from Table B .... $_____
19. **Total Assets.** Add Lines 16 through 18 .... $_____
20. Asset Protection Allowance. From Table E .... $_____
21. Discretionary Net Worth. Line 19 minus Line 20 .... $_____
22. **CONTRIBUTION FROM ASSETS.** Multiply Line 21 by 7%. .... $_____
23. Adjusted Available Income. Add Line 15 and Line 22. .... $_____
24. **TOTAL CONTRIBUTION.** From Table D. If negative, enter 0. .... $_____
25. Number in College Adjustment. Divide Line 24 by the number in college
    at least half-time at the same time. Quotient is the contribution/student ... $_____

■■■■■■■■■■■■■■■■■■■■■■■■■■■■

INDEPENDENT STUDENTS WITHOUT DEPENDENTS (2010/2011 ACADEMIC YEAR)

Contribution from Income (Student's and Spouse's)

1. Student's (and Spouse's) Adjusted Gross Income .... $_____
2. Student's (and Spouse's) Tax-exempt Interest Income .... $_____
3. Student's (and Spouse's) Earned Income Credit .... $_____
4. Student's (and Spouse's) Other Untaxed Income and Benefits.
   This may include child support received,untaxed portions of pensions and
   IRA distributions, workers' compensation, disability payments, housing,
   food and living allowances for military, clergy or others .... $_____
5. Deductible IRA, KEOGH, 403 (b) and 401(k) payments made by
   student (and spouse) .... $_____
6. **Total Income.** Add Lines 1 through 5 .... $_____
7. US Income Taxes paid .... $_____
8. State Income Taxes paid .... $_____
9. Social Security/Medicare Taxes paid .... $_____
10. Income Protection Allowance of $7,780 for single student or
    married student if spouse is also enrolled in college at least half time;
    $12,460 for married student if spouse is not enrolled at least half-time .... $_____
11. Child Support paid by you for another child .... $_____
11. Hope Tax credit, Lifetime Learning credit, AmeriCorps awards, taxable
    earnings from Federal Work-Study (or other need-based work program)
    and other student financial aid that may have been included in Line 6. .... $_____
13. Employment Expense Allowance. If the student is single, enter $0. If the
    student is married and both the student and spouse are working, enter 35%
    of the lower income or $3,500, whichever is less. Otherwise, enter $0 .... $_____
14. **Total Allowances.** Add Lines 7 through 13 .... $_____
15. **Available Income.** Line 6 minus Line 14 .... $_____
16. **Contribution from Income**. Take 50% of Line 15 .... $_____

Contribution from Assets (Student's and Spouse's)[2]

17. Cash, savings and checking accounts .... $_____
18. Net Worth of real estate (excluding primary residence), investments, stocks,
    bonds, trusts, commodities, precious metals, college savings plans .... $_____
19. Business and/or Commercial Farm Net Worth (excluding family farms
    and family-controlled small businesses) from Table B .... $_____
20. **Total Assets.** Add lines 17 through 19 .... $_____
21. Asset Protection Allowance. From Table E .... $_____
22. Discretionary Net Worth. Line 20 minus Line 21 .... $_____
23. **CONTRIBUTION FROM ASSETS.** Multiply Line 22 by 20%.
    If negative, enter $0 .... $_____
24. **TOTAL CONTRIBUTION.** Add Line 16 and Line 23 .... $_____
25. Number in College Adjustment. Divide Line 24 by the number in college
    at least half-time at the same time. Quotient is the contribution/ student .. $_____

Table A—Income Protection Allowance

Family Members (Incl. Student)	Dep. Student Allowance	Indep. Stdnt Allowance
2	$16,230	$19,690
3	$20,210	$24,510
4	$24,970	$30,280
5	$29,460	$35,730
6	$33,460	$41,780
Each Addit'l	$3,890	$4,710

Note: *For each student over one in college, subtract $2,760 from the appropriate maintenance allowance (for dependent students) or $3,350 from the appropriate maintenance allowance (for independent students).*

Table B—Adjustment of Business/Farm Net Worth

Net Worth of Business/Farm	Adjustment
To $115,000	40% of Net Worth
$115,001 to $345,000	$46,000, plus 50% of NW over $115,000
$345,001 to $580,000	$161,000, plus 60% of NW over $345,000
$580,501 or more	$302,000 plus 100% of NW over $580,000

Table C—Asset Protection Allowance, Dependent Student

Age of Older Parent	Two-Parent Family	One Parent Family
40-44	$43,300	$17,100
45-49	48,900	19,100
50-54	55,500	21,500
55-59	63,500	24,300
60-64	73,200	27,800
65 +	80,300	30,100

Table D—Parent and Independent Student Contribution

Adjusted Available Income (AAI)	Parent Contribution
To minus $3,409	-$750 (negative figure)
Minus $3,409 to plus $14,500	22% of AAI
$14,501 to $18,200	$3,190 plus 25% of AAI over $14,500
$18,201 to $21,900	$4,115 plus 29% of AAI over $18,200
$21,901 to $25,600	$5,188 plus 34% of AAI over $21,900
$25,601 to $29,300	$6,446 plus 40% of AAI over $25,600
$29,301 or more	$7,926 plus 47% of AAI over $29,300

Table E—Asset Protection Allowance, Independent Student

Age	Single	Married
25 & Under	$ 0	$ 0
26	1,100	2,800
29	4,400	11,100
32	7,700	19,400
35	10,900	27,700
38	14,200	36,000
45	18,300	46,600
50	20,500	52,900
65+	30,100	80,300

CALCULATIONS

College Planning Guides from Octameron

Don't Miss Out: The Ambitious Student's Guide to Financial Aid **$14.00**

Hailed as the top consumer guide to student aid, Don't Miss Out covers scholarships, loans, and personal finance strategies. It will save readers hundreds, if not thousands of dollars in college costs.

The A's and B's of Academic Scholarships **$13.00**

Money for being bright! This book describes 100,000 awards offered by nearly 1200 colleges. Best of all, most of these (which must be used at the sponsoring school) are not based on financial need.

Loans and Grants from Uncle Sam **$8.00**

Increase your eligibility for federal student aid. This guide describes it all—the aid application process as well as loans and grants for students, parents and health professionals.

Financial Aid FinAncer: Expert Answers to College Financing Questions **$8.00**

Learn how special family circumstances impact on student aid.

The Winning Edge: The Student-Athlete's Guide to College Sports **$9.00**

It's all here. Scholarship opportunities. NCAA rules and regulations. Advice from coaches. Sample athletic resumes. Strategies, timetables, and worksheets—all to help you take your sport to college!

Behind the Scenes: An Inside Look at the College Admission Process **$8.00**

Who get is, and why? Through questions and answer sections and case studies, you can view the admission process from the inside. Originally written by Ed Wall, former Dean of Admission at Amherst College; updated by Janet Adams-Wall, Director of College Counseling at The Governor's Academy.

Do It Write: How to Prepare a Great College Application **$8.00**

Personalize your essays so they stand out from the crowd. Author Gary Ripple is the former Admission Director at Lafayette College and the College of William and Mary

College Match: A Blueprint for Choosing the Best School for You **$12.00**

Author Steve Antonoff combines dozens of easy-to-use worksheets with lots of practical advice to make sure you find schools that meet your needs and your preferences.

Campus Pursuit: Making the Most of the Visit and Interview **$7.00**

Nervous about your interview? In his companion book to Do-It Write, Gary Ripple gives advice to help you shine, as well as show you how to maximize the benefits of a campus visit.

College.edu: On-Line Resources for the Cyber-Savvy Student **$12.00**

Lost in Cyberspace? College.edu takes you to hundreds of useful sites on admission and financial aid, giving you Internet tips and warnings along the way.

Campus Daze: Easing the Transition from High School to College **$8.00**

Learn what to expect during your first year of college and how to succeed starting on Day One. Author George Gibbs is the former Dean of Admission and Freshmen at Muhlenberg College.

College Majors That Work **$10.00**

Get in. Get out. Get a job. Worksheets help match a student's goals and expectations with the right college major and explores how that choice plays out in the real world—influencing both career and lifestyle options. Written by Michael P. Viollt, President of Robert Morris College (IL).

Desk Set **$85.00**

One copy of each of the above publications.

Ordering Information

Send Orders to: Octameron Associates, PO Box 2748, Alexandria, VA 22301, or contact us at: 703-836-5480 (voice), 703-836-5650 (fax), octameron@aol.com (e-mail).

Order Online: www.octameron.com.

Postage and Handling: Please include $3.00 for one publication, $5.00 for two publications $6.00 for three publications and $7.00 for four or more publications (and for Desk Sets).

Method of Payment: Payment must accompany order. We accept checks, money orders, American Express, Visa and MasterCard. If ordering by credit card, please include the card number and its expiration date.

64041425R00044

For information address:

SAGE Publications, Inc.
2455 Teller Road
Newbury Park, California 91320

SAGE Publications Ltd.
6 Bonhill Street
London EC2A 4PU
United Kingdom

SAGE Publications India Pvt. Ltd.
M-32 Market
Greater Kailash I
New Delhi 110 048 India

Printed in the United States of America

Library of Congress Cataloging-in-Publication Data

Main entry under title:
Harrison, Michael I.
    Diagnosing organizations.

    (Applied social research methods series ; v. 8)
    Bibliography: p.
    Includes index.
    1. Organizational behavior.   2. Organizational change.
I. Title.   II. Series.
HD58.7.H3697   1986   302.3'5   86-13078
ISBN 0-8039-2626-X
ISBN 0-8039-2627-8 (pbk.)

93   94   15   14

DIAGNOSING ORGANIZATIONS

Methods, Models, and Processes

Michael I. Harrison

Applied Social Research Methods Series
Volume 8

 SAGE PUBLICATIONS
The International Professional Publishers
Newbury Park   London   New Delhi

D0327598

HARBINGERS 18

Interesting Times

Jeff Gerke

Angela Hunt, Alton Gansky,
and Bill Myers

Published by Amaris Media International.
Copyright © 2017 Jeff Gerke
Cover Design: Angela Hunt
Photo credits: © *flexire* —fotolia.com

ISBN-13:978-1543118896
ISBN-10:1543118895

For more information, visit us on Facebook:
https://www.facebook.com/pages/Harbingers/705107309586877
or *www.barbingersseries.com.*

HARBINGERS

A novella series by
Bill Myers, Jeff Gerke, Angela Hunt,
and Alton Gansky

In this fast-paced world with all its demands, the four of us wanted to try something new. Instead of the longer novel format, we wanted to write something equally as engaging but that could be read in one or two sittings—on the plane, waiting to pick up the kids from soccer, or as an evening's read.

We also wanted to play. As friends and seasoned novelists, we thought it would be fun to create a game we could participate in together. The rules were simple:

Rule #1

Each of us will write as if we were one of the characters in the series:

Bill Myers will write as Brenda, the street-hustling tattoo artist who sees images of the future.

Frank Peretti will write as the professor, the atheist ex-priest ruled by logic.

Jeff Gerke will write as Chad, the mind reader with devastating good looks and an arrogance to match.

Angela Hunt will write as Andi, the brilliant-but-geeky young woman who sees inexplicable patterns.

Alton Gansky will write as Tank, the naïve, big-hearted jock with a surprising connection to a healing power.

Rule #2

Instead of the five of us writing one novella

3

together (we're friends but not crazy), we would write it like a TV series. There would be an overarching storyline into which we'd plug our individual novellas, with each story written from our character's point of view.

If you're keeping track, this is the order:

Harbingers #1—*The Call*—Bill Myers
Harbingers #2—*The Haunted*—Frank Peretti
Harbingers #3—*The Sentinels*—Angela Hunt
Harbingers #4—*The Girl*—Alton Gansky

Volumes #1-4 omnibus: *Cycle One: Invitation*

Harbingers #5—*The Revealing*—Bill Myers
Harbingers #6—*Infestation*—Frank Peretti
Harbingers #7—*Infiltration*—Angela Hunt
Harbingers #8—*The Fog*—Alton Gansky

Volumes #5-8 omnibus: *Cycle Two: Mosaic*

Harbingers #9—*Leviathan*—Bill Myers
Harbingers #10—*The Mind Pirates*—Frank Peretti
Harbingers #11—*Hybrids*—Angela Hunt
Harbingers #12—*The Village*—Alton Gansky

Volumes 9-12 omnibus: *Cycle Three: The Probing*

Harbingers #13—*Piercing the Veil*—Bill Myers
Harbingers #14—*Home Base*—Jeff Gerke
Harbingers #15—*Fairy*—Angela Hunt
Harbingers #16—*At Sea*—Alton Gansky

Volumes 13-16 omnibus: *Cycle Four: The Pursuit*

Harbingers #17—*Piercing the Veil*—Bill Myers
Harbingers #18—*Interesting Times*—Jeff Gerke

There you have it, at least for now. We hope you'll find these as entertaining in the reading as we are in the writing.

Bill, Jeff, Angie, and Al

JEFF GERKE

Chapter 1

I have hooves.

I'm a stallion—what else? —and I'm trotting along a pebble beach. My hooves sink in the little rocks and water fills every footprint.

It's a dream, of course, or maybe a vision. Or else maybe I'm remote viewing and can't remember. One time, I fell asleep while casting my spirit around the South Pole. You can imagine how messed-up *those* dreams were. *A dweam wiffin a dweam* . . .

So I squish-clomp up to this thing in the water and I see it's the body of a pony. I think it's dead, the way the water rocks it and it doesn't stir. It's got a big hole in its back, but there's no blood.

Suddenly there are other horses around us. Not nearly as regal and beautiful as me, of course, but

horses all the same. I know there are three others there for sure, but sometimes there's a fourth, and over us all is this big half dome of flying mermaids— almost like a fishy band shell.

I know, right?

The other horses nuzzle the pony, but it doesn't move. Amateurs. I whinny at them (it sounded cooler in the dream—real manly and commanding) and they back away, awed by my splendor. I whisper into the pony's ear, and it springs right up.

No one thanks me, as usual. I'm about to complain, but a warm feeling comes over me and I decide it's okay this time. I look at the flying mermaids and, in the air above them, I can see the outline of a big ol' blue whale just floating there like it's swimming in air. Somehow, knowing the whale is there is really, really comforting.

The ground shakes below my hooves, and without looking, I know it's the bear. I couldn't tell you what bear, but in my dream, I know it's *the* bear. I look anyway.

It's one of those massive Kodiak brown bears. It's stomping around on the water way out at sea. We all know it's looking for something, and I realize before the rest of them that it's looking for us.

No, not us, exactly. The pony.

Everyone runs—er, gallops—away. Somehow we all know we have to get back to the classroom so I can find my backpack. As we're running, I see the hole in the pony's back, and I know it will heal in time and with help.

We're running in the school hallways. Our hooves clatter on the tile. People look at us as we gallop by. We try to get their help or warn them about the bear,

but they just look at us like they don't understand horse.

We get back into the classroom and I find my pack. The others get their packs too, and we all run out onto the kickball field.

The bear is already there, so we horses interpose ourselves between it and the pony, just daring the beast to make a move. We've got our packs now, after all.

Though I don't look up, I know the dome of mermaids is still over us and the blue whale is floating above our standoff as if the concerns of bears and ponies attract its attention but don't cause it any anxiety.

That gives me courage, so I stamp forward and rear up against the bear in challenge. The other horses do too, and this time there really are four others with me. The pony paces nervously behind us.

The giant brown bear rises on his own rear legs, and he towers over us. He gives us a slavering roar, his mouth held hideously wide open. Yellowed fangs block my vision and I hardly even notice when he lashes out with his claws. I hear heavy bodies falling around me and I reach into my backpack for the item of power.

Searing pain erupts on my neck and chest, and I fall to the dirt. The other horses writhe around me, all bleeding, all trying to get up to protect the smallest of us. But we can't.

The Kodiak bear drops to all fours with a deep *humph* and saunters forward, as if he's late for his nap and we were no more obstacle to him than a quintet of honey bees.

The pony backs away but bumps into the mesh

fence backstop. The bear closes in.

This is it. In the end, all we did was buy the little guy a few more minutes.

I feel my own life dwindling. The others are with me on this cosmic elevator going slowly up or down.

My vision dims, but now I see it's because I've been overshadowed. Not by the mermaids or the whale but by the pony, which is growing as I watch. It's already as tall as the bear and is expanding proportionately like someone scaling up an object in a 3D rendering program.

The pony is still young, but he's no longer weak. He lifts up his front hoof and holds it over the bear. The bear rises on his rear legs and claws at the air over him. The pony's nostrils flare and he brings the hoof down like he's executing a rattlesnake.

All I can see of the bear, as my vision dims for real this time, is a bit of brown fuzz at the edges of the hoof. The pony looks down at me, at all of us, and just stares.

Then he blinks and strides away, and I—

* * *

… I wake up.

Whew.

I was on my bed in the presidential suite of the DFW Grand Hyatt. Nothing seemed amiss. The green marble behind my headboard reflected the pink Texas sunrise. The crazy zigzag carpet still looked weird in here, though it was probably quite posh and stylish. Sounds of a trickling brook still piped from the white noise generator beside my king-sized bed. I felt drowsy and I was lying under the covers.

So, a dream, after all.

Not dead. That was good.

I threw on a plush white robe and slippers and padded out into the central suite. Early October sunlight gleamed off the hardwood floors, the dining table, the vase table, and the grand piano I'd had installed. Nobody in our group played keyboard, but it looked classy. Besides, nothing beat Daniel—or Tank—playing "Chopsticks" on a beautiful grand piano.

An image from the dream twinged my thoughts. The soothing presence of the floating whale, maybe. Whatever.

I spread out my awareness and located the other team members. As usual, they were all just about to—

The door to my suite opened, and all of them tramped in: Bjorn (a.k.a. "Tank," a.k.a. "Cowboy," a.k.a. "the Troll"), Brenda (a.k.a. "Ghetto," a.k.a. "Pain in My Buttocks"), Andi (a.k.a. "Sweet Cheeks," a.k.a. "Andrea"), and Daniel (a.k.a. "the kid").

A.K.A. The Pony.

I didn't know whose idea it was—certainly not mine, and I didn't remember ever agreeing to it—but somehow it had been decided that my suite was public property and the site for all group meetings, meals, and after-hours hangouts. Of course, I'd picked the very best spot in the entire Grand Hyatt for my room and their suites were middle class by comparison and I wouldn't have agreed to slum it in theirs anyway. But that was just it: I'd picked the best spot *for me*.

Whatever.

"Good morning, rookies," I said, quite politely. "Whose turn is it to fix my breakfast?"

Normally, that got a round of scowls and "Fix your own &%$@ toaster pastries." But this time, they

11

formed a semicircle around me in their robes and PJs and stood there as if waiting for something.

"What?" I could've read their little minds, but I hadn't had my coffee yet.

Andi folded her arms, which I thought was a shame, and blew one of those gorgeous red hairs out of her face. "We all had a dream. More or less the same dream. We're wondering if you did, too."

I sighed. "Oh, that." I walked through their circle and toward the couch, which sat beyond the piano. "You mean you all saw a floating whale and flying water nymphs too?" I plopped on the L-shaped couch and looked back at them. They seemed confused.

"If he didn't dream what we did," Tank said, "doesn't that mean . . . ?"

Brenda scowled. "That it wasn't really a message."

Tank hooted with relief and went to the piano bench. "You guys had me worried for a minute. Don't do that." He put the index fingers of both hands on side-by-side keys and started to play you know what.

I wished for the telekinetic ability to slam the lid down on his fingers.

The others drifted toward the couch, looking dazed.

Daniel dropped onto the coach beside me, a tablet in his hands. He seemed engrossed by whatever game he was playing, but he spoke to me. "They didn't see the whale or the mermaids, but it's the same dream." He sneaked a look at me. "Aren't you gonna tell them?"

The kid was good, no doubt. "All right, my little pony," I said. "I'll tell."

"Okay, you yokels," I said in a louder tone, "gather 'round Uncle Chad, and I'll tell you a story of knapsacks and schoolyards, and of horses and bears."

The lovely strains of "Chopsticks" came to an abrupt halt, though the lingering harmonics worked their way into my cranium.

Andi sat on the L couch, tucking her white bathrobe around her knees. Brenda, in her plaid house pants and black sleep shirt, settled in beside Daniel and pulled him closer.

Tank put both meaty hands on the back of the couch and leaned on them, just about toppling all of us backward. "Sorry," he said, letting go. "So you dreamed about the bear, too?"

"I did." I gave them a quick recap of my dream.

"Hey, Pretty Boy," Brenda said when I was through, "feeling superior and uncongratulated in your own dreams is pretty sad."

I shrugged. "There could never be enough appreciation in this life, so I do what I can to get along."

Andi rubbed both sides of her head irritably. "So what does it mean? We all dreamed about a big bear coming after—" she looked at Daniel— "one of us, and we're all horses that try to save him but can't, and then he gets huge and saves himself."

"*After* we're all dead." I nudged Daniel. "Thanks for that."

He smirked and tilted his head as if to say, *It's no bother, really.*

"What about what I saw in the clouds?" Brenda asked. "I saw tattoos in the clouds."

I chortled. Seriously, around these guys, I chortle a lot. I've become a chortler.

"Yes, tattoos," Brenda said. "Hey, shapes in the clouds make a whole lot more sense than flying mermaids, beluga boy."

"Fair point."

"I saw geometric shapes in the clouds," Andi said. "Tank?"

His cheeks shot with red and he froze.

"Duh," I said to Andi. "He saw you. Again. Probably naked."

That snapped the troll from his paralysis. "No! Not naked!" His eyes widened and he looked with fear at Andi. "I mean— You—" He waved a finger in the air vaguely. "Um, anybody want orange juice?" He turned and strode toward the kitchen.

"What about you?" I asked Daniel. "What did you dream about?"

He kept playing his game. "Nothing."

I cocked my head. "Nothing?"

Daniel shook his head.

"Huh."

We took a break to fix breakfast, then we sat around the dining table and ate.

Tank conspicuously bowed his head and prayed silently. It kind of ticked me off. I'd seen him eat alone before, and he didn't make such a big show of his prayer—if he even gave one—so why the big "Hey, look at me: I'm praying!" when we were around? When *I* was around.

I knew he prayed. He and I had even prayed together, back in Ye Olde Eden Towne. Plus, I thought praying to be *seen* praying was kind of a no-no in Jesus's book. But what did I know?

Actually, if I could be serious a minute, I had been asking that question a lot lately. But…not now.

There we sat, munching on toast or cereal or yogurt or Danish, as the sunlight went through the spectrum to a glaring white. Not many of us were morning people, so these meals were always subdued, but today seemed unusually quiet.

"So," Sweet Cheeks said, her milky skin and copper hair looking resplendent in the white light and white robe, despite the droplet of milk on her upper lip. "What does it mean?"

Tank spoke through a mouthful of toast and orange marmalade: "Which part?"

"All of it." Brenda reached for Daniel's tablet, which he was still playing with at the table, but he turned it off and tucked it under his legs. "The horses, the bear, the clouds—"

I chortled. "It doesn't have to mean anything. If the Watchers want to send us a message, they usually do it through e-mail or a stack of airline tickets or something. They don't generally use dreams. Some things *are* just coincidences."

Nobody seemed convinced.

"Bears are talked about in the Bible," Daniel said. "Sometimes they're used as a curse by God, like when the kids mocked the prophet Elisha and called him an old baldy."

Brenda's eyes went wide. "Where you getting this, boy?"

"And in the prophet Daniel's vision, one of the empires looks like a bear," he said. "The Medo-Persians, I think."

I pondered the kid's words, and the others seemed to be spinning their little mental hamster wheels, as well. "Yeah," I said, "but I really don't think the Medes and Persians are after us."

Andi raised a finger. "*Us?* So you think the horses were us."

"Duh."

"You know, that is really annoying," Brenda said, scrunching up her face at me.

I blew her a kiss.

"Also," Daniel said, "when you dream about a bear, it might mean you've got a pushy mother." He shrugged at Brenda. "One site said it could be some feeling about to break out. Or it could mean being strong or alone."

"I know you didn't just say *a pushy mother.*"

"Hey," I said, "don't argue with the literature."

"I'll push you both, you watch."

Tank pursed his lips. "I think it's the Antichrist."

We all stared at him.

"Say *what* now, big guy?" I said.

Tank shrugged those massive shoulders. "What else could it be?"

"Um...last night's chili?" I suggested.

Daniel shook his head at me. "We had lasagna."

"Shut up, kid."

"Think about it," Tank said. "I know you guys don't like it when I go all Bible on you, but seriously, am I the only one who remembers that we went to Iraq and just barely managed to not release the four angels of the Apocalypse chained under the Euphrates? You all sure believed in the Bible then. And what about the demons? And what about how 'Be Thou My Vision' drove away the devils? Don't stop there. What about all the things we've been dealing with since we first came together? You can cook up your fancy theories all day long, but nothing explains the Gate and those fog creatures and

everything else like a straight up reading of Revelation."

No one moved. No one made eye contact.

Finally, Andi adjusted herself in her chair. "Okay, Tank, just for the sake of discussion, let's say you're right and all of this is foretold in your New Testament."

"It's not just *my* New—"

"Sure, sure. But let's say you're right. What would the dream mean?"

Tank swallowed and focused on a spot above the maple syrup bottle. "It's weird. I mean, the Bible talks about the Antichrist as 'the beast from the sea,' and our bear was definitely out on the ocean. But this one was looking for something."

"You mean looking for *us*," Brenda said.

"It sure seemed like it, Miss Brenda. See, that's the weird part. Because the only time the Bible might be talking about the Antichrist looking for someone is when he's after the Two Witnesses."

I rolled my eyes. "Seriously?"

That got a chorus of *Shut ups* from the peanut gallery.

"Tank, honey," Brenda said, "pretend I skipped a whole lotta Sunday School. Who are the two witnesses? Like Jehovah's Witnesses?"

"The Two Witnesses," Daniel said, surprising us, "are in the end of the world. They rise up against the Antichrist and fight him. But he comes and kills them both. They lie dead on the street for a while, then God brings them back to life and takes them up to heaven."

Brenda's mouth dropped open. "Since when you know all this Bible, boy?"

He brought out the tablet from under his legs. "I'm not always playing games."

I shook my head and stood up to take my plates to the sink. "Well, while you guys are playing Bible Bingo, I'm going to start thinking about real possible explanations."

Tank looked sullen. "I thought you said it was last night's chili."

"I don't think that anymore," I said.

"Really?" Andi spun in her chair. "Why not?"

"Because last night...we had lasagna."

She stuck her tongue out at me.

Daniel's tablet emitted a triplet of musical tones.

"Turn that off," Brenda said.

Daniel stared at it. "It *is* off, Mom."

As we looked at the obviously powered-off device, it began to sing a nonstop line of musical triplets, until it was more irritating even than "Chopsticks."

"Make it stop!" I said, coming back to the table.

Daniel shook it and rotated it and finally turned it on. But instead of the lock screen I'd seen so many times—of an anime girl Daniel wouldn't admit he was hot for—an image appeared that shocked even me.

It was the professor.

Professor James McKinney looked like he'd spent the night in a dumpster. His left cheek and the side of his forehead were smeared with black grease—or something worse—and his hair was matted flat and wide like a political cartoon of Donald Trump's hairdo. I couldn't tell what he wore. Burlap rags, maybe? I'd never seen the guy in the flesh, just in that vision on the cruise ship. But I'd seen photos and video, and of course I'd heard Andi rave about him in her bouts of hero worship.

The question, of course, was why he was Skyping us from the netherworld.

"Omigosh, Professor?" Andi cried, leaping from her chair and coming to stand over Daniel to look

into the tablet. "Is that you? Can you hear us?"

Halfway through her words, as if there had been a distance delay, the professor's face registered recognition. "Andrea!" he said, overlapping her. "Is that you?"

The others shouted sundry blather at the screen, and for a while they exchanged inanities.

In the eventual lull, he looked at me. "Ah, Chad Thorton. In the flesh."

I bowed. "Doctor Who, I presume."

He looked at Andi. "Dr. Who?"

She waved the question away. "Where are you? How is this possible?"

The professor began to answer, then seemed to hear something and looked behind him. I noticed he was in what appeared to be a long, dark hallway, with shafts of light slanting in from the upper left of the screen. An abandoned horse barn somewhere in the Twilight Zone?

"I can't stay long," he said, "and I don't know if I'll ever be able to reach you like this again. But I think our friends gave us this because . . . Well, I should probably just begin."

"Let's move to the couch," I said, "so we can all see."

They took my suggestion—natch—and soon we were arrayed comfortably in the overstuffed L-shape. Somewhere along the way, Andi had seized the tablet and was holding it like a steering wheel on an icy road.

"I assume you all got the dream last night, about the bear."

It was surreal, hearing him talk about this unexplained phenomenon as if it were a TV show

we'd all watched. Par for the course, these days.

"We did," Andi said. "Everyone but Daniel."

"Good," he began, but then the delay intervened and he interrupted himself and listened. "Oh, Daniel—you didn't get the dream?"

"No, sir."

Lags in communication and reaction always made a person seem dense. I knew this man wasn't stupid, so I made myself keep ascribing intelligence to him. That, I found, was an underdeveloped practice .of mine, assuming people were intelligent who didn't seem like they were. It didn't help that he looked like a street bum.

The professor folded his arms and brought one hand up to pinch his bottom lip in thought. "How very odd." After a moment, he seemed to shake it off and lowered his arms. "I'm glad to see all of you, and to see you hale and well. That's good. You'll need that for what is to come." His eyes strayed to Daniel, and he fell silent.

"Professor," Andi said, "what did the dream mean? Are we in danger? Who or what is the bear?"

He started to answer a couple of times, but the delay got him, so he waited out all her questions before responding. "Are you in danger? Yes. Yes, I'm afraid you're in the greatest imaginable danger. The whole world is. Your entire dimension has come to a precipice none of you can see. The key moment is not this second, not this week, but so very soon." This time, his eyes went to Andi, and he smiled sadly. "It's wonderful to see you."

"Yeah, yeah," I said. "Let's get back to our doomed dimension, can we?"

"Professor," Tank said, "the bear in our dreams—

it's the Antichrist, isn't it?"

Even accounting for the delay, the professor paused a long time before responding. "As you know, I haven't always ascribed to such things. But as I told you on the ship, I've had a change of heart. Besides, here in this . . . where I am . . . things are different. The Gate, the Watchers, the creatures you've seen, the bear—even you all and the other teams, all of these are complex and colored from my perspective. Everything is partially this and somewhat that and altogether this other thing, except for those times when it's utterly not."

I caught Brenda mouthing *Other teams?* to Andi, who shrugged.

"From what I can gather," the professor said, "the Gate is comprised of beings you would call aliens. Extraterrestrials. Except for those times when they are spirits like ghosts or ghouls or, yes, even demons. Except not always. And they don't come from another world but another dimension. Not this one, thankfully, but the one next door, perhaps. The Watchers are very different but exactly the same, if you follow. They're from another dimension and they're spirits, and they're very much living beings.

"The two groups are at war—a war that's gone on a long time, I gather—and both groups are preparing for an end game. They both talk about the next phase of history, though 'history' is entirely the wrong word. The Gate is always trying to advance to this next phase. To force things forward. They've tried again and again across the millennia. Very nearly made it a couple of times, from what I've seen. But something always thwarts them.

"The time is nearly ripe for them to try again, and

this is why you have seen the massive uptick in paranormal and other bizarre behavior in your dimension. Indeed, the Gate's readiness for their latest attempt to push us across the threshold to the End is the single reason your team was summoned and brought together. It was your group's genesis." Something about that struck him as amusing and he all but grinned.

Oh, I got it: Genesis and Revelation, beginning and end.

"So the bear isn't the 'beast from the sea,'" I said. "It's just the boss for this level."

The professor cocked his head. "I'm sorry: *boss?*"

"Oh, you know," I said, "the eight-hundred-pound gorilla they're bringing this time to squash all resistance so the aliens-that-are-sometimes-demons can have their way with the world and move to the next level of dimensional beautification."

Andi sent me a mean look. "Stop wasting his time! We have no idea how long we'll have him."

I gave her a hands-off gesture.

"It's quite all right, Andrea," the professor said. "Chad, as I understand it, the Gate has had, over the centuries, many of what you might call antichrists. More accurately, they have had many *potential* antichrists, or many antichrist *candidates,* over the millennia. The usual list: Nero, Genghis Khan, Hitler, Saddam Hussein, etc. It seems the first thing the Gate must do before making any move to shove time into the next phase is to secure their Antichrist nominee. Once they've got him—or her, I suppose—they can concentrate on taking action."

"Wait," Brenda said. "You said the bat-crazy stuff we've been seeing is because they're ready for their

next big shove, right? Don't that mean—"

The professor inserted his "That's correct" at the appropriate moment when he heard her comment on his end, but by the time it reached us, it seemed like a rude interruption.

Brenda just kept going. "Don't that mean they've already got their guy? Their wanna-be beast?"

I thought, but did not say, *Wanna-beast*.

"Yes, of course they do," the professor said. "And you've already heard his name. I've given you a file on him."

I instantly remembered the mysterious silver folder the professor had given Andi, and it looked as if the others remembered it too.

"Ambrosi Giacomo," Daniel said.

The professor pointed at him. "That's the one."

"He has a human mother and some kind of 'higher reality' father," Tank said. "He's their Antichrist . . . candidate? So he's the bear?"

"Y—" the professor began, but the delay got him so he waited. "Yes, I think it's a fair conclusion that Giacomo is the bear in your dream and that he's looking for you." He looked over his shoulder again and leaned forward. "The Gate is nearly ready to strike. Only one more piece to move into position. But this is our chance to stop him."

I thought he was going to keep explaining, but he stopped. Belatedly, I wondered how he was communicating with us. He didn't seem to have a phone or anything. I shrugged. "So . . . ?" I prompted.

"Well," the professor said, as if surprised he needed to say more, "you've got to find him and kill him, of course."

* * *

We sat in silence. I stared at the fish in the big aquarium in the wall of my suite. Find a half-spirit/half-human übermensch who has the aid of supernatural minions, corner him somehow, and bring an end to his dreams of dimensional domination?

I had been born for this.

I clapped my hands, startling the mares and gelding. "Finally! When do we start?"

They all gave me verbal forms of "What?" but I leaned into the tablet's camera lens.

"How do we find him, Prof? And how do we kill him?"

Tank waved his hand. "Wait just a minute. Nobody's killing anybody. I didn't get into this to become an assassin."

"Oh, shut up," I said. "We've killed scores of times just since I joined."

"Yeah," Brenda said, taking up the cause, "but those were machines and monsters and demons. This is—"

I squeezed my eyes shut. "So what? Seriously, you people. This Ambrosi Giacomo is a half-alien, half-human chimera. You don't get more monstrous than that."

"Everybody, be quiet!" Andi wrested the tablet from me. "Professor, what can you tell us? How can we do this? Where do we even start?"

But the professor seemed not to have heard, and his image flashed with digital fuzz. I got the feeling we were about to lose him.

"If you fail, the world will be plunged into a

darkness so deep it will never recover. Even if you thwart the Gate's plans but fail to kill Giacomo, he will unleash a terror on the level of Hitler and Stalin combined. If you would prevent disaster, you must kill Ambrosi Giacomo. Doing so will . . ." fuzz covered bits of his sentence . . . "set them back . . .—ty years, at leas . . . —ust kill . . .—como!" He leaned back as if spent.

The others shouted questions at him, but the screen strobed fuzz now and I was left with an image of the professor looking at all of us with sadness, especially Andi, and then a piercing look at Daniel.

The connection failed at last, and the tablet displayed Daniel's lock screen picture.

"Okay," I said. "I need to get busy on this. Which means you people need to get out of my way. Come on, up you go. Out, out, out. Back to your rooms."

Brenda folded her arms and, I think, willed herself to gain about three tons. "I ain't goin' nowhere. The professor said this was *our* job. All of ours. Not just your skinny butt's."

"But we're not seriously talking about killing anyone, right?" Tank asked. No one replied, so he touched Andi's shoulder. "Right?"

She turned to me. "If I understood him correctly, that may be our job. Maybe the only job, in the end, that we were assembled to do."

The big guy looked like he might actually break down and cry.

We sat in a state of communal thoughtfulness. The fish drifted placidly in the tank.

Andi spoke again. "I mean, think about it: If our team hadn't been gathered in the first place, we wouldn't know about the Gate and all the

supernatural things going on in the world. And Dr. McKinney wouldn't be where he is, so he wouldn't have discovered what the Gate was planning, which would mean *we* wouldn't have discovered what they were planning. We might not have had any warning at all, and Ambrosi Giacomo and the Gate might've succeeded in . . . doing that thing he described about the next phase of time. But now we know and have a chance to do something about it before it's too late."

Brenda shook her head. "Y'all really believe that?"

"Which parts?" I asked.

"The end of the world. The sea beast. A dude worse than Hitler."

"And—" Tank said, striding around the room with his fingers to his forehead— "that now we're suddenly freaking assassins! Is that seriously what you guys signed up for?"

"Get over it, Muscles," I said. "So we kill another supernatural monstrosity, so what?"

"So what? We're not killers, that's so what."

"Pansy."

Tank rounded the couch and came at me. "I've had enough out of you, fancy . . . mouth."

I backed away but couldn't keep from grinning. "Fancy mouth? You don't threaten people much, do you?"

Andi leapt between us. "Guys, stop it!"

Daniel said something but I didn't catch it. I was more worried about the troll in his PJs bearing down on me.

"What, Daniel?" Andi said, both hands on Tank's chest, which I'm sure he loved. "What did you say? Something defusing, maybe?"

We all turned to look at him.

Daniel shrugged. "I said it's different this time."

"What is, sugar?" Brenda asked.

"I mean, usually, we get airplane tickets or a car comes for us or something, right? Or at least an e-mail. But this time . . ." He gestured to his tablet.

"He's right," Andi said, escorting/pushing Tank to the couch.

I relaxed a smidge. "Don't you think the Skype call from beyond was our message?"

"Yes and no," Andi said. "Daniel's right: This one's different. We have no destination. We don't know where to go, so how can they send a plane ticket?"

Brenda swore and pulled her legs up under her on the couch. "Don't that mean *they* don't know where he is?"

"Of course that's what it means," I said. "For the first time, the Watchers don't see. Our advisors can't advise because *they don't know.* The quarry is mobile and unpredictable. It's up to us to find him. If we can predict his movements and guess where he'll be in time to intercept him, we can save the world from the next Hitler-Stalin madman."

Tank glared at me from beneath a Neanderthal brow. "And just how are we supposed to do that?"

At least they were seeing the need for me to lead them. "We try the easy ways first," I said. "We check the news and Google for announcements about where he's going to be in the next few days. We also ask the Watchers if they can provide any clues at all." I put my hands in the pockets of my bathrobe and wished I could hit the shower. "But I'm guessing we're going to have to pool our meager skills and solve our last great puzzle or . . . bear the

responsibility for the destruction of the world."

They looked at me with wide eyes.

Except for Brenda, who rolled hers. "Drama much?"

Chapter 3

"It's a valley with low hills. Fog spilling into a bowl or depression. I see a ski lift, but no snow. Not much of a slope, either. Beautiful grey hills covered with orange ground growth of some kind. Where does grass turn orange in fall?"

I was in my third hour of bilocating, and I had managed to get a fix on our favorite Antichrist candidate. I was hovering and flitting all around him like a remote viewing hummingbird.

Once I'd found his spiritual location, it wasn't hard to know which aura was Ambrosi Giacomo's, since nobody else I'd ever encountered seemed to be half earthborn, like a regular human, and half fluid, like the spirits I regularly saw when I bilocated. Dozens of regular human auras surrounded him as he gave a speech. Everyone was bundled up, but they were definitely outside.

Now all we had to do was determine where on earth this was.

The ski lift suggested it probably wasn't a Third World country, and that helped. The fact that this ski resort had no snow on the ground today, October 3, suggested it was not high in any mountains.

I could see signs and placards all around Giacomo and his group, but the ether made a mockery of written language, and this time I couldn't understand what I was looking at. Sometimes, I was able to read perfectly, even if later I found out the language was one I didn't speak and wouldn't even be able to read—Korean or Farsi and the like. And sometimes, words and letters were impossibly jumbled and exploded, though I later found out it had been English. This time, impossibly jumbled and exploded. But that didn't necessarily mean English.

I swooped back down around Giacomo's head. I hoped to hear what language he was speaking in. But to my surprise, he paused in his speech and turned to look directly at me.

I flinched. Maybe it was a fluke. I floated over the crowd. His gaze tracked me perfectly. I felt a change in the air around me. Bad things suddenly aware of me and coming to deal with me. I sped around the scene, trying to spot something that would pinpoint this location. An especially vicious creature of teeth and hate floated near and Giacomo pointed at me, which caused the creature to lunge for me. I decided it was time to make good my escape, so I sped away until I felt he wasn't watching me anymore.

Maybe Tank was right that remote viewing was something that belonged to the bad guys more than the good. Maybe that's why I'm always outnumbered

when I'm floating around in there and why monsters and devils and antichrist pupils seem at ease there.

The whole thing hurt my head, and I decided it was time for a bladder break anyway, so I ascended from my bilocating trance and made the jump back to the physical world.

For the second time today, I awoke in my king-size bed in the presidential suite at the DFW Grand Hyatt. Judging by the angle of the sunlight and the time on the white noise machine clock by the bed, it was time for lunch.

To my great joy, I found Andi sitting in a chair at my bedside, working on a netbook on her lap. She'd changed into a white blouse and khaki capris, and there she was, attending to my needs.

"Andrea," I said, "be a dear and fetch my lunch, hmm? Some of that Steak Oscar from last night would be divine." I decided to keep to myself the fact that our quarry might've seen me.

Andi didn't even look up from her screen. "I'm not your servant. Get your own lunch."

So much for attending to my needs. I swung my legs over the edge of the bed and rubbed my face. "Do you at least know where he is?"

"Based on your references? Hardly." Andi used her finger to scroll up on her screen, and I could see lots of her typed notes. "It's not nothing, and at least you finally found him, but—"

"Finally? *Finally?* Know anybody else who could've found him at all?" In my most comfortable jeans, I stood and walked barefoot toward the door. "Whatever. If your supposedly legendary skills in pattern recognition worked as advertised, you would've found him without my help at all. And I've

given you extra bonus clues, too."

She glared at me. "I have a theory. I'm forming a theory, anyway."

"Pssht." I dismissed her and went out to find some steak and hollandaise.

In the common area of my suite, I found the rest of Mystery Incorporated. Tank was raiding the fridge—shocker—and his grey shorts and sweaty, rust-colored t-shirt suggested he'd been doing his thing in the hotel fitness center again. *Like a dozen eggs with that, Gaston?*

Brenda sat on the other side of the big room in the grey chair facing the L-couch, drawing intently on a sketch pad in her lap. And I could tell from sundry bleeps and clangs that Daniel was over there too, probably flat on his back playing some game on his tablet.

I padded into the kitchen, careful to avoid Fancy Mouth, and put a plate of Steak Oscar into the microwave. I took the steaming plate to the dining table and sat.

A minute later, Brenda looked up from whatever she was sketching. "Hoo, that smells good. Tell me you didn't take it all."

I shook my head.

"I'm gonna *have* to get me some of that." She closed her sketch pad and put it under the chair— mysteriously, I thought—and nudged Daniel. "You hungry, Danny?"

Tank sat at the glass table with his greasy room service burger and steak fries. Andi came into the room from behind me, mumbling about something smelling good, and in seven minutes, we were all gathering around the table again.

"I should go to *your* suites to get some privacy," I said.

Tank nodded earnestly. "Yeah, you totally should."

"Be nice, Tank," Andi said, pulling her own bit of Steak Oscar from the microwave and bringing it over.

Brenda moaned over her bite of beef and crab. "Okay," she managed around her chewing, "what do we know?"

"You're the one supposed to be tracking his past locations," I said. "You and the kid. Found much?"

Daniel brought his tablet up and fingered around until it displayed a world map. There were dozens of virtual pins on the map: blue, green, yellow, orange, and red. Many of them clustered in Europe, which would make sense for an Italian, but there were several pins in Africa, North America, South America, India, Turkey, Japan, New Guinea, Australia, and New Zealand.

"Red means recent and blue means longer in the past?" I didn't need to see Daniel nod, because I knew that's how he would do it. "How far in the past?"

The kid took a bite from his chili in a microwavable cup. "Blues are six months ago. Reds are less than seven days ago."

I nodded. "Most recent?"

Brenda slid the tablet to her and scrolled the map around. She landed on a red pin in Madagascar. "Here. That's where his sorry self was four days ago. Latest we could find." She slid the tablet back to the middle of the table.

I swallowed a luscious lump of lemon-and-butter-drenched beef. "Well, I saw him at a ski resort, so he's sure not in the rain forest anymore."

"Did you ask the Watchers?" Tank asked, looking at me, his eyes still hooded.

"Of course. They got bupkis." I studied the map. Pins of all the colors were everywhere. It wasn't like Giacomo was on an African world tour or anything that would indicate where he would go next. The man—well, the whatever-he-was—seemed to bounce around the globe like the pope.

"Andi," Tank said sweetly, "what do you see, honey?"

Sweet Cheeks didn't seem to notice what he'd called her. "Just the obvious, of course."

"The obvious?" Brenda asked. "Girl, *obvious* for you ain't always obvious for us. Why don't you let us in on your obvious?"

Andi looked around as if only just realizing she'd spoken aloud. "Huh? Oh, yes, sure. Well, it's obvious he gets around. It's obvious something is taking him all over the world. It's obvious his base is Italy. And it's obvious he's extremely rich or at least well-funded, to be able to do this globetrotting. Do we know any more about him other than he's supposed to be an Italian businessman?"

"You're the one who saw the bio in the silver folder," Brenda said.

Andi shook her head. "It just said he'd grown up in Italy and was an Ital—" She stopped herself and went into what looked like a thinking trance. She pulled the tablet closer and used her fingers to zoom out.

"You got something?" Tank asked, ever solicitous.

Andi brought her right hand to her forehead and made an odd pinching gesture with her fingers, as if trying to pull a strand of thought from her brain.

I waved a hand in front of her face, but she took no notice.

"Leave her alone," Tank said, all gentleness gone from his voice. "I've seen her like this before. She's onto something. She'll have the answer, I know it. . . if you leave her alone."

"Listen, bruiser—"

Brenda, Tank, and Daniel shushed me.

Andi snatched up the tablet and walked out the front door of my suite.

"Huh," I said. "Daniel, I think she just stole your tablet."

We continued with our lunch. I wanted to get back to the bed to start my bilocating search again. But I did have to admit that it felt different—nice, even—to think that Andi might be able to get us the information we needed. Thanks to me, of course, and not diminishing my input in the least. Still, occasionally these lesser horses did manage to earn their hay and oats.

Poor Daniel looked forlorn without a device to play on. He took his plate to the sink and helped himself to *my* TV. Tank picked up Andi's plate and glass and combined them with his own.

"So, Brenda," I said, since we were the only two still at the table, "what were you drawing over there?"

She drank from her glass and raised an eyebrow at me. "None of your business, pretty boy."

"Had another of your visions? Thinking of maybe letting us in on your tiny possible contribution to our efforts?"

"Nope."

"Figures." I shrugged. "I'm sure we'll save the world without you."

She shook her head at me. "Remember when I punched you in the face?"

I stood and grabbed my plates.

"*I* remember it," she said with a smile like someone stepping into warm sunshine. "I remember it so well."

"Whatever." I turned toward the kitchen.

"I'll let y'all see it," Brenda said, "when it's finished and when I know what it is. Danny's right: Everything's different this time. My visions usually come fully formed, but this one didn't. I'm getting pieces. Right now, it's just a bunch of lines and tones. I keep—I keep thinking it has meaning, but when I look at it, my mind don't give me anything."

I really wanted to fire off a retort to that, but with Ghetto reminding me of physical violence in the past, the troll threatening physical violence in the present, and Sweet Cheeks off on her vision quest, I thought it prudent to zip my lip for now.

I walked to Daniel, who was sitting on the couch watching the big screen. "Hey, kid, wanna trip the lights fantastic with me? See what we can see?"

"My mom told me to say no to drugs."

I thwacked him on the back of the head. "You know what I mean."

He turned the TV off. "Okay."

I flopped onto the couch next to him and began the descent into remote viewing, but then the front door flew open and Andi strode in.

"Found him!"

We all more or less came running. She stood in front of the grand piano and handed the tablet not to Daniel, but to me. "He's in Scotland."

I frowned at her. "There's no ski resorts in

37

"I'm telling you, it's *bay-zheeng*," Andi said to me. "That's how it's always pronounced everywhere I've ever heard it. It's got the fancy 'j' sound, like the French *bon jour.*"

We were on an Air China 777, mercifully near the end of our 14-hour nonstop flight from DFW to Beijing. The plane was luxuriously wide, with four seats in the middle section and three seats across both side aisles. We'd slept, eaten multiple times, watched more current-release movies than I would normally watch in a year, crossed one or more date lines, and tried very hard to understand the English spoken over the loudspeakers, supposedly for our benefit but not comprehensible to me. Happily, I didn't need the translation.

The flight was packed with Chinese. When I sat on my knees backward in my seat and looked down the rows and rows toward the back of coach class, I saw nothing but black hair and sleeping people with brown skin. Correction: A couple of Chinese teenagers here and there played games on the seat-back monitors. I turned and sat back down.

Brenda and Daniel sat across the aisle to my left, while Andi, Tank, and a tiny Chinese grandmother type—who had spoken to Tank in Mandarin for two hours straight, beginning at takeoff, before realizing he didn't understand her—sat on our row in the middle section. Perhaps partially as an act of self-defense, Tank had fallen asleep and had awakened only long enough to eat. He breathed heavily beside Andi and his arms took up both armrests.

Andi flipped through a tourist guide book, as if pointing to the spelling of the word "Beijing" would cause me to agree with her incorrect pronunciation of it.

"That's because you've only ever heard it pronounced wrong," I said. "By Americans. By *laowai*. Look, the word is made of two symbols: *Bey*, meaning northern, and *Jing*"—I came down with a hard *j* as in *jelly*, to emphasize my point—"meaning *capital city*. It's pronounced *bey-Jing*."

Andi growled at me and slammed the book shut. She reached up and pressed the flight attendant call button. "Let's settle this."

Presently, a very slender and pretty flight attendant arrived in my aisle and turned off the call button. "Yes, may I help you?" Her accent was deep but intelligible.

"Yes," Andi said, leaning across me, "I wonder if

you can help me settle an argument with my seat buddy here."

The woman looked instantly worried. "Yes, of course, ma'am. Would you like to be reseated?"

Andi and I chuckled. "You have no idea how much," Andi said. "But no, it's a friendly argument."

"Oh, I see."

I intervened. "Nǐ hǎo," I said.

"Nǐ hǎo ma?" she replied with a smile and a slight bow.

"Hǎo. Wǒ jiào Chad." I extended my hand to shake. *My name is Chad.*

She shook it and giggled. "Hěn gāoxìng jiàn dào nǐ." *Nice to meet you.*

"Wait," Andi said. "You speak Chinese? Since when?"

"I speak *Mandarin.* Be specific. And I spent five years in China as a kid. Now be quiet." I turned back to the flight attendant. "Xièxiè." I wagged a thumb at Andi. "Qǐng gàosu zhè wèi wàiguó rén rúhé fāyīn Běijīng." *Please tell this foreigner how to pronounce Beijing.*

"Okay," she said, making even that sound like a Mandarin word. She turned to Andi. "Our capital city pronounced 'bey-JING."

I smirked at Andi. Then, to the flight attendant: "Not *bey-zhing,* like French *bon jour?*"

Her smile implied that she'd made this correction a million times. "No, sir. I'm very sorry, but we say *jing,*" she said it with a hard *j,* "for word meaning—"

"Northern capital," I said.

"Yes, sir." She picked up some trash from our

trays. "We will be landing soon." She looked at Andi. "In what city?"

Andi rolled her eyes. "Bey-JJJJJJJING."

"Zuò de hǎo." The flight attendant patted Andi's shoulder and went on down the aisle.

I nudged Andi with my elbow. "She said you did a good j—"

"Shut up."

I chortled.

* * *

"It looks like three flying saucers landed on top of each other."

I nodded at Daniel's description of the Temple of Heaven. "Kind of does."

The five of us stood near the wide, white courtyard surrounding the four-story high Temple of Heaven, which itself was on a wide circular base with steps leading up on all sides. It was ten minutes to noon on a Thursday in early October, and the crowds were here en masse. Almost all the tourists appeared to be Chinese, but there was one tour group we'd passed that had looked Western and had been speaking German.

The temple grounds were impressive. Wide, flat pavement with long, low, red-walled, blue-roofed buildings on three sides of the temple tower. The open space here, with the looming tower in the middle, was about as wide and long as a football field. Visitors thronged the pavement in groups and couples, with a line waiting to walk through the bottom floor of the temple itself. A wedding couple posed for a photographer in front of the temple, and several bridesmaids in blue dresses stood by. It had rained earlier in the morning and the sky looked like it

could rain some more—or maybe that was just the infamous Chinese pollution. The pavestones were slick and people walked around with umbrellas. And selfie sticks. Hundreds of selfie sticks.

The entire complex was surrounded by forested parkland, though it was in the center of Beijing. We'd entered along pavement paths designed to give a view of the tower ahead. Today, the paths were all wet, providing excellent reflections of the tower. Intriguing side-paths branched off the main avenue, including one leading to the Seven Meteorite pavilion, which I really wanted to visit. But we weren't here to sightsee.

We were here to kill the Antichrist.

I thought the others wouldn't shut up about that particular fact all the way across the Pacific. I think most of them figured it wouldn't come to that. I suspected it would come to exactly that.

We stood under the porch roof of one of the three low buildings. I walked to the railing to look out over the grounds and to watch the people streaming up the base upon which the tower sat. The rest of the group followed my lead, as was only right.

Andi had her head in the guide book. "Says here the Temple of Heaven is one of the few monuments from ancient China dedicated to a monotheistic God. The emperor came here to make sacrifices to the One God so the harvest would go well that year." She touched Tank's arm softly. "See? The One God is with us, even here."

Tank had been uncharacteristically morose ever since we'd figured out, way back in my hotel suite, that we needed to come here. And he didn't seem about to snap out of it now. "Andi, do you really

think the One God is going to be happy to watch us commit murder?"

Andi shot me a worried look. I didn't know what she was thinking—didn't want to expend the energy to find out, either—but my chief concern with having the troll in the doldrums was that he wouldn't bring his bulk to bear in the fight if we needed him.

Brenda, for her part, had gone full-on tourist and was already wearing a bright yellow dragon t-shirt and five jade necklaces and bracelets, plus she was carrying a small sculpture of a section of the Great Wall, a carved box with "special" chopsticks, a plush panda doll, and a flag she'd been told said, "Lucky Year of the Rooster" but which I'd told her had said, "I'm a stupid American and I want to get rid of all my money."

Daniel stood beside her, munching on some chicken-related meat on a wooden stick.

I shook my head. What had we been thinking? It was all well and good to track this guy down and be in position to confront him, but then what? I hadn't brought a gun, despite the Chinese airport customs agents attempts to find something of interest in my bags, nor had the rest of the group. So unless we were going to pelt him with twenty-yuan plastic Buddhas, I didn't know how we thought we were going to assassinate him.

Now, if I were on my own and didn't have to worry about these other clods, I could . . .

Hmm, not a bad idea, Chad, my boy. Keep it in your back pocket.

I did more than that: I submerged the idea beneath a shield of mundane thoughts, hoping that would keep it hidden, should anyone come snooping

through my mind.

The Chinese curse came to my mind: *May you live in interesting times.* Truly it was a curse. How much better to live in boring, safe times when the universe wasn't in danger.

Nah.

Andi turned Tank around and we formed a huddle. "So here's what I'm thinking. Once we find him, we get his attention and demand he immediately cease and desist from all activities related to the Gate and the end of the world." She shifted her weight back and forth and scowled, as if she were about to go into the octagon to fight for the welterweight title. "You know, show 'em we're onto him and are sick of it."

The rest of us looked at her incredulously.

"Girl, you trippin'."

Even Tank broke out of his torpor. "Andi, are you being serious?"

All I did was raise my eyebrows and tilt my head at her.

Andi's hands splayed. "Well, I don't know. I'm not exactly experienced at this. Maybe Tank holds him down and we . . . Chad could . . . I saw a loose tile with a really sharp. . . Oh, I don't know! What's *your* plan?"

"I'll tell you a plan," Tank said. "We give up any thought of killing this guy and we—"

A black wave washed over me like I was having a stroke. "Shut up! Shut up, shut up, shut up." The image of a bear's gaping maw and saliva strung between yellow fangs consumed my mind.

"He's here."

* * *

A group of twenty men and women in black crossed the pavement from our right and began to ascend the central steps of the base beneath the tower. They looked like New Yorkers in their black leather jackets, black slacks or skirts, and black shoes. They were clearly Westerners, with their white skin, and a few of the women were striking blondes with long legs and high heels. Brawny, serious looking men in dark sunglasses and long black coats comprised the meaty center of the group. Chinese men in black, long-sleeve shirts walked the perimeter of their clutch, unapologetically brandishing automatic rifles. Five armed Chinese soldiers in Mao green uniforms and green caps with a red star strolled behind them like tolerant babysitters.

At the head of the phalanx ascending the steps was a figure I recognized even at a distance of fifty yards. I probably would've recognized him by appearance, having seen him in remote viewing. But there was a magnetism about him, an aura I could feel even in my waking life, that made him unmistakable.

Ambrosi Giacomo reached the midpoint of the steps to the Temple of Heaven and turned to look directly at us. From more than sixty yards away, with him at the head of the group in black and the others arrayed below him, it looked like a staged group photo with the chief man at the top of the hierarchy.

I felt his eyes on me. Just as he'd seen through the ether when I hovered near him in Scotland, now he somehow knew me despite the others around us.

Or perhaps there was a different explanation entirely.

Perhaps he'd seen me all along.

I felt as though a trap door was about to open beneath me. "Um," I said aloud, "we may have miscalculated a little."

Giacomo's gaze held me as if it was his turn to float between dimensions and I was standing in the quick-drying cement of reality.

Tank spun around. "What are you saying, Chad? What do you mean, you 'miscalculated'?"

I must've been backing away, because my heels and head struck the wall behind me. "Remember when I said we needed to figure out where he was going to be so we could catch up to him?"

"Of course we do," Andi said, right up in my personal space. "What about it?"

"Well," I said, not taking my eyes off Giacomo, "that might not be exactly what was going on."

Brenda clutched her Great Wall statuette. "What you think *is* going on, then? Is that him?"

"I don't think we came here so we could kill him," I said, trying to step backward but hitting the wall again.

Tank grabbed the front of my shirt. "Then what?"

I opened my mouth to answer, but the kid beat me to it.

"He found *us,*" Daniel said. "It's a trap. He's the bear, we're the horses, and he's brought us here to kill *us.*"

There was a rush of air and suddenly we were standing at the base of the stairs, with Ambrosi Giacomo standing over us.

"Buongiorno, i miei amici." Though he spoke in Italian, I presumed, it was perfectly intelligible in my mind: *Good day, my friends.*

Giacomo was an impossibly handsome man. In the diffuse light of the cloudy day and the white pavement and steps around us, his face seemed almost vampire pale, especially against bushy, black hair perfectly styled, and a trimmed black beard and mustache. His face was long and rugged and his jaw almost comically square. Thick eyebrows drew together as he examined us, and a concentration crease appeared in his forehead.

His shoulders, beneath his long, tailored black

coat, were broad, and he held himself easily, with one shoulder slightly higher than the other, as if he were a martial artist evaluating the fastest way to get us to the ground.

I realized belatedly that, though I appeared to have full freedom of movement along with rest of our team, everyone else within the scope of my vision had turned to statues that shimmered with unreality. Were we bilocating or was this happening in physical space?

"What do you call yourselves?"

My brain had trouble taking everything in, so it wasn't until about the last word of his question that I realized he was even asking one. "What? Who? Oh, us? You mean like, 'the Harlem Globetrotters' or something?"

Giacomo tilted his head back and to the side in an unusual, unassuming manner, and he smiled. When he did, his cheeks swelled and the rugged lumberjack image gave way to the look of a cherubic rogue. "You are the globetrotters, yes? Yes, I see."

I looked left and right to assess my doltish team, and they still seemed stunned.

"Actually, the team had no name until I joined, only recently. But under my leadership, we are now known as 'Mystery Incorporated.'"

Giacomo's right eyebrow went up and he stuck out his bottom lip as if impressed by our fearsome title.

I couldn't tell if he caught the joke or what. "I'm Fred, and this is—" I pointed at Andi, Tank, Brenda, and Daniel— "Daphne, Shaggy, Velma, and Scooby Doo."

He swung his head to the other side. "Now I know you are playing me on."

It was bizarre, talking about Scooby Snacks with the Antichrist on the steps of a Chinese temple. All we needed now were flying monkeys.

Speaking of which: I sensed dark spirits gathering in the ether around us.

"Be gone!" Tank yelled, his right arm flying forward to point up at Giacomo. "In the name of Jesus, be gone, foul creature!"

Giacomo looked at him with wide eyes. Then he turned to me and pointed his thumb at Tank, who seemed to be locked in his last pose. "Is he all right?"

I chortled. "I really don't think so. But he's not so bad. Small brain, big heart. Long on faith."

"I see. What about the others?"

"Oh, they have their uses." I decided to see if I really did have freedom of movement. I climbed the steps and passed Giacomo, as if I were interested in the temple tower above us. He turned to face me, which, if we had brought weapons of any kind, would've offered a great opportunity for the morons to use them. At the very least, the troll could've jumped him. But he didn't.

I sighed. "Sometimes."

Giacomo looked at the sky and sniffed the air. "You know, you and your Mystery Incorporated team have deeply aggravated my friends. You've really been quite a bother."

"Your friends? You mean the Gate? The creatures bent on terrorizing, enslaving, and/or destroying the human race?"

He looked aggrieved. He tsked at me. "Oh, shame, shame, Chad . . . or do you prefer *Fred*? You misunderstand. My friends are great humanitarians. Indeed, the greatest humanitarians the world has ever

seen. Oh, by your face I see you do not believe me. But yes, it is true. For humanity to become what they were intended to be, they must evolve. They must move beyond this—" he looked around— "ancient, outdated existence. If they are to receive the final gift of wholeness, which I alone can bring them, then yes, certain measures must be taken. How do you Americans put it? To make an omelet, one must break some eggs, yes?" He shrugged.

Final gift of wholeness? Nah, that didn't have an Orwellian ring to it at all.

"Cease." It was only a whisper from Andi, but it seemed to give her courage so she said it again. "Cease! Cease and desist! I know what you are, and you disgust me. You are a plague on humanity, and I demand that you—"

Giacomo made a tiny flicking gesture with his right index finger, and Andi was flung high into the sky. Her scream of surprise began at my ear and continued, fading as she rose.

That broke the others from their trance. Tank gasped and ran in broad circles on the pavement, looking up and spreading his arms.

Brenda brought her hand up to shield her eyes as she searched the overcast sky. She pointed. "There! She's right there. She's—" She cocked her head.

"Don't worry, Tank," Daniel said. "She's not falling. Not yet."

Tank shot his eyes back and forth between the Andi spot in the sky and Giacomo. "What did you do to her? Bring her down—softly—or, so help me, I'll— I'll—"

"You'll *what*, Bjorn?" Giacomo skipped lightly down the steps and circled around Tank. "Your team

has come here to kill me, but you don't want to do it. No stomach for it. But if I don't drop your sweetheart into your tender embrace, you'll what? Kill me? Ha!" He rapped Tank's shoulder and leaned closer. "She could never love you, by the way."

"What?"

Giacomo clucked and wagged his head. "Oh, you have given her your heart. But she will not give you hers. Come, come, Bjorn—how could a woman like that ever even think about being with a troglodyte like you?"

"Hey," I shouted, "leave him alone. He may be a troglodyte but he's my troglodyte, and if anyone's going to run him down, it's going to be someone who likes him. More or less."

Brenda shrieked like a serial killer and ran at Giacomo with her Great Wall statue lifted over her head.

When she was ten feet from him, he blew a kiss at her, and she stopped short, dropping the statue and clutching her throat.

Daniel ran to her and clung to her side. "Let her go! Stop it! Leave her alone!"

Giacomo heaved a great sigh and walked away from Tank, who was still watching the sky, and Brenda and Daniel. "What a pretty group of pretenders you are."

The air around us was boiling with dark spirits now, though I didn't expect anyone else to be able to see them. There was another presence in the area, too, and the dark spirits didn't seem to like it. I didn't know how to use that to our advantage, but it had to be a good sign.

I stepped down to the courtyard level and

approached Brenda and Daniel. "Mr. Giacomo, please release her."

Immediately, Brenda drew in a great breath and collapsed.

Giacomo smiled. "In Italy, we say, 'Politeness from the mouth is high in value and low in cost.'"

"Thank you," I said. "Now, about our floating girl"

. . .

Giacomo squatted beside Daniel. "Hello, young man."

Daniel seemed suddenly shy. "Hello."

The man examined the boy thoughtfully, as if contemplating a painting by Caravaggio. "It is a shame you and I must be enemies."

By way of reply, Daniel moved closer to his fallen mother and hugged Brenda's shoulders.

"You really are quite gifted," Giacomo said. "Ah, the things I could teach you. The things you could achieve. You could sit beside me when I come into my inheritance."

Brenda put up her hand. "Just stay back!" She scrambled to her feet and pulled Daniel away, keeping him behind her.

"So is this all we're going to do?" I asked, approaching him. "You're going to monologue and posture and threaten and then kill us off one by one?"

Giacomo turned to face me. He stood a good five inches taller than me, and all roguish charm vanished. "You would prefer to all die together, perhaps? In one enormous, glorious explosion?" He thrust his lower lip out again and shook his head. "We could do it that way. Why not?"

"Actually, I had something else in mind."

I retrieved that idea I'd hidden beneath mundane

thoughts and descended halfway into a waking bilocation. I pushed into the hijacked mind of one of the Chinese soldiers and broke Giacomo's control. The man animated as if escaping stasis and looked around as if in a daze. Giacomo didn't seem to notice. I pressed again and re-hijacked the soldier's mind, but this time for our team. He raised his rifle and switched the safety off.

"Something else?" Giacomo's left eyebrow rose.

"And what might that be?"

I shrugged. "It's probably just a shot in the dark."

The soldier fired, and the bullet struck Giacomo square in the back. The soldier fired again and again, and we scattered out of danger zone. Giacomo spun around and turned toward the soldier, who kept shooting until his cartridge clicked dry.

Giacomo clutched his torso and pulled bloody hands away. "That was . . . un . . . unex . . . pected."

He crumpled to the wet pavement, now speckled and smeary with blood.

The people around us snapped back to life, and the courtyard flooded with a cacophony of confusion. Through the noise, a woman's cry of alarm reached us from above, and too late I realized my oversight.

"Andi!"

I spotted her falling, but she was coming too fast and I was too far away. Tank was beneath her, arms held wide, but at the rate she was falling, he might as well have been hoping to catch a piano. I squeezed my eyes shut against the inevitable.

The crowd gave a collective cry, and I knew she was dead. Maybe they both were. God, how is it fair for them to end like this?

Then the crowd's cry turned to a gasp of fear or

wonder, and I made myself look.

Andi was not dead. She hovered in the air just above Tank, who looked up, blinking in astonishment. As I watched, Andi lowered gently into his arms.

In that moment I discovered that the Mandarin expression of "What the %*&# is going on?" sounds almost identical to the same expression in English.

What *was* going on?

I felt something in my mind like a cello string plucked, and I realized I'd forgotten about my soldier. I caught a glimpse of movement through the crowd as he woke up and tried to figure out what had happened.

Another section of the crowd shrieked and people hurried away from something on the ground.

Giacomo's body. Had to be.

As they pulled away, Giacomo's men-in-black army moved in to surround him. Would they try something now?

I heard a deep voice shout as Tank spun Andi around in celebration. Brenda and Daniel ran to them, and I took a step in that direction, too.

But the black wave passed over me again, and I found myself on the pavement looking up at shreds of dark grey clouds. An image filled my mind—the professor's face on Daniel's tablet.

It's not over.

* * *

As I lay on the pavement, I heard a triple pop with a long echo, as if someone had dropped three boards at a lumber yard. I heard it again and then yet again, from slightly different locations around me.

The crowd screamed and people ducked. That's

when I realized what I was hearing.

Gunfire.

I sat up and would've stood, but at that moment the crowd closest to me bolted away like a startled flock of birds. A woman in a bridesmaid's dress knocked down a child and both of them collided into me, putting us all in a heap. Panicked people tried to avoid us as they ran for their lives.

I lifted the child—a spindly Chinese boy with a shaved head—and ran for the nearest building. My only thought was to get behind something that people would avoid in their flight. Something that might block the enemy's view, if not his bullets.

The gunfire continued behind us, and I heard shrieks of pain and fear. The triple-fire sound had to be automatic rifles on some sort of burst mode, which was definitely better than full auto.

A rush of people squeezed between us and the building, heading toward the front entrance to the monument, then the boy and I reached the edge of the porch. I realized, as I pounded up the steps with the squirming boy in my arms, that my right ankle was throbbing.

I fell on the polished stone floor behind the largest cylindrical pillar I could find. The boy was crying for his baba and mama. "Liuli," I said. *Stay down.*

The boy looked at me in even more terror, if possible, and sprang off the porch and away from the buildings in the direction the other people were fleeing.

"God," I said, not really intending to pray, "keep the boy safe. And . . . we could use some help here."

Then I felt stupid about saying it. Whatever. The gunfire seemed more sporadic now, and the

sound of the crowd's panicked flight had diminished. It couldn't be long before sirens blared and Chinese police came, could it?

I wanted to peek up and see if my frien— If the people I'd been living with—were safe. But I didn't want to risk my skull. So I decided to look around in my own way.

I settled my mind and began to bilocate.

I found myself in a black tornado. Dark spirits swarmed me like piranhas. I switched into defense mode, zipping away, lashing out, darting for areas of lesser darkness. Only tangentially could I see the architecture of the Temple of Heaven, but finding the locations of my . . . colleagues . . . was not happening.

I found one particular spirit, though. It was unmistakable, and clearly not dead.

Ambrosi Giacomo stood at the top of the steps under the tower. His outstretched arms were swathed in shreds of black energy like banshee cloths flapping in a spectral blast. He was a dark god come to earth. The cloud of spirits danced at his whim, moving with his gestures like extensions of his hands.

"Daniel!" Giacomo roared, and his voice was like a hungry beast of metal and flesh. "Daniel, come to me."

I scanned the area, searching through the intervening spirits as best I could, and managed to find the auras of Tank and Andi close to one another. I found Brenda, apparently alone beneath a pile of dying and dead tourists. Her aura shone faintly, and I knew what she was doing.

She was trying to hide Daniel's presence from the bear. She wouldn't be able to hide him much longer, but I liked her idea. I concentrated on adding my own

essence to her masking effort. We wouldn't last forever, but our masks should keep him hidden until I could figure out what to do.

A pulse of suffering and fear struck me, and I was forced to acknowledge the horror of what had happened and was still happening. So much death. So many innocents, like that boy. I felt dampness on my face and realized it had started to rain again. And that I was weeping.

I also sensed more enemies converging on this spot. It was a hot spot and about to get much hotter. I felt a presence at my side. My first thought was that God had arrived to answer my stupid prayer. Then I saw it was someone slightly more believable: the professor. He looked much better here in the spiritual plane than he had on Skype.

"Only together."

I was still dodging spirits and shielding Daniel, so my brain wasn't exactly available to solve riddles. "What do you mean, old man? Speak clearly."

But even as I said it, an image formed in my mind. It was a moment from a movie—*Guardians of the Galaxy*, maybe—in which the heroes stood hand in hand to fight the bad guy. Could we do something like that? Pool our powers?

Just then, Giacomo's allies arrived. First, the meaty men in black who had been part of his entourage took off their sunglasses and revealed empty eye sockets. I knew all about those guys.

Second, half a dozen shiny golden spheres burst through the trees on all sides of the tower and floated toward us like deadly Sputniks.

Third, swimming in a low cloud of their own

making came creatures that were part lamprey eel and part severed tentacle with big heads and lots of sharp teeth: the fog creatures the Gate loved so much.

Finally came a busload of black-eyed children, who stepped out of the central door of the three-tiered tower that was the Temple of Heaven.

Apparently, shooting the Antichrist was like kicking a hornet's nest. One way or another, this was going to be a very short battle.

Luckily, I'd had an idea.

I was already near Brenda and Daniel, so I started with them. "Brenda, it's Chad. I'm helping you hide with them. Daniel. Don't try to talk; just listen. We're in big trouble, Daniel, I need you too. The five of us have to combine our energies into some kind of weapon or attack. We've got only seconds to do this, so listen up. Our only chance is to take out the big guy, okay? You get ready while I go tell the others. When I leave, he's probably going to see you, so . . . try not to die."

I located Tank and Andi behind an overturned souvenir cart. I zipped toward them.

Sure enough, as soon as I moved my consciousness, Giacomo roared like a beast from a horror film. He spun the spiritual torrents toward me. Fog creatures left their cloud and darted at me like knife jabs. Eyeless thugs and black-eyed peas ran after my metaphysical presence. The golden orbs changed direction with disturbing quickness and loomed closer. All of that was bad for me, but at least for the moment they weren't attacking Brenda and Daniel.

Except they *were* following me to Andi and Tank. I neared those two and danced around them, trying to dodge the spiritual projectiles being hurled at me. "You guys, this is Chad. We have to unite our

powers and create a bomb to send at Giacomo. I know you haven't done this much, but you do have weapons to use. Tank, I know you know how to bring it. You've done it for me so many times. I hope now you've decided it's okay to kill him, because I need you. Andi, bring some of that righteous anger you've got saved up. Wait for my signal, and then shoot everything right at him."

I started to zoom away, but I paused. "If this doesn't work, it's been . . . nice getting to know you."

Again, stupid.

Okay, Porky, time for a roast.

I rose through the black storm, hoping I looked like an angel from the ninth heaven coming to strike down the beast. Demon children and nightmarish monsters nipped at my heels, but I soared above it all. Giacomo laughed and turned rolling arms of demonic spirits toward me. But this time, that was exactly what I wanted.

"Ambrosi," I said, laughing too. "What kind of name is that? Didn't your mother love you? Oh, right, your mother was a slut who did it with a devil. I forgot."

His features, already hideous in his spiritual form, contorted in anger, and the sound from his mouth was pure outrage. All his anger—and all his army—focused on me.

Really? He was that easy of a mark? Okay, then.

"Buddy, it's not your fault she was a demon's ho, you know?" I sensed Brenda and the others coiling their energies. We were going to have only one shot at this, so I needed to play it right.

I flew behind Giacomo and, as before on the steps, he turned toward me. This time, at least, my

team actually had weapons. "Ambrosi—can I call you that? —what's the plan, then? You and the Gate, you think you're going to, what, sow chaos and stuff like that? Create a hell on earth? Genocide, of course— that's a given. What else? I don't know what you think you can do. I mean, it's not like you and your demon buddies can force God's hand or anything. Pfft. Was that seriously your plan?"

The beast slashed a black arm at me and growled.

The spiritual Giacomo was a lot less articulate than the physical one. This one was more *Hulk, smash* than uber-villain conversationalist. But all I really needed to do was distract him.

Giacomo seemed to notice something. He turned away from me and looked directly at Daniel and Brenda.

Not good.

He lumbered across the pavement toward them.

The black winds swirled away from everything else and concentrated on Daniel. Already, the spirits had pummeled Brenda and were pulling her away from him. My vision cleared, and I could see all the enemy's creatures converging on them.

The soldiers and bodyguards opened fire, and Brenda spun to the ground, a mist of blood hanging in the air.

Light flashed, and a shield appeared around Daniel. Somehow I knew it was the professor, and somehow, I knew that shield wouldn't last for more than an instant. I felt as much as saw the professor's eyes pleading with me. *Now.*

I flung my presence across the courtyard. "Now, people, shoot now!"

I had no idea if they could do anything at all, so I

launched my own attack. I coiled my energy into a fist and flung it—and myself—directly into Giacomo's face.

It struck him like a slow punch. He reared back, but he wasn't hurt. Then I felt another force join mine, Brenda's. My "arm" strengthened, and I drove it into his face again.

A new propulsion joined us—Andi—and then another—Tank.

I sneered at Giacomo. "Here's your final gift of wholeness, freak!"

My aim became hard to control. The fist was like a torpedo now, pushed from behind, but easily sent off course. I yanked to keep it on target, and I felt the professor's arm steadying me. The spirits shrieked. The spheres fired energy bolts. The children screamed with nightmare mouths. All around were empty eye sockets, biting jaws, demonic howls, crashing bodies, flinging guns. Giacomo turned aside from our fist with a titanic cry, and the point of our forceful beam slipped under his chin and onto his throat.

That was when Daniel added his energy.

The blunt torpedo became a sharpened spear and opened Giacomo's neck with a swift, hideous puncture, shredding muscle, trachea, esophagus, and spine, and flying on through like a missile, leaving a gory gap. The energy continued forward into the tower, penetrating a support structure beneath the middle saucer. The left half of the Temple of Heaven toppled onto the ground in a billowing cloud of paint, tile, and ancient dust.

Giacomo, kept erect by some force of his spirit, leaned back, but caught himself. He was again only a man, and he might've enjoined me in verbal sparring

if it weren't for the blood pouring from his mouth, nose, ears, and the horrific hole in his neck.

With a bubble of blood on his lips, he fell forward onto the steps, bumping down in a sickening rhythm until he came to rest like a rag doll at the bottom.

A squeal like a tortured whale flooded my spiritual ears and resounded off the walls of heaven.

The black spirits vanished as if they'd never been there. The gold spheres lost power and crashed to the ground in burst of black smoke. The fog creatures coiled as if electrocuted and fell to the pavement in steaming chunks. The black-eyed children and empty-eyed gunmen and soldiers and bodyguards and minions beheld their mortally wounded master and fled, tripping over each other in a second panicked stampede.

The doomed squeal continued. I couldn't bear the assault of sound. I had to return to my physical body. I did, but in my fleshly ears I could still hear the echo. I sat up, still sitting on the porch behind the pillar.

The courtyard was a macabre assemblage of the dead and dying. The squeal became the sound of sirens, and the crushing *whump* of spiritual wind became the sound of rotors on a police helicopter.

I struggled to my feet, again feeling the pain in my ankle, and limped toward the tower, which was still shedding bits of plaster and stone from the portion that had collapsed. The area was a national disaster and a human travesty, but all I could think about was Brenda, shot and possibly dead, and Daniel, and Andi, and Tank.

There were survivors, I noticed as I crossed the distance. Tourists. Family members. I spotted Brenda

on the ground. Already, Daniel was draped over her, crying. Andi shouted, and I saw her and Tank running toward them.

When I was twenty feet away, I saw Brenda's hand rise to caress Daniel's face. But that could have been a last goodbye. When I was five feet away, I saw her glance at me, and the angry face she gave me was the most beautiful thing in the world.

I fell to my knees, laughing and crying, and took the sorry tattoo artist into my arms for a painful hug. Andi and Tank arrived, and I saw that she was bloody and he was holding his arm awkwardly and seemed in some sort of new pain. But we were alive. Somehow, we'd made it. Somehow, we had done something amazing.

My friends and I.

I felt a nudge in my spirit, and I recognized it as the professor. "Thanks, man. Thanks for what you did. But did we do it? Did we defeat the Antichrist and beat the Gate and save our dimension for another twenty years?"

I couldn't catch his answer. He was fading. How had he managed what he'd done here?

"Thanks, Professor. You did good. I approve."

But instead of the tendrils of warm fuzzies I'd expected to feel from his direction as he departed, I felt a wave of sudden alarm. But his exit seemed unavoidable somehow, and in seconds he was gone.

I looked around, fearing some new danger, but everything seemed settled. The sirens wailed nearer and I could hear the beat of booted feet running our way. The helicopter held station with a police sniper sitting with his legs and rifle barrel sticking out the door.

Our group still clustered around Brenda. Her wound didn't seem as serious as I'd thought at first. Andi was applying pressure to both sides of Brenda's bloody shoulder and Daniel sat still, breathing steadily. But then I saw what had seemed amiss: The tableau was too small.

"Where's Tank?"

* * *

Tank knelt over the ravaged body of the Antichrist candidate, Ambrosi Giacomo.

I was thirty feet away, but already I knew I wouldn't be able to get to him in time, even without a sprained ankle. I ran for him anyway. "Tank! Don't do it!"

I had crossed half the distance before I read in the minds of the others that they had begun to grasp what was happening. But Brenda couldn't move, and Andi and Daniel would certainly stay with her.

How was it, after defeating this chimera against all odds, it was again up to me to save the world? I only hoped, as I limped, that the sniper wouldn't shoot me in the back.

"Tank! For the love of God, stop what you're doing!"

Tank had his back to me, but despite the other noise in the courtyard, somehow I heard his soft reply. "It wasn't his fault. He was only a kid once. He didn't ask for any of this."

I reached him and pulled at his shoulder. "Maybe not, but he sure embraced it. He wasn't a victim, Tank. Not in the end. Don't even think about—"

I was too late. The appalling wound in his neck had closed under angry red skin, and Tank's right hand glowed as he pressed it against Giacomo's chest.

"Tank, no!" I pulled his hand away.

Ambrosi Giacomo's eyes flew open and he shouted in fear and anger. He reached forward with both hands as if grasping something that was leaving him.

Then he seemed to come to himself. He looked at us. Astonishment dawned on his face, then he sat up and backed away. His hands went to his throat, as if he'd just remembered the wound. He patted the skin and found no gash. He looked at us in complete confusion and seemed about to speak, but his eyes landed on something and he gave us a look of surprise and incomprehension.

Tank turned his hand this way and that, and slowly the golden glow diminished.

We entered an eternal moment. Emotions marched across Giacomo's face: wonder, suspicion, broken-heartedness, resolve, indecision, and finally, fatigue.

His eyes met Tank's and his shoulders rose. "Why?" He shook his head in bewilderment. "Why would you?"

Tank stood until he towered over us both. "Because you were a kid once. And because all of us—*all* of us—need the love and forgiveness of Jesus Christ."

I couldn't believe what I was hearing. "Tank, what the &*#$@ have you done?"

A male voice spoke Mandarin over a bullhorn behind me, and I raised my hands and turned around. Tank didn't follow suit, so I turned to tell him what to do. In the corner of my eye, I saw Giacomo, half spirit and half human, rise and run away from the Temple of Heaven.

And back to wherever he would go to plan his next move.

Epilogue

What was there to be said?

We had triumphed against all odds and killed the Antichrist before he could come into his power. And then we had healed him. Had *freaking* up and healed him, so he *could* come into his power.

I paid a fellow passenger two hundred yuan to switch seats with me so I wouldn't have to sit with Tank or the others.

God, is that how You are? I don't . . . I don't understand. Is that what You wanted? Tank was wrong, wasn't he? Next, are we supposed to go find

out what the devil wants and see if we can help him do it? I thought we were supposed to destroy the Gate, not move them closer to their goals. I don't get it.

I threw a wadded-up paper napkin into my plastic cup and reclined my seat to try to sleep through the trans-Pacific flight.

Andi had seemed stunned by Tank's actions and Brenda had been as mad as I was. Only Daniel had seemed unfazed by it all. Maybe he was resigned to the idea that, sooner or later, that monster was going to kill him.

Whatever.

I must've fallen asleep, because when I awoke, people around me were eating again. I sat up and tried to identify what was being served. We were deep into that time of unnatural quiet on long-endurance flights.

Brenda appeared beside my seat and knelt in the aisle. "Don't get the pork."

I gave her a half smile. "I like pork."

She looked unusually amicable. I saw a hint of white gauze peeking from beneath one of her jade necklaces. "Hey, I just wanted to say—" She paused and blew out a nervous puff. "In all that with the police and our embassy and the news coverage—" She shook her head. "Anyway, I never had the chance to thank you."

I felt my eyebrows rise. "You—"

"Let me finish."

I chortled.

Brenda rolled her shoulder and winced. "I wanted to thank you and say you did a really good job. Leading us, I mean. If you hadn't stepped up, I don't

know what would've happened." She sighed. "Daniel is everything to me, and you . . ." She nodded firmly and continued: "You saved him. Saved us all." Her expression turned mock serious. "But don't get any ideas. Our team doesn't have a leader. We all lead. That's what's up. Next time, maybe it'll be me who knows what to do, so don't let that big ol' head get any bigger than it already is—hear me, pretty boy?"

I saluted. "Sir, yes, sir."

She stood to let a flight attendant pass, and I thought she was going to go back to her seat. But she knelt again, and when she did, she had her sketch pad out. She looked at the image on the page but kept it hidden from me.

"I haven't shown this to the others yet. Didn't finish it until the flight over. Thought it had meant something else, actually. But because you'd seen me working on it in Dallas, and because . . . Well, I figured you should see it first." She laid it on my lap.

It was a drawing in Brenda's distinctive style. At first, I thought it was an illustration of a moment from the dream we'd all shared, and I suppose it sort of was. But this was notably different.

A man all in black, with dark hair and beard and a deep gash in his neck, floated above a range of snow-covered mountains. Below, in front of a cave leading inside the largest mountain, stood a boy who looked a lot like Daniel. He wasn't large at all, as in our dream, but small and frightened, with the black figure's shadow falling over him. No brave stallions surrounded him protectively. Instead, lying about him in the snow, in broken and stiff poses, were the lifeless bodies of Tank, Andi, Brenda, and me.

I looked into Brenda's eyes and she returned the

gaze.
What was there to be said?

JEFF GERKE

Don't miss the other books in the Harbingers series which can be purchased separately or in collections:

CYCLE ONE: INVITATION
The Call
The House
The Sentinels
The Girl

CYCLE TWO: MOSAIC
The Revealing
Infestation
Infiltration

JEFF GERKE

The Fog

CYCLE THREE: *The Probing*
Leviathan
The Mind Pirates
Hybrids
The Village

CYCLE FOUR: *The Pursuit*
Piercing the Veil
Home Base
Fairy
At Sea

OTHER BOOKS BY JEFF GERKE

NOVELS

Virtually Eliminated
Terminal Logic
Fatal Defect
Operation Firebrand—Origin
Operation Firebrand—Crusade
Operation Firebrand—Deliverance

FICTION HOW-TO BOOKS

Plot Versus Character
The First 50 Pages
Write Your Novel in a Month
The Irresistible Novel

For more information about Jeff, visit JeffGerke.com

CONTENTS

PREFACE

This book introduces the methods, models, and processes of organizational diagnosis. It is intended for advanced undergraduates, graduate students, and other readers having a basic knowledge of behavioral science methods and concepts but limited exposure to the fields of organizational behavior and organization development. Organizational diagnosis involves the use of behavioral science knowledge to assess an organization's current state and to help discover routes to its improvement. Professional consultants (and occasionally participants in an organizational self-study) conduct diagnoses to develop recommendations for handling a particular challenge or problem (e.g., rapid employee turnover) or to contribute to organization development programs aimed more broadly at improving processes (e.g., decision making) and structures (e.g., division of responsibilities) and enhancing organizational effectiveness.

Although this book is mainly directed at would-be practitioners of diagnosis, it develops several themes of concern to professional consultants and applied researchers:

(1) Practitioners need to be as attentive to the relationships that develop between them and the members of the organization being studied as they are to their methods and diagnostic interpretations.

(2) Diagnosis can benefit from using an open-systems approach stressing external relations and resource dependencies, the interdependencies of system parts, and the impacts of structural and organization-level factors. This approach recognizes that many internal and external contingencies determine what managerial practices work best.

(3) Practitioners must acknowledge the political nature of organizations and come to terms with the implications of influence struggles and power relations for consulting practice.

My students at Bar Ilan University and Boston College contributed significantly to this project through their course participation and their reports on organizations in which they worked and conducted research. Yaacov Ben Dor, the head of the consulting firm, TIL, and Nisan Hadas of the Israeli Air Force provided opportunities to engage in diagnostic work, to help others build their diagnostic skills, and to develop my own approach to diagnosis and consulting. Yizhak Samuel of Rafael, Bruce Phillips of General Motors, and my wife, Jo Ann, of Bar Ilan's School of Education, generously shared their consulting experiences with me. The groundwork for this book was laid during a sabbatical spent at the Harvard Business School and Boston College's School of Management. My thanks to the academic and administrative staffs of these institutions and of Bar Ilan for providing me with congenial and stimulating work environments. In particular, thanks to Arthur Turner, who sponsored my visit to Harvard, provided valuable feedback on my work, and contributed greatly to my understanding of the impact of interpersonal processes on consulting. Thomas Backer, Jean Bartunek, Leonard Bickman, Jo Ann Harrison, Dafna Izraeli, Debra Rog, and one anonymous reader read the entire manuscript and made invaluable suggestions for its improvement. I also benefited from my all-too-brief association with the late Ed Huse. Judy Gordon, Jim Bowditch, Dal Fisher, Jack Lewis, Bill Torbert, and my other colleagues at Boston College and at Bar Ilan also gave valuable advice and encouragement. Hadassah Rahab, Kumiko DiSalvo, and Clare White-Sullivan provided invaluable secretarial assistance. Yoshio Saito and members of the Audio-Visual Department at Boston College kindly prepared the figures in Chapters 2, 3, and 4.

Finally, I want to express my appreciation to my wife, Jo Ann, who is a never-failing source of support and inspiration. She and my son, Natan, helped me keep this project in perspective. This book is dedicated to them, to my father, my brother, and to the memory of my mother Joan Kant Harrison.

1

Diagnosis:
Approaches and Methods

This chapter examines the main features of diagnosis and its uses in organization development and other forms of behavioral science consulting. Three critical facets of diagnosis are introduced; (1) *The Consulting Process*—working with members of an organization in planning and administering a diagnostic study and providing feedback on the findings; (2) *Interpretation*—defining the problems presented by members of the organization, framing issues for study, and interpreting the findings; and (3) *Methods*—collecting and summarizing diagnostic data.

INTRODUCTION

Organizational diagnosis is the process of using concepts and methods from the behavioral sciences to assess an organization's current state and find ways to increase its effectiveness.[1] Diagnosis can take many forms:

Case 1: Members of a private behavioral-science consulting firm study the overall structure of a large transport company in response to a request from its senior management. The managers were overburdened with minor problems originating in the firm's branches and sought advice on reducing the decision-making burden on top management and improving the coordination of field operations.

Case 2: The head of a national charitable agency asks a member of the agency's Human Resources Department to help top executives learn to work together more effectively. The human resources specialist interviews members of the executive committee in preparation for off-site workshops designed to improve teamwork within the executive committee.

1. The term "behavioral science" refers to both the social and behavioral sciences. Unless otherwise noted the cases in the text are based on actual cases drawn from my own experiences, those of my colleagues, and from the business press and other published sources.

Case 3: A professor of psychology conducts a survey of workers in a manufacturing plant as part of a program cosponsored by union and management to make work more satisfying and rewarding.

All of these cases involved requests by some client for advice from a consultant. *Clients*—like the senior management group in the first case and the union and management representatives in the third— are the people who sponsor a consultation and bear most of the responsibility for implementing its recommendations. The clients thus play a critical role in defining the goals of the consultations and shaping relationships between the consultant and the organization. In these three cases, the clients turned to consultants trained in the behavioral sciences because the clients assumed that the problems or challenges facing their organization related to people, groups, and organizational arrangements rather than involving mainly business or technical issues. Clients often refer initially to problems like these:

—Employee turnover, stress and health problems, low morale, poor work quality, neglect of equipment, and low productivity
—Conflicts and tensions that are polarizing people and groups, mis-understandings, and communication failures
—Disruptions of work flows between groups, tasks falling between the cracks, frequent delays and crises, red tape, and wasteful overlapping of responsibilities
—Missed opportunities (e.g., failure of a marketing campaign), lack of innovation and new ideas, dissatisfaction with the organization among powerful external groups (e.g., major clients) or supervisory bodies (e.g., boards of directors), inability to adjust to changing external conditions (e.g., technologies, markets)

In other cases clients may request an assessment of how well the organization is functioning in some area—such as meeting the career needs of its skilled employees—or they may seek advice on how to improve performance in areas such as technological innovativeness, creativity, productivity, quality, or flexibility in the face of techno-logical change. Concerns and problems like these have led to consul-tations and change projects in public sector organizations such as schools, hospitals, city governments, and the military; private firms in areas such as manufacturing, banking, and retailing; voluntary groups such as charities and religious groups; and cooperative businesses and communities.

The behavioral science *consultants* to whom clients turn are specialists in organization development, applied research, human resources, or related fields who provide advice and other services to members of the organization when requested to do so (see Steele, 1975; Tilles, 1961; Turner, 1982, on the consulting process). Besides being skilled at understanding and investigating organizational life, these consultants are usually skilled at giving feedback and working with groups. The consultants can be located within advisory units of a large organization (e.g., the Human Resources Department in case 2 above) or may be hired from outside on a contractual basis (e.g., cases 1 and 3). External consultants are usually members of management consulting firms or are university faculty members specializing in organizational research and consulting.

In each of the cases described above the consultants (or *practitioners*) conducted a diagnosis to understand the nature and causes of the problems or challenges initially presented by clients, to identify additional organizational problems and opportunities, to discover ways to solve these problems, and to improve *organizational effectiveness*. During diagnosis they compared the *current state* within the client organization to some *preferred state* (e.g., improved coordination of field operations, improved teamwork) and assessed effectiveness in terms of some standard (e.g., employee satisfaction). Moreover, each diagnostic study involved a search for ways to narrow the gap between the current and the desired state of affairs.

In light of the diagnostic findings consultants may recommend changing one or more of the key features of the organization. These include managerial goals or strategies (e.g., to develop a new product); members' skills, knowledge, and attitudes (e.g., interpersonal skills needed for teamwork); interpersonal and intergroup processes (e.g., leadership patterns); organizational structures (e.g., division into departments); and work technologies. Moreover, they may recommend a wide range of *interventions* to accomplish these changes—including training programs and workshops, conflict mediation, redefinition of job responsibilities, changes in pay and other reward systems, and the redesign of work techniques (see "Organization Development Interventions" below).

PLAN OF THE BOOK

This first chapter describes diagnosis and explains its contribution to behavioral science consulting. Then it shows how effective diagnosis depends on managing the *processes and relationships* that develop as consultants work with members of an organization, making appropriate *interpretations* of organizational problems and diagnostic findings and choosing appropriate *methods* for gathering and summarizing diagnostic data. Chapter 2 presents a model of organizations as open systems and shows how the model can help practitioners choose topics for diagnosis, develop criteria for assessing organizational effectiveness, and decide what steps, if any, will help clients solve problems and enhance organizational effectiveness.

Chapters 3 through 5 explain how to diagnose *individual* attitudes and behavior (e.g., work effort), *group-level* factors (e.g., decision making, interpersonal relations), and broader *organizational* patterns. Exercises for students are provided at the end of Chapters 1 through 5. Chapter 6 discusses diagnostic goals and conditions for their attainment and examines ethical and professional issues that confront practitioners of diagnosis. The appendices give more details on diagnostic instruments and suggest ways that readers can further develop their diagnostic skills and learn more about organizational consulting. A more detailed overview of the book can be obtained by reading the overviews at the start of each chapter and the section, "Diagnostic Goals," in Chapter 6.

THE USES OF DIAGNOSIS

Diagnosis and Organization Development

Diagnosis is a crucial part of *organization development*—a term that includes programs of *action research* and *planned change* (Huse & Cummings, 1985). These terms refer to efforts by consultants to use behavioral science knowledge to help clients improve organizational effectiveness. Organization development consultants work with clients and other members of an organization to plan a diagnostic study, gather and analyze data, provide feedback on the findings, and plan actions in response to this feedback (Nadler, 1977). The diagnoses in the cases cited at the beginning of the chapter were all parts of organization development activities. As these cases suggest, organization development consultants usually seek to enhance basic organizational features, such as communication and employee motivation, rather than just trying to solve short-term problems. Thus they seek to build the organization's capacities to handle *future* problems and challenges (see Chapter 6, "Diagnostic Goals").

Stages in organization development. Although organization development activities overlap and interact in practice, it is helpful to distinguish seven main stages that occur in full organizational development projects (Kolb & Frohman, 1970):

Scouting—The consultant(s) and client(s) get to know each other without contracting to carry out a project. The consultant seeks to determine how ready and able the client and other members of the organization are to follow through on a project and to change their behavior and their organization, if necessary. In addition, the consultant forms a first impression of the organization's needs, problems, and capacities and decides whether they fit his or her resources (e.g., time and staff), abilities, and interests.

Entry—The consultant and the client negotiate about their expectations for the project and formalize them in a contract specifying the timing and nature of the consultant's activities; staff and facilities (e.g., computer time) to be supplied by both parties; forms of collaboration; and the expected benefits to all participants in the project.

Diagnosis—The consultant gathers information about the nature and sources of organizational problems and challenges, analyzes this information, examines possible solutions, considers ways to improve effectiveness, and provides feedback to clients (and sometimes to other members of the organization); diagnosis may precede or be intertwined with the next two steps.

Planning—Consultants and clients jointly establish objectives for the project's action phase and plan any steps (interventions) to be taken to solve problems and improve effectiveness.

Action—Clients implement these plans with the help of the consultant.

Evaluation—Clients and consultants assess the impacts of the action phase and consider further actions. Under ideal circumstances an independent researcher evaluates project outcomes.

Termination—The project terminates if no further action is planned. The project may break off earlier if clients or consultants become dissatisfied with it.

Organization development interventions. In light of the diagnostic findings, clients and consultants choose among a wide range of possible interventions during the planning stage of organizational development (see Beer, 1980; Bennis et al., 1976; Burke, 1982; Huse & Cummings, 1985; Tichy, 1983 for surveys). These interventions may aim at one or more of the following types of targets:

where one enters:

Members—changing or selecting for skills, attitudes, and values through training programs and courses (e.g., the management development program in the Southwestern Hospitals case below); recruitment, selection, counseling, and placement, stress management and health-maintenance programs.

Behavior and processes—changing interaction processes, such as decision making, leadership, and communication through sensitivity training, team building (e.g., case 2), process consultation (see below), third-party intervention for conflict resolution; feedback of survey data for self-diagnosis and action planning.

Organizational structures and technologies—redesigning jobs (e.g., case 3), administrative procedures, reward mechanisms, the division of labor, coordinating mechanisms (see Chapter 4), introducing new work procedures (e.g., work teams instead of assembly line in automobile plant).

Organizational goals, strategies, and cultures—promoting goal clarification and the formulation of strategies for coping with markets and other external conditions through workshops and exercises (e.g., "Open Systems Planning" in Chapter 5); changing corporate culture (values, norms, beliefs) to fit strategies and environmental conditions.

A case study. The following case describes the diagnostic stage of an organization-development project and the recommendations made during the planning stage. It illustrates the methods used, the ways in which consultants may redefine the problems presented to them, and the way that diagnosis can lead to recommendations for action.

Southwestern Hospital System (SHS), a nonprofit chain of 12 hospitals, was in serious financial trouble when its top management turned for help to a team of university-based organizational consultants (Tichy, 1978, 1983). SHS asked the consultants for help after their chronic financial problems had become acute as a result of changes in a local employer's health program that had supplied nearly 30% of SHS's revenues. The consultants suggested that they conduct a broad diagnostic study, instead of concentrating on the immediate crisis. Once agreement was reached on the scope and character of the study, the consultants framed their diagnostic study to include underlying managerial and organizational problems that might threaten SHS's long-term viability. Guided by a broad analytical framework (similar to the one described in Chapter 2), they gathered data on SHS's financial and organizational environment and on its major organizational components, including

—management's view of SHS's mission, objectives, and long-term strategy

—SHS's management style (participativeness, flexibility, openness of communication)

—managerial structures and processes (such as conflict resolution-procedures, decision making, communication patterns, mechanisms for coordinating work)

—SHS's performance and outputs

The consultants interviewed the hospital heads, directors of nursing, chiefs of the medical staffs, and 14 members of the staff at SHS headquarters. They also studied organizational documents, observed administrative meetings and managerial work, and conducted a questionnaire study among employees. The questionnaire dealt with satisfaction with work, the goals of SHS, conflict resolution techniques, and informal (unofficial) work relations.

After analyzing these data. the consultants concluded that the administrators at SHS needed to become more skilled at analyzing external developments and planning to deal with them. They also found that SHS needed a more flexible organizational structure so that it could better handle the many uncertainties in its environment (see Chapter 4). Hence they recommended that SHS introduce new forms of coordination between the hospitals and the headquarters, create a program of strategic planning, and start a management development program to train administrators to handle their tasks more professionally.

Diagnostic activities outside of the diagnostic stage. Many organization development projects shift back and forth between stages rather than proceeding sequentially. In addition, consultants often engage in diagnostic activities during other stages in a consultation. In the *scouting stage*, for example, to get a feel for interpersonal processes, consultants may closely, but informally, observe interactions between clients and other members of the organization that occur in the consultants' presence. Similarly, they may tour the organization's physical plant and note any unobtrusive indications of working conditions, morale, and performance. On a walk through a corporate headquarters, for instance, an experienced consultant might notice that office workers have not personalized their workspaces with pictures of their families and desk ornaments, as so often occurs. The consultant would then make a mental note to check whether this tendency reflects low identification with the workplace among office workers or a corporate policy forbidding personalization of work stations. During scouting consultants may also conduct a few interviews or discussions with important members in order to become familiar with the organization and to assess the members' attitudes toward the proposed consulting project. They will also read any available documents on the organization's history, purposes, and current operations.

Based on this information consultants usually make a *preliminary diagnosis* of the organization's needs and strengths and its capacity for improvement and change. This preliminary diagnosis is critical to the further development of the project. The experienced practitioner will seek to determine as early as possible whether members of an organization are likely to cooperate with a more formal diagnostic study and how willing and able they are to reach decisions and act in response to feedback. By discussing these first impressions with clients, practitioners can adjust their expectations and those of their clients and avoid entering into a relationship that will become an exercise in frustration for both parties.

In a sense, diagnosis also forms a part of the *action stage* of organization development because it is an *intervention* into the routine life of an organization (Argyris, 1970). The process of asking people about their work and their organization encourages them to examine their own feelings, to think about the way their organization is run, and may lead them to expect that management will act to change things. In *process consultation* (Schein, 1969), for example, the practitioner provides feedback on group processes to heighten awareness of these processes and help improve them. Similarly in Open Systems Planning (see Chapter 5), the consultant helps managers diagnose their organization's environmental position in order to aid decision making and strategy formulation. Many of the issues that arise during diagnosis also become important when consultants and clients move into the *evaluation stage* and try to determine what effects some intervention has had. In light of this evaluation, clients and consultants may negotiate entry into another cycle of diagnosis, planning, and action.

Participation in Diagnosis by Members of the Organization

Advantages and disadvantages. Many organization development projects and other consultations can be described as *consultant-centered* because the consultant takes on most of the responsibility for guiding the project from diagnosis through the planning of proposed actions and may even conduct any interventions or supervise their implementation. Because diagnosis requires technical skills, it often becomes very consultant centered. Once the proposed study is approved, clients and other members of the organization may not be actively involved until they receive feedback on the findings. Practitioners often prefer this type of diagnosis because it seems simpler and more suitable to objective, rigorous research. However, they often discover after giving feedback that their clients regard the study's findings as irrelevant or overly threatening and are unwilling to act upon them (Block, 1981; Turner, 1982; see also Chapter 6).

In contrast, *client-centered* diagnoses involve clients or members appointed by them in as many phases of the study as is feasible (Lawler & Drexler, 1980; Turner, 1982). One benefit of this approach is that members can more readily contribute their insights and expertise about organizational life as they participate actively in gathering and analyzing diagnostic data. In addition, participation often increases members' commitment to the importance of the study and makes the feedback more believable and salient for them. Participation also enhances the possibility that members will develop the capacity to assess their own operations. This capacity for routine self-assessment can help organizations cope with the rapid pace of social, technological, and economic change (Nadler et al., 1976; Torbert, 1981; Wildavsky, 1972). On the other hand, the active involvement of members in diagnosis may raise questions about the study's objectivity and may lead people to fear that their responses or observed behavior will not be kept confidential.

Self-Diagnosis. Members of an organization may be able to conduct a self-diagnosis without the aid of a professional consultant, if they are open to self-analysis and criticism, and if some members have the skills needed for the gathering and interpretation of information. Here is an example of a modest self-diagnosis (Austin et al., 1982, p. 20):

> The executive director of a multi-service youth agency appointed a program-review committee to make a general evaluation of the services provided by the agency and make recommendations for improving its effectiveness. The committee included clinical case workers, supervisors, administrators, and several members of the agency's governing board. The director of the agency, who had technical knowledge of how to conduct such a study, served as an advisor to the committee. She asked the committee members to look first at the agency's intake service, because it was central to the operations of the entire agency

and suffered from high turnover among its paid staff. Besides examining intake operations, the committee members decided to investigate whether clients were getting appropriate services. They interviewed both the paid and the volunteer intake staff and surveyed clients over a three-month period. Their main finding was that there were substantial delays in client referral to counseling. They traced these delays to the difficulties that the half-time coordinator of intake had in handling the large staff, many of whom were volunteers, and to the heavy burden of record keeping that fell on the intake workers. This paperwork was required by funding agencies but did not contribute directly to providing services to clients. In order to increase the satisfaction of the intake staff and thereby reduce turnover, the committee recommended that the coordinator's position be made full time and that the paperwork intake be reduced. The executive director accepted the first recommendation and asked for further study of how to streamline the record-keeping process and reduce paperwork.

As this example suggests, during self-diagnosis members of the organization temporarily take on some of the tasks that would otherwise have been the responsibility of a professional consultant. Many of the interpretive models and research techniques described in this book and in other guides to diagnosis (e.g., Lauffer et al., 1977, 1982; Weisbord, 1978) could be used in such self-studies. People who want to conduct a self-diagnosis or act as consultants should be skilled at handling the interpersonal relationships that develop during a study and at giving feedback to groups and individuals, as well as at gathering and interpreting diagnostic data.

Comparisons to Other Types of Organizational Research

Another way of understanding diagnosis is to contrast it to other forms of investigation into organizational life. As defined here, diagnosis does not include investigations of programs by governmental bodies, comptrollers, ombudsman, journalists, and bodies granting professional certification (e.g., of schools). These studies are not ordinarily grounded in the methods and models of behavioral science and differ from diagnosis in their sponsorship, goals, assumptions, and in the relationships between investigators and members of the focal organization.

Diagnosis has more in common with *evaluation research* (Rossi & Freeman, 1982), in which behavioral science research contributes to the planning, monitoring, and assessment of the costs and impacts of social programs in areas such as health, education, and welfare. Like diagnosis, evaluation is practically oriented, and it may focus on effectiveness. But diagnosis

—uses many definitions of effectiveness, rather than concentrating on project impacts on some target population (e.g., impact of reading readiness program on preschoolers)
—focuses more on the organizations delivering goods and services than on their impacts on clients and customers
—examines operations, processes, and structures more fully, rather than concentrating on whether projects were conducted according to plans

The term *organizational assessment* is sometimes used to describe the gathering of useful data about organizations through social science research techniques (Lawler et al., 1980). Diagnosis is one use of assessment data, but assessment can also refer to other uses, such as helping public and private agencies formulate policies and allocate funds (e.g., to help reduce stress at work) or conducting academic research on organizational variables (e.g., determining the causes of job satisfaction).

Diagnosis differs substantially from *nonapplied, academic research* on organizations in its emphasis on obtaining results that will be immediately useful to members of a client organization (Block, 1981, p. 142). Unlike academic research, diagnostic studies

—concentrate on the causes of a problem or condition that can be changed most readily, even if these are not the most important or interesting from a researcher's point of view
—may encourage the members of the organization under study to become involved in the research
—may have to use impressionistic, unsystematic research methods to conform to practical constraints and client preferences
—need to rely on hunches, experience, and intuition, as well as scientific methods when analyzing data and formulating conclusions and recommendations
—cannot remain neutral about the impact of their study on the organization and needs and concerns of members of the organization

These and other differences between diagnosis and nonapplied research can create serious dilemmas for diagnostic practitioners who seek to maintain academic research standards (see Chapter 6).

THREE FACETS OF DIAGNOSIS

To conduct a diagnosis, consultants have to deal simultaneously with issues of *process, interpretation*, and *method* and try to achieve an appropriate match between them. Thus, for example, consultants may choose a data-gathering technique, such as observing work on a shop floor, because that method is less likely than others (e.g., questionnaires) to encourage speculations that changes will soon occur in the plant. The discussion that follows highlights important features of the three facets of diagnosis and the relations among them.

Process

Phases in diagnosis. In some diagnoses consultants simply provide feedback on the state of the organization and leave decisions about appropriate actions up to clients, whereas in others they recommend one or more specific interventions. In either case the diagnostic tasks, techniques, and the relationships between clients and the organization shift as the diagnosis moves through a series of phases that are roughly analogous to the stages of organization development discussed above (see also Nadler, 1977):

Scouting—Clients and consultants explore expectations for the study, client presents problems, challenges; consultant assesses likelihood of cooperation with various types of research, probable receptiveness to feedback, makes a preliminary reconnaissance of organizational problems and strengths.

Contracting—Consultants and clients negotiate and agree on the nature of the diagnosis and the consulting relationship.

Study design—Methods, measurement procedures, sampling, analysis, and administrative procedures are planned.

Data gathering—Data are gathered through interviews, observations, questionnaires, analysis of secondary data, group discussions and workshops.

Analysis—The data are organized and summarized; consultants (and sometimes clients) interpret them and prepare for feedback.

Feedback—The consultants present their findings to clients and other members of the client organization. Feedback may include explicit recommendations or more general findings to stimulate discussion, decision making, and action planning.

As the following case suggests, these phases may not occur sequentially in practice and may overlap:

[handwritten annotation: biases of consultant may make client aware of something not really a problem or[13] doesnt exist — self-fulfilling prophecy]

The owner and president of 21C Scientific Instruments, a small manufacturing firm, asked a private consultant to examine ways to improve efficiency and morale. They agreed that a set of in-depth interviews would be conducted with divisional managers and a sample of other employees. The first interviews with top managers suggested that their frustrations and poor morale stemmed from the firm's lack of growth and the president's failure to include the managers in decision making and strategy formulation. In light of these findings the consultant returned to the president, discussed the results of these interviews and suggested refocusing the diagnosis on the relationships between the managers and the president and on planning and strategy formulation within the firm.

In this case analysis and feedback began before the data gathering phase was completed. In addition the diagnosis shifted back into the contracting phase when the consultant sought approval to redefine the diagnostic problem and change the research design.

Key process issues. The relationships that develop between practitioners and members of a client organization can greatly affect the outcomes of an organizational diagnosis, just as they affect other aspects of consulting (Block, 1981; Turner, 1982). Although clients and practitioners should try to define their expectations early in the project, they will often have to redefine their relationship during the course of the diagnosis so as to deal with issues that were neglected during initial contracting or arose subsequently.[2] To manage the consulting relationship successfully, practitioners need to handle the following key process issues (see Nadler, 1977; Van de Ven & Ferry, 1980, pp. 22–51) in ways that promote cooperation between themselves and members of the client organization:

> *Purpose*—What are the goals of the study, how are they defined, and how can the outcomes of the study be evaluated? What issues, challenges, and problems are to be studied?
>
> *Design*—How will members of the organization be affected by the study design (organizational features to be studied, units and individuals included in the data-gathering, and types of data collection techniques)?
>
> *Support and cooperation*—Who sponsors and supports the study, and what resources will the client organization contribute? What are the attitudes of other members of the organization toward the study?

2. Suggestions like these that are addressed to consultants (or practitioners) are intended for would-be and beginning practitioners as well as more experienced ones.

Participation—What will be the role of members of the organization in planning the study, gathering the data, interpreting them, and reacting to them?

Feedback—When, how, and in what format will feedback be given? Who will receive feedback on the study and what uses will they make of the data?

The challenge of successfully handling these issues will become apparent as we elaborate on them below and in subsequent chapters.

Interpretation

The second facet of diagnosis involves defining the diagnostic problems, choosing topics for study, and interpreting the results. The importance of *interpretation* was illustrated in the Southern Hospital Systems case, in which the consultants went beyond the initial definition of the organization's problem as an immediate financial crisis and *redefined* that problem as a chronic failure to cope with external conditions. As is often the case, this redefinition contained an image of the organization's desired state, helped specify the issues that should be studied in depth, and even suggested ways that the clients could deal with the problem. In formulating their recommendations the consultants also had to consider which possible solutions were more likely to be accepted and successfully implemented by their clients (see Chapter 2, "Assessing the Feasibility of Change. . .").

Interpretive questions. The following summary of questions that consultants can ask themselves (based partly on Beckhard, 1969, p. 46, and Block, 1981, p. 143) highlights this process of interpretation. The term "problem" is used here to cover any kind of gap between actual and ideal conditions, including challenges to enter new fields, raise standards, and so on.

(1) *Interpreting the initial statement of the problem*—How does the client initially define the problems, needs, and challenges facing the organization or unit? How does the client view the desired state of the organization?

(2) *Redefining the problem*—How can the problem be redefined so that it can be investigated and workable solutions developed? What assumptions about the preferred state of the organization and definitions of organizational effectiveness will be used in the diagnosis? How will solving the problem contribute to organizational effectiveness? What aspects of organizational life will be the focal points of the diagnosis?

/Stakeholders

(3) *Understanding the current state*—What individuals, groups, and components of the organization are most affected by this redefined problem and most likely to be involved in or affected by its solution? What is their current state? How is the problem currently being dealt with? How do members of the relevant groups define the problem and suggest solving it? What organizational resources and strengths could help contribute to solving the problem and improving effectiveness?

(4) *Identifying the forces for and against change*—What internal and external groups and conditions create pressure for organizational change and what are the sources of resistance to it? How ready and capable of changing are the people and groups who are most affected by the problem and its possible solutions? Do they have common interests or needs that could become a basis for working together to solve the problem?

(5) *Developing workable solutions*—Which behavior patterns and organizational arrangements, if any, can be most easily changed to solve problems and improve effectiveness? What are the best ways to introduce these changes?

In some diagnoses responsibility for the fourth and fifth task is left entirely up to clients and members of the organization (see Chapter 6). Even in such cases, however, the analysis and feedback may reflect practitioners' assumptions about how to improve the organization.

Level of analysis. A major interpretive issue facing consultants concerns the level of analysis at which they will examine a problem and suggest dealing with it. Questions about people's attitudes, motivations, and work behavior focus on the *individual level*. Those dealing with face-to-face relationships are at the *interpersonal level*. At the *group level* are questions about the performance and practices of departments or work units, like those raised in the case of the youth agency self-study. Then come questions at the *divisional level* about the management of major subunits (divisions, branches, factories) within large organizations and about relations between units within divisions. Finally, some investigations, like the study of Southwestern Hospital Systems, examine the *organization* as a whole and its relation to its environment.

Many important phenomena show up at more than one level of analysis. In a manufacturing division, for example, the main technology (work methods and techniques) might be an assembly line. At the group level, each work group would have its own assembly techniques and equipment. At the individual level there are specific assembly procedures and the equipment used by each particular employee.

Certain other phenomena, like the aggressiveness of a firm's pursuit of new markets, can best be observed at a particular level—in this case the organizational level of analysis.

The choice of levels of analysis in diagnosis should reflect the nature of the problem, the goals of the diagnosis, and the organizational location of the clients. To facilitate the diagnosis and increase the chances that recommendations will be implemented, practitioners should concentrate on organizational features over which their clients have considerable control. Changes in the departmental structure of an entire division, for example, could be made only with the support of top management. In addition consultants should focus their diagnosis on levels at which interventions are most likely to lead to organizational improvement. For example, if managers asked for a diagnosis of problems related to employee performance, consultants would examine the rules and procedures for monitoring, controlling, and rewarding performance, if these *design tools* (see Chapter 4) could be readily changed by managerial clients. Other influential factors, such as workers' informal relations and their expectations about how hard they should work, might be more difficult to change.

Sometimes by raising or lowering the level of analysis consultants and clients can discover relationships and possibilities for change that were not previously apparent. For instance, rather than concentrating exclusively on leadership, group norms, and relationships within a single, underproductive work group, consultants might look at the work flow of the entire division in which the group was located and examine divisionwide mechanisms for coordinating and controlling performance.

Scope. Practitioners must also decide on the scope of their study. An individual-level diagnosis of broad scope, for example, would try to take into account all of the major factors related to the performance and feelings of the people within a focal unit (see Chapter 3). In contrast, a more narrowly focused individual-level diagnosis within the same unit might look only at those factors that are related to employees' plans to leave their current jobs.

Guides to interpretation. To decide what to study and how to interpret the diagnostic findings, consultants draw on their own professional experience, that of other consultants (as reported in conferences and in print), and on behavioral science methods, findings, and models. Analytical models like the one used in the Southwestern Hospital Systems diagnosis and those presented in the next four chapters can help consultants define and measure organizational effectiveness and identify conditions promoting effectiveness (Tichy, 1983).

Although research-based models can help guide diagnosis, they cannot specify in advance exactly what practitioners should study, how to interpret diagnostic data, or what interventions will work best in a particular client organization. The research behind these models shows that the managerial practices and organization patterns that promote effectiveness for one organization may not do so for another one facing different conditions. The kinds of rules and clear definitions of responsibilities that produce efficiency and high productivity in a state employment agency, for example, probably would not produce these results in a private job placement agency providing custom services to professionals and high-level managers. The chapters that follow point to some of the important *contingencies* that determine what practices work best, but a book of this length cannot adequately discuss all of them (see Fottler, 1981; Kanter & Brinkerhoff, 1981; Khandwalla, 1977; Lorsch & Morse, 1974; Miles & Snow, 1978; Mintzberg, 1979). Among the contingencies that may affect the sources of organizational effectiveness and the appropriateness of particular interventions are the following:

—organizational size and complexity
—overall purpose (e.g., profit versus service)
—sectoral or institutional setting (e.g., social welfare military, manufacturing, banking)
—technological type (individual unit, small batch, mass production; continuous production, e.g., chemicals)
—routineness of procedures
—workforce composition (e.g., occupational, educational, and skill levels)
—degree of bureaucratization
—stage in the organizational life cycle (starting up, established, declining, etc.)
—strategy for coping with the environment
—environmental predictability and competitiveness

In addition, because effectiveness can be defined in many ways (see Chapter 2), there is no single, ideal state for all organizations. Hence, consultants use many divergent models in diagnosis and recommend a wide range of intervention techniques for promoting effectiveness. So far, the virtues of most of these models and interventions have only been demonstrated in a preliminary fashion (see

Alderfer, 1977; Katz & Kahn, 1978; Strauss, 1976). In view of this situation, the chapters that follow seek to convey the range of choices open to practitioners of diagnosis. Models that take account of important contingencies and allow for different definitions of effectiveness (e.g., Lawrence & Lorsch, 1969) are preferred to those advocating some "one best way" to achieve effectiveness (e.g., Blake and Mouton, 1964; Likert, 1967). Special emphasis is given to models for examining organizational and division-level factors, such as organization-environment relations and the fits between organizational structures and technologies (see Chapters 4 and 5). This emphasis reflects the growing recognition in organizational studies (e.g., Miles, 1980) of the powerful impact of such factors on organizational effectiveness.

Methods

Table 1 provides an overview of the data-collection techniques frequently used in diagnosis and provides references for further study. As the table suggests, when choosing techniques for gathering and analyzing data consultants need to consider their implications for the consulting process and their appropriateness to the interpretive questions being asked, as well their practicality and their suitability from a more purely methodological standpoint. Consultants can use some techniques, such as interviewing and the conducting of workshops, to build an understanding of the purposes of the consulting project and sympathy with it. The impact of particular methods on the consulting process will depend, of course, on the ways in which members of the client organization react to them. In some cases, for example, methods like unstructured observations or the conducting of group interviews that do not yield quantified results may be regarded as unscientific. In others, the use of questionnaires or other techniques that lend themselves to quantification may be regarded as too impersonal and overly academic.

Key interpretive issues for consideration include the appropriateness of the method to the topic under study and to the level of analysis. Questionnaire data, for example, lend themselves most readily to examining individual-level attitudes and behavior, whereas observations and interviews can more readily be used to obtain data on interpersonal, group, and organizational factors (see Chapters 3–5).

More strictly methodological considerations concern the degree to which the gathering and analysis procedures are *structured* and *rigorous.* Structured techniques, like fixed-choice questionnaires and observations using a standard coding scheme, follow detailed rules and procedures that facilitate the summarizing of results according to precisely defined categories. Structured data-gathering and measurement procedures usually produce higher levels of reliability (i.e., reproducibility) between investigators, but it is very hard to structure techniques for assessing many complex phenomena, such as the degree to which managers accurately interpret external developments. Rigorous methods (which need not be quantitative) follow accepted standard of scientific inquiry. They have a high probability of producing results that are valid and could be replicated by other trained investigators. Nonrigorous approaches may yield valid results, but these cannot be evaluated or replicated by other investigators. Organization-development consultants may nonetheless use nonrigorous methods because of constraints on resources and access to data or because they feel that the nonrigorous methods contribute to the consulting relationships—for example, by facilitating a more client-centered diagnosis or by enabling them to draw on their professional judgment.

TABLE 1
A Comparison of Methods for Gathering Diagnostic Data*

Method	Advantages	Disadvantages
Questionnaires Self-administered schedules of questions with fixed-choice responses (see Chapter 3; App. B; Bowditch & Buono, 1982; Selltiz et al., 1981).	Easy to quantify and summarize results; quickest and least costly way to gather new data rigorously; suitable for large samples; useful for repeated measures over time, comparisons between units or to norms; standardized instruments contain pretested items and reflect diagnostic models; well-suited for studying attitudes.	Hard to obtain data on structure, behavior, etc., little information on contexts, situations shaping behavior; not suited for subtle or sensitive issues; impersonal; risks of nonresponse, biased answers, invalid questions; requires skills in constructing instruments and quantitative analysis; danger of over-reliance on standard instruments.

Interviews
Interviewer poses open-ended questions according to fixed schedule, interview guide (list of topics) or on-the-spot judgment (see Chapter 2, 3, 5, App. A; Cannell & Kahn, 1968; Schatzman & Strauss, 1973; Selltiz et al., 1981).

Readily cover wide range of topics and features; can be modified to fit needs before or during interview; can convey empathy, build trust; rich data; provide understanding of respondent's own viewpoint and interpretations.

Expensive, require skilled interviewers; sampling problems in large organizations; respondent and interviewer bias; noncomparability of responses in unstructured or semistructured interviews; difficult to analyze and interpret results.

Observations
Observations of people and their work settings (see Chapter 3; Lofland, 1973; Perkins et al., 1981; Schatzman & Strauss, 1973).

Data on behavior are independent of people's generalizations, feelings, opinions; information on effects of situations; flexible, rich data on range of hard-to-measure topics; generate insights and new hypotheses.

Constraints on access are (timing, distance, secrecy, participants' objections); sampling problems; costly, require trained observers; observers bias/reliability; may affect behavior of those observed; problems of interpretation, analysis, reporting; may seem unscientific.

Secondary Analysis
Use of organizational documents, reports, files, unobtrusive measurements (e.g., rate of suggestion box use) (see Chapter 2; Selltiz et al., 1981; Webb et al., 1966).

Unobtrusive, members do not feel or react to measurement; often quantifiable; repeated measures can show change; members of organizations can help gather, analyze data; validity and believability of familiar measures (e.g. wastage); often cheaper and faster than collecting new data; can provide data on total organization and environment.

Access, retrieval, analysis problems can raise costs and time requirements; validity and believability may be low and interpretation difficult when data are not used for original purpose; need to interpret in context; limited coverage of many topics.

Workshops and Group Discussions Discussions on group processes, history, challenges directed or facilitated by consultant or leader; simulations and exercises (see Chapter 5; Schein, 1969).	Useful data on complex, subtle processes; interactions can stimulate thinking; data available for immediate feedback and analysis; high involvement of members of organization; self-diagnosis possible; can feed directly into action planning; consultant can convey empathy, build trust.	Biases due to group processes (e.g., stifling of unpopular views) and leaders' influence; requires group skills; depends on high levels of trust and cooperation within group; impressionistic, not rigorous, may produce superficial, biased results.

*Derived in part from Bowditch & Buono (1977, pp. 32–33). Nadler (1977, p. 119). Sutherland (1978, p. 163).

No single method for gathering and analyzing data can suit every diagnostic problem and situation, just as there cannot be a universal model for guiding diagnostic interpretations or one ideal procedure for managing the consulting process. By using several methods to gather and analyze their data, practitioners can compensate for many of the drawbacks associated with relying on a single method. They will also need to choose methods that fit the diagnostic problems and contribute to cooperative, productive consulting relationships.

EXERCISE

It will be easier and more satisfying for you to base all of the exercises in this book on the same organization. In addition to organizations where you work or where you know someone who can help you get access to information and people, consider the possibility of studying some part of the university, such as the housing office or the student union, or one of the many voluntary organizations found on campus and in the community. Once you have located an organization or unit (e.g., department, branch), discuss the possibility of studying it with a person who could give you permission to do so and could help you learn about the organization. Explain that you want to do several exercises designed to help you learn how behavioral science consultants and researchers can help organizations deal with issues and challenges confronting them and contribute to their improvement. Promise not to identify the organization and explain that your reports will only be read by your instructor.

If your contact expresses interest in becoming a client—in the sense of wanting to get feedback from your project—explain that you will be glad to provide oral feedback to the contact person only, provided that the anonymity of the people studied can be preserved. During these discussions try to learn as much about your contact person's job, his or her view of organizational affairs, degree of interest in your project, and how much help you can expect from this person. If possible, ask your contact person to take you on a tour of the organization's headquarters or physical plant, and to try to give you an overview of the organization's operations.

Next, imagine that you are going to conduct an organizational diagnosis. What have you learned during your "scouting" that bears on items 1 and 2 in the Interpretive Questions listed in the chapter? Pay particular attention to the way your contact person defined the organization's problems and strengths. Do any alternative interpretations occur to you? Summarize your experiences and understandings so far in a report on the following topics:

(1) Description of the organization and the contact person (including source of access to them)

(2) Initial contacts—including your feelings and behavior and those of the contact person

(3) Your contact peron's view of the organization's strengths, weaknesses, current problems, desired state (see topic 1 of the Interpretive Questions)

(4) Your understanding of these issues (see topic 2 in the Interpretive Questions)

(5) Preliminary thoughts about conducting a diagnosis—topics, methods, groups and individuals to be included

2

Using the
Open System Model

A model of organizations as open systems is presented that can help practitioners choose topics for diagnosis, develop criteria for assessing organizational effectiveness, and decide what steps, if any, will help clients solve problems and enhance organizational effectiveness. A list of Basic Organizational Information to gather at the start of a diagnosis is provided, and methods are discussed for gathering and analyzing data in both broad and focused diagnoses.

THE ORGANIZATION AS
AN OPEN SYSTEM

The open systems approach provides practitioners with an abstract model that is applicable to any kind of organization and to divisions or departments within them (Beer, 1980; Hall, 1982; Katz and Kahn, 1978; Kotter, 1978; Miles, 1980; Nadler & Tushman, 1980). One useful version of this model is shown in Figure 1.

System Elements

Here are the main elements in the model and their key subcomponents:

> *Inputs (or resources)*—This includes the raw materials, money, people ("human resources"), information, and knowledge that an organization obtains from its environment and that contribute to the creation of its outputs.
> *Outputs*—This includes the products, services, and ideas that are the outcomes of organizational action. An organization transfers its main outputs back to the environment and uses others internally.
> *Technology*—This includes the methods and processes for transforming resources into outputs. These methods may be mental (e.g., exercising medical judgment), as well as physical (e.g., drug therapy), and mechanical (e.g., computerized data processing).

23

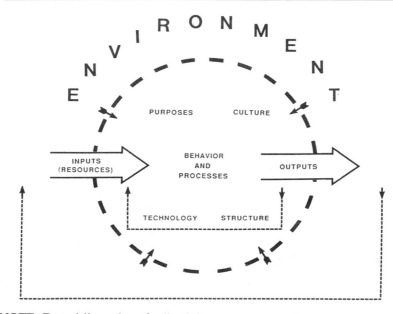

NOTE: Dotted lines show feedback loops.

Figure 1: Organizations as Open Systems

Environment—The *Task Environment* includes all the external organizations and conditions that are directly related to an organization's main operations and its technologies. They include suppliers, unions, customers, clients, regulators, competitors, markets for products and resources, and the state of knowledge concerning the organization's technologies. The *General Environment* includes institutions and conditions that may have infrequent or long-term impacts on the organization and its task environment, including the economy, the legal system, the state of scientific and technical knowledge, social institutions such as the family, population distribution and composition, the political system, and the national culture within which the organization operates.

Purposes—This includes the strategies, goals, objectives, plans, and interests of the organization's dominant decision makers. *Strategies* are overall routes to goals, including ways of dealing with the environment (e.g., strategy for expanding operations into the construction business); *goals* are desired end states (e.g., becoming the leading construction firm in the South), whereas *objectives* are specific targets and indicators of goal attainment (e.g., 5% growth per year). *Plans* specify courses of action toward some end. Purposes may be explicit or implicit in the decision makers' actions. They are the outcomes of conflict and negotiation among powerful parties within and outside the organization.

Behavior and processes—This includes the prevailing patterns of behavior, interactions, and relationships between groups and individuals—including cooperation, conflict, coordination, communication, controlling and rewarding behavior, influence and power relations, supervision, leadership, decision making, problem solving, planning, goal setting, information gathering, self-criticism, evaluation, and group learning.

Culture—This includes shared norms, beliefs, values, symbols, and rituals relating to key aspects of organizational life, such as the nature and identity of the organization, the way work is done, the value and possibility of changing or innovating, and relationships between lower and higher ranking members.

Structure—This includes enduring relations between individuals, groups, and larger units—including role assignments (job descriptions; authority, responsibility, privileges attached to positions); grouping of positions in divisions, departments and other units; standard operating procedures; established mechanisms for handling key processes such as coordination (e.g., committees, weekly meetings); human resources mechanisms (career lines, reward, evaluation procedures); actual patterns (e.g., informal relations, cliques, coalitions, power distribution) that may differ from officially mandated ones.

Key Features of the Model

The model contains several important ideas for diagnosis:

(1) *External conditions influence the flow of inputs (resources) to organizations, affect the reception of outputs, and can directly affect internal operations*—for instance, when regulatory agencies define production standards. Figure 1 depicts the possibility for direct impacts on internal operations by showing a broken, permeable boundary around the organization. Feedback from outputs to inputs occurs when responses by customers or clients to products or services affect resource flows—for instance, when demand for cigarettes dropped among American men because they recognized the health hazards of smoking.

(2) *Organizations use many of their products, services, and ideas as inputs to organizational maintenance or growth* (as shown in Figure 1 by the feedback loop within the organizational boundary). A computer firm, for example, may use its own machines and software, and a university may employ its doctoral students as instructors. The

human consequences of work—including members' satisfactions with the quality of their working life and their motivations to contribute to the organization—are another form of output that has important *internal* impacts (see Chapter 3).

(3) *Organizations are influenced by their members as well as their environments.* The employees and clients who enter an organization may contribute to its operations, resist them, or change them from within. In organizations in which the main job involves educating, classifying, or treating people, the same people who enter it are ultimately transferred back to the environment—hopefully healthier, wealthier, or wiser. While these clients are being treated or receiving services, they may change or shape the very practices that were designed to influence them. Current values and standards increasingly urge managers to consider what is good for their employees and clients and not to treat them as inanimate resources (e.g., Business Week, 1981a).

(4) *The eight system elements and their subcomponents are interrelated and influence one another.* An organization's culture and structure affect members' behavior, but their behavior also shapes the structure and the culture. Environments shape purposes, but organizations also shape their environments. Practitioners should therefore be on the watch for nonobvious relations between system features so that they can better anticipate the likely impacts of changes in some part of the organization. They should consider the possibility, for example, that managers may acquire a new computer system to enhance efficiency in record-keeping and accounting, but that once the system is installed, people will start looking for new ways to use it. Thus, technology may shape objectives as well as responding to them.

(5) *Organizations are constantly changing as relationships among their system elements shift.*[1] An organization's responses to internal and external changes depend on members' interpretations of these changes and their decisions about how to deal with them. Information about internal and external developments flows through both official and unofficial channels. Small changes in one part of the system may not require more than routine adjustments in other elements, but major changes in one element can set off a series of changes in others. For instance, if a firm hires people with somewhat less training than past recruits, current procedures for placing and training new employees may still be used with slight adjustments. On the other hand, if the firm sets up a branch overseas and begins to hire people who have radically different backgrounds than those employed at home, major shifts may be needed in the technology, structure, and processes in order to adapt to the employees' skills, experience, and work styles.

---

1. The assumption that systems seek a state of "balance" has been widely criticized (e.g., Abrahamsson, 1977) and has been avoided here.

(6) *An organization's success depends heavily on its ability to adapt to its environment—or to find a favorable environment in which to operate—as well as on its ability to tie people into their roles in the organization, conduct its transformative processes, and manage its operations* (Katz & Kahn, 1978). These "system needs" do not necessarily correspond to the interests or priorities of top management (see "How to Choose Effectiveness Criteria," later in this chapter).

(7) *Any level or unit within an organization can be viewed as a system.* So far the model has only been applied to the total organization, but a major division or branch within an organization can also be viewed as a system having all of the elements and features mentioned above. Even a single department or work group within a department can be analyzed as a subsystem embedded within the larger systems. The broader organizational conditions shape the operations of such subunits but do not fully determine them.

Using the System Model

The open system model provides practitioners with a comprehensive yet flexible guide to examining the main features of an organization and understanding their relationships.

Basic organizational information. Drawing on the model (and on Levinson, 1972, pp. 55–59), we generated the following list of basic information about a client organization (or subunit) to gather at the beginning of a diagnosis. After obtaining the overview provided by this information, consultants can decide what topics, if any, they want to study in greater depth. The basic information that is most readily available should be gathered during scouting, and the rest of this information should be collected as quickly as possible after contracting to conduct a diagnosis.

Basic Organizational Information.

(1) *Outputs*—main products or services, volume of sales, production, services delivered etc.; human "outputs" (indications of satisfaction and commitment such as absenteeism, turnover).

(2) *Purposes*—official statements of goals and mission; actual priorities as indicated by budget allocations to divisions, programs (e.g., percentage of budget allocated to research and development).

(3) *Inputs*—financial assets, capital assets including real estate, physical plant, equipment (amount, condition, e.g., age, degree of obsolescence, state of repair); revenues and allocations from funding sources (e.g., for public agencies); human resources—numbers of employees by job category, social and educational backgrounds, training and previous experience.

(4) *Environment*—affiliation and ownership (public, versus private, affiliation with larger bodies and nature of regulation by them); industry;
task environment, including major markets, customers, clients;
suppliers, competitors, regulators, distributors etc.; availability of
funds for growth and expansion (internal and external borrowing,
grants and budget prospects for public agencies); physical and social
surroundings (e.g., city center versus suburban location, transportation, access to services, neighborhood safety).

(5) *Technology*—type of production (unit, batch, mass, continuous process), level of automation, use of sophisticated information-processing
technologies; main procedures used to treat or process people in
service organizations; data on operational failures, accidents, waste,
down time, etc.

(6) *Structure*—major divisions and units; number of levels of hierarchy;
basis for grouping of units (e.g., by functions, markets, see Chapter 4),
coordination mechanisms; spans of control (number of subordinates
reporting directly to each supervisor); spatial distribution of units,
employees, and activities; unions and other forms of employee repre-
sentation, grievance procedures; human resources policies and procedures (recruitment, selection, orientation, training, placement and
promotion, pay, health, safety, benefits); recent union contracts and
other obligations affecting human resources management (e.g.,
directives relating to hiring minorities); informal power blocks
and coalitions.

(7) *Behavior and processes*—main processes for high-level decision making,
strategy formulation, and planning; major types of conflicts—e.g.,
labor relations, conflicts between divisions; strength of unions and
degree of militancy, union involvement in issues other than compensation; communication styles (e.g., oral, written, meeting oriented).

(8) *Culture*—symbols of organizational identity (logo, slogans, current
advertising campaigns, physical appearance of corporate headquarters and branches); myths (stories of founders, historic successes);
rituals (outings, sporting events, celebrations, annual reviews and
plans); jargon (frequently used terms and phrases); dominant styles
of dress, decor, life style; clients' working styles (e.g., taking work
home, working overtime).

(9) *System dynamics*—overall financial condition—profits, losses, deficits;
growth and contractions (e.g., layoffs, consolidations of units) of
inputs, outputs, operating budget; major changes in any of above
features.

Using the system model in broad diagnoses. Practitioners who intend
to conduct a broad diagnosis can first obtain as much of the Basic
Organizational Information as possible and then gather data in

greater depth on each of the eight system elements and their relationships. The consultants in the Southern Hospital Systems case (see Chapter 1) used a systems approach like this to decide what topics to study. Then they assessed the degree of fit between system elements like structure and environment (see Chapter 4, "Diagnosing System Fits").

Using the model in focused diagnoses. To apply the model to more narrowly focused diagnoses, practitioners should first gather the Basic Organizational Information so as to better understand the context of the focal problem or issue. Then they can choose the appropriate level(s) of analysis, the system elements most directly related to the focal problem, particular subcomponents within these elements, and the units in which data will be gathered. In data gathering and analysis, practitioners should examine the impacts of *all* eight system elements on the focal problem. Suppose, for example, that the head of a firm that was having trouble retaining top quality engineers in its research and development division asked an internal consultant to study the division's compensation policies. Focusing on the division as a whole, the consultant could examine current compensation policies (a subcomponent of its structure) and the relations between these policies and all eight system elements. Important relations to environmental factors, for instance, would be evident in the ability of the current benefits package to compete with that of other firms recruiting from the same labor pool. Processual impacts would show up in the kinds of behavior and activities that were rewarded (e.g., were promotions going to more innovative engineers or to those who just met deadlines and handled routine problems?).

Redefining presented problems. The systems model can also help practitioners redefine the problems or challenges initially presented by clients. Redefinition occurs whenever consultants assume that presented problems may be symptomatic of broader, underlying conditions and then examine these conditions. In broad studies, like the Southwestern Hospital Systems diagnosis, the decision to examine all system elements and their relations implies an assumption that presented problems, such as falling revenues, reflect complex relations between system elements and will probably require interventions that change these relations. In more focused diagnoses as well, the examination of the links between a presented problem and all system elements can reveal underlying causes or suggest ways to solve the problem that were not considered by the client. The division manager struggling with high turnover among engineers, for example, may not have considered the possibility that a reward system that discouraged innovation and initiative could cause the more creative engineers to look elsewhere for challenging work.

By discovering such unrecognized linkages, consultants can help clients break out of familiar ways of interpreting and responding to problems and may discover solutions that are more feasible than those previously considered (e.g., reward creative work, rather than raising salaries across the board). Although helpful, the open systems model will not suggest exactly how to redefine a problem or how to go about solving it. Insights will typically derive more from past consulting experience and training, from ideas generated by members of the organization, and from the leads provided by some of the more explicit diagnostic models discussed in subsequent chapters.

Data collection. Practitioners can begin gathering the Basic Organizational Information listed above during site visits and initial meetings with clients during scouting (see Chapter 1). Statistics on topics such as budgets, work force composition, financial position, and the scope of operations can be found in organizational documents or can be prepared for the practitioner as soon as the contracting stage has been completed. Official statements of purpose and charts of the organizational structure should also be obtained. Site visits can provide some impressions of the organizational culture, such as the corporate image presented to visitors and employees by buildings, equipment, and furnishings (e.g., "high-tech" versus "tried and true" communications equipment; signs of prosperity and expansion versus signs of retrenchment and cost-cutting). Subsequent investigations will be needed, however, to determine whether these images reflect everyday practice. Bulletin boards and newsletters provide additional unobtrusive indications of organizational culture and processes. For instance, notices about sporting teams whose membership cuts across ranks point to informal contacts between ranks and may indicate a deemphasis of status differences among employees.

High-level managers or their assistants are usually asked to provide basic information. Then further interviews with top managers, department or division heads, and a sample of other members can provide more adequate data on those system features that were not adequately covered initially, such as organizational processes or members' assessments of how well things work in the organization. A schedule like the General Orientation Interview in Appendix A could be used to cover characteristics of units and some broader organizational factors, or a schedule could be created that concentrates on organizationwide features. Interviews with informed outsiders (e.g., journalists or customers) and external documents (newspapers, government reports, etc.) can provide additional data sources on the organization and its external relations.

Measurement problems. Because some of the factors covered in the Basic Organizational Information list and the General Orientation Interview are abstract and hard to measure, practitioners must often content themselves with nonrigorous measures. For instance, when analyzing basic information about the organizational culture of a firm, a practitioner might make a judgment as to the orientation toward employees conveyed in newsletters or other documents (e.g., hard-nosed and competitive versus caring and supportive) without systematically coding the contents of the documents or interviewing managers and employees about human resources policies. Use of more rigorous but time-consuming methods could only be contemplated if the topic were particularly critical to the diagnosis. In like manner, practitioners often have to settle for global assessments of very complex conditions. When interviewing top management, for example, practitioners may ask for general assessments of the organization's overall financial condition (ranging from excellent down to critical), the competitiveness of the environment, and its degree of threat or munificence.

Consultants can learn a great deal about their respondents' viewpoints and can identify controversial or problematic issues for further study by comparing their respondents' interpretations of such complex organizational and environmental conditions. They can also gain insights of this sort by comparing respondents' descriptions of ostensibly objective phenomena, such as the lines of authority and reporting. If, for example, departmental managers draw different organization charts of the same division, this diversity points to ambiguity and possibly to conflict about the lines of authority and the division of labor in that division. By using two or more types of data on the same topic (e.g., descriptions of corporate goals in the report to stockholders and in interviews) practitioners can also illuminate the perspectives and concerns of individuals and groups and can develop their own independent judgments about topics on which participants hold divergent views.

Summarizing and analyzing data. The lists of Basic Organizational Information and of System Elements can serve as accounting schemes within which consultants can organize and summarize their diagnostic findings. One straightforward approach is to make a separate card or file for each system element and then to enter information into appropriate files, cross-referencing them as needed, and noting the source of the information. A typical entry in the Technology file for a diagnostic study of a high school might read as follows:

Teaching techniques—most classes are lectures and discussions conducted by teacher, supplemented by homework exercises and projects. Remedial help available in Math and English. Labs in sciences. Microcomputer lab for word processing after school and for elective course in Programming. Two language labs per week in French and Spanish. Minimal use of audiovisual equipment, field trips, and so on.

Administrative: All filing is manual; electric and manual typewriters, photocopier; mimeograph in office; two phone lines.

Source: Assistant Principal.

To summarize responses to interviews based on a schedule like the General Orientation Interview, practitioners may group together responses to each question that make the same point and then record each type of response and the number of people giving it. If, for example, eight employees in a branch of a fast-food chain were interviewed, a typical entry in the summary might read as follows:

Are there any difficulties and barriers to getting work done here or doing it the way you'd like to?

—annoying customer complaints about food—taste, quality, and so on (3)
—pressures from supervisor to work faster, come in on weekends (2)
—none (2)
—we often run out of buns (1)

Practitioners may choose to present the entire range of responses as feedback in order to stimulate analysis of the operations and suggestions for their improvement, or they may summarize findings about organizational strengths and problems in a feedback report. In the hypothetical case above, if feedback was to be provided to the supervisor, the former method would probably be preferred, so that the two people who complained about the supervisor would not be singled out for attention.

The system model itself can also be used to analyze and present data about relationships between elements. A graphic approach that aids both analysis and feedback is to place all eight elements in a circle, list their important subcomponents, and draw color-coded lines between those elements or subcomponents that promote some focal condition, such as job satisfaction, and those that hinder it. Data supporting the inferences in the figure can be recorded separately and used appropriately in feedback.

CHOOSING EFFECTIVENESS CRITERIA

The systems model can also help consultants choose criteria for assessing an organization's current state and develop measures of effectiveness.

Types of Criteria

Output, system state, and adaptation criteria. Table 2 groups the many criteria that have been used to assess organizational effectiveness into three broad categories (see Cameron, 1980; Campbell, 1977; Kanter & Brinkerhoff, 1981). These criteria derive from clients' and consultants' images of some preferred organizational state and from their assumptions about the organizational conditions that can facilitate the achievement of those states. *Output-goal criteria* correspond to many of the specific targets toward which members of organizations strive. Sometimes they are expressed in terms of the success or failure to achieve some end, such as the design of a solar-powered bicycle or a city commission's development of a workable rezoning plan. Criteria dealing with output goals are most appropriate where goals can be defined in terms of clear, measurable objectives and members of the client organization agree about the meaning and importance of these goals. In contrast, this type of criterion is hard to use if members disagree about goals or if goals cannot be readily defined and measured, as is often the case in service and cultural organizations. Even if members of these organizations agree on some abstract goal, such as improving public health, they are likely to differ on its operational meaning and its measurement. An additional drawback of defining effectiveness solely in terms of output goals is that this approach tends to confine the consultant to a technical, evaluator's role.

TABLE 2
Effectiveness Criteria

Type	Operational Definitions
(1) Output Goals	
Goal Attainment	Success/Failure (e.g., rocket launching).
Quantity of Outputs	Productivity (units produced, hours of services provided, values of sales, services—sometimes per work unit or per time period); profits (revenues minus costs); revenues as percentage of investment; percentage of target group reached by services, messages.
Quality of Outputs	Number of rejects, returns, complaints; client, customer satisfaction; expert rating of services (e.g., in health education) or work performance (e.g., in manufacturing, military); impact of services or products on target population (e.g., impact of antilitter campaign).
(2) Internal System State	
Costs of Production or Services	Efficiency (ratio of output value to costs—e.g., labor, equipment—with constant quality); wastage, downtime.
Human Outcomes	Employee satisfactions with pay, working conditions and relationships; motivation (disposition to work); work effort (observed, reported); low absenteeism, lateness, and turnover; health and safety of workforce.
Consensus/Conflict	Agreement on goals and procedures; cohesion (mutual attraction, and identification with work group, and organization); cooperation (reported/observed) within and between units; few strikes, work stoppages, disputes, and feuds.
Work and Information Flows	Smooth flow of products, ideas and information; few snags, foul-ups, misunderstandings; rich, multidirectional communication, accurate analysis of information.

Interpersonal Relations	High levels of trust; open communication of feelings, needs between ranks; de-emphasis of status differences.
Participation	Subordinates participate in making decisions affecting them; diffusion of power and authority.
Fit	Compatibility of requirements of system elements.

(3) *Adaptation and Resource Position* - *combe used for eval. org/surviv rel.*

Resources-quantity	Size of organization (employees; cash, physical assets); resource flows (e.g., investment, grants and budget support in nonprofit organizations).
Resources-quality	Human capital (experience, and training of employees); desirability of clients (e.g., selectiveness of college admissions); reputation of staff.
Legitimacy	Support and approval by community and public bodies; public image; compliance with standards of legal, regulatory, professional bodies (e.g., government pollution control standards, accreditation of college).
Competitive/ Strategic Position	Market share, ranking among competitors in size, volume of business; reputation within the field or industry; full use of capacities to exploit external opportunities.
Impact on Environment	Ability to shape demand, government action, behavior of competitors, suppliers.
Adaptiveness	Adjustment to changes in inputs and demands for outputs; flexibility in handling crises, surprises.
Innovativeness	Number, quality of new products, services, procedures; incorporation of new technologies, management practices.
Fit	Compatibility of internal system elements with requirements, constraints of environment.

Many of the criteria in the second category refer to *internal organizational states and processes* that can contribute to achieving output goals, whereas others, like efficiency or employee satisfaction (see Chapter 3, "Quality of work life outcomes"), are sometimes regarded as ends in themselves. Efficiency and cost-related criteria are hard to apply to nonprofit organizations because of the difficulties of measuring all of the important aspects of outputs and inputs. In contrast, the system criteria relating to internal relationships and processes can be applied to any type of organization. They can be viewed as desirable states or as indicators of some more global state of organizational "health" (e.g., Beckhard, 1969) that facilitates coping with organizational challenges. Criteria relating to internal system states are also useful in the diagnosis of departments or subunits that have little control over their environments.

Many of the *adaptation and resource-position criteria* are applicable to nonprofit organizations, which may have unclear output goals, as well as to commercial firms. Even nonprofit organizations operate as open systems that compete for funds, personnel, and other scarce resources and face pressures to adapt to changing external conditions (see Chapter 5).

Comparison standards. In choosing and developing working definitions of effectiveness, consultants must decide what time frames and comparison standards to use (Cameron, 1980). They may compare

—current and past levels of effectiveness, e.g., rates of growth, development

—the effectiveness of units within the same organization, e.g., comparisons of efficiency ratings, accidents, quality

—the client organization's effectiveness to that of others in the same industry or field, e.g., comparisons of profitability or sales to industry figures

—the organization's current state to some minimum standard, e.g., conformity to federal environmental standards

—the current state to an ideal standard, e.g., innovativeness or community service

The time frame used may vary from hours or days to several years, depending in part on the organizational feature being assessed. Different time frames can also be applied to the same phenomenon. A manufacturing firm's performance may seem impressive, for example, if we look at its current quarterly profits or return on investment. In contrast. if that firm is achieving the results by cutting costs and aggressively marketing current products, it may be unable to sustain these results for more than a year or two because of lack of investment in new product development (Hayes & Abernathy, 1980).

Conflicts among effectiveness criteria. Although all the effectiveness criteria listed in Table 2 may seem reasonable at first glance, there actually are many contradictions and tensions among them. For example, growth usually indicates that an organization is successful in obtaining needed resources, but growth can also lead to less participation in decision making, reduced efficiency, and less ability to adjust to environmental change. The same manager may have conflicting priorities and evaluative criteria without being aware of the conflicts, because the criteria are not evoked simultaneously or their operational implications are not spelled out fully.

An additional problem is that few effectiveness criteria equally suit the interests and priorities of all members of an organization. The many groups and individuals who have a stake in an organization often have conflicting interests and engage in recurrent bargaining and influence struggles to promote their own goals and interests. In pursuing their own purposes, these *stakeholders* (or *constituencies*) typically advocate the use of divergent effectiveness criteria (Pennings & Goodman, 1977). In an industrial firm, for example, stockholders may want more short-term profits, while the research and development people favor investment that will support innovation and growth in the long run, and the unions press for better wages and working conditions. Hence, those effectiveness criteria that best reflect the interests and needs of one subgroup, such as the dominant decision makers within the top management, will probably neglect the priorities of less powerful managers, external clients, production workers, government regulators, and so on.

How to Choose Effectiveness Criteria

If the various effectiveness criteria are not mutually compatible and applicable, how should consultants choose appropriate criteria and incorporate them into diagnosis? To make these decisions they need to consider three sets of questions (Campbell, 1977; Goodman & Pennings, 1980):

(1) Who are the main clients for the study, what do they regard as the preferred state of the organization, and what criteria reflect the

degree of attainment of this state? How can the consultant help them resolve conflicts and ambiguities among their stated preferences?

(2) What other states or conditions will help promote client goals or are otherwise appropriate as effectiveness criteria?

(3) How can consultants encourage clients to adopt these additional priorities?

Identifying clients and clarifying their priorities. The main clients for a diagnosis are those people who will have responsibility for deciding what actions (if any) should be taken in light of the diagnostic findings and for planning and implementing such actions. These individuals are usually, but not always, the ones who originally solicited and sponsored the study.

One way for consultants to deal with conflicts between clients and other stakeholders about effectiveness is to ask clients to develop a working consensus with guidelines for choosing effectiveness criteria (e.g., Beckhard & Harris, 1977). Clients can then meet to define their priorities for the diagnosis with or without the help of the consultant. If this approach is impractical, consultants may simply accept the goals and priorities of the most powerful clients and then seek to find ways of achieving them that will bring benefits to the broadest possible spectrum of members and stakeholders (see Chapter 6, "Who Benefits?").

Consultants may also press clients to set priorities when the clients hold ambiguous or internally inconsistent views of what is best for the organization. To help resolve such conflicts and ambiguities, consultants should carefully examine data on the priorities reflected in actual practice (see Chapter 4), rather than relying solely on stated priorities. For example, consultants can examine how much top management has invested in research and development and whether they have recently promoted anyone who bucked the tide to champion a new product or administrative procedure, rather than relying on management's declarations of good intentions in these areas. When practitioners examine the priorities underlying major decisions, resource allocations, and patterns of rewarding and evaluating performance, they may find that operative goals and priorities diverge greatly from stated purposes.

If consultants discover major discrepancies between declared and operative priorities early in a diagnosis, they may present their findings to clients and help them to rework their priorities and conceptions of effectiveness in light of the feedback or help clients redouble their efforts to achieve their initially stated goals. This process of providing feedback about group goals and priorities can sometimes become a major focus of intervention that can help clients clarify their goals, priorities, policies, and evaluative criteria. In more client-oriented studies, the process of examining and clarifying priorities can occur quite naturally as consultants and clients collaborate in choosing effectiveness criteria during the design and analysis phases.

Choosing additional criteria. In most diagnoses consultants introduce additional effectiveness criteria that do not derive directly from initial client priorities but point to conditions (such as teamwork or flexibility) that can contribute to the achievement of clients' goals or are generally compatible with the clients' image of the desired state of the organization. Sometimes consultants also lead clients toward a radically different image of what is good for their organization—for example, by suggesting that if the organization does not become more innovative, it will ultimately encounter problems of adapting to its environment.

By introducing effectiveness criteria relating to the organization's internal system state and to its ability to obtain resources and adapt to its environment (see Table 2), practitioners can often help their clients redefine specific problems and challenges in terms of needs for improving broader, underlying forms of effectiveness. If these broader aspects of effectiveness can be enhanced, the organization will be better able to handle future problems, as well as coping with current ones. For example, enhancing the satisfaction and motivation of workers can help reduce such immediate symptoms of dissatisfaction as rapid employee turnover, absenteeism, and noncompliance with minimal performance requirements. But improving quality of work life, satisfaction, and motivation can also yield long-term benefits, such as a loyal, flexible work force.

In like manner, the criteria related to smooth, cooperative internal relationships and processes need not be applied only in cases of rancorous conflict or poor work flow. They are appropriate whenever work requires high levels of mutual consultation and cooperation—for instance, in professional and administrative teams. The major drawback of criteria that assume the need for fits among system parts and for smooth, trustful relations among employees is that they may lead practitioners to underestimate the potential contribution of tension and conflict to organizational change and adaptation. Conflict may be too low rather than too high if work standards are lax, if members automatically submit to authority, or if they avoid confronting the challenges and problems facing their organization (Robbins, 1978).

Criteria relating to resource position and adaptation are especially relevant when the task environment is changing very rapidly (e.g., in high-technology industries), is highly competitive, or poses a serious challenge to the client organization's viability (e.g., in social services faced with budget cuts). These criteria are especially suited for work with high-level administrators who have both the authority and the willingness to work for change in their organization's (or their division's) relation to its environment.

Clients are likely to reject findings that reflect priorities and evaluative standards that they do not understand or with which they disagree. Hence, consultants should reach an understanding with clients as soon as possible after agreeing to conduct a diagnosis about the effectiveness criteria, time frames, and comparison standards that will be used.

Problems of Measuring Effectiveness

In principle, the procedure for developing systematic measures of effectiveness is identical to that of developing any kind of measure (e.g., Selltiz et al., 1981). After clarifying the concept conceptually, the investigator specifies concretely what phenomena will be considered indicative of effectiveness and chooses measures that fit this operational definition. Here is an example that shows how the initial conceptualization of effectiveness affects subsequent choices:

Conceptualization A: Effectiveness refers (in part) to the absence of rancorous conflict among the people and groups who contribute to work flow
  Operational definition: absence of conflicts that interrupt work flow
  Possible measures: number of days lost to strikes and number of work stoppages
Conceptualization B: Effectiveness refers to smooth work flow
  Operational definition: absence of all types of interruptions in the work flow
  Possible measures: amount of time that units are idle while waiting for inputs; number of interruptions; total time to produce a product or complete some operation (e.g., develop marketing plan)

In practice, consultants may have to define and measure effectiveness in ways that allow them to engage in secondary analysis of data that are available or can be gathered quickly and inexpensively. Unless they keep clear conceptual and operational definitions of effectiveness in mind when working with these less-than-perfect data, they may interpret their findings incorrectly and overlook important phenomena that are not covered by these measures. For example, data on pupils' performance on standardized achievement tests might be readily available to consultants conducting a diagnosis of an elementary school. Unfortunately, these tests do not measure many important educational outcomes, such as the ability to engage in self study, critical thinking, and creativity. Yet these kinds of outcomes and the social and educational processes occurring within the school may actually be more relevant to the diagnosis than the outcomes on which data are available. A further problem arises when data were originally designed to evaluate the performance of employees or units. In such cases, members may have learned to perform in ways that make them look good on the measured criteria, such as the number of sales completed, while neglecting other desirable forms of behavior—such as customer satisfaction or service—that are less closely monitored (Lawler & Rhode, 1976).

Another issue in measuring effectiveness is the value of using objective, behavioral measures of effectiveness (such as the number of strike days), as opposed to subjective measures reflecting the judgements of participants of experts (e.g., descriptions of the quality of labor relations in the plant). In practice, this distinction often turns out to be far from clear cut (Campbell, 1977, p. 45). For example, the number of units manufactured in a plant during a month is apparently an objective measure, but we must have a standard in order to decide whether the figure is too high, too low, or just right. Even comparing the figure to past performance does not resolve the problem. Is a 5% growth over last year substantial or lackluster, in light of the efforts and investments made? In the final analysis, the kinds of objective data that managers collect and pay attention to and their evaluations of these figures all depend heavily on their subjective priorities and standards.

ASSESSING THE FEASIBILITY OF CHANGE
AND CHOOSING APPROPRIATE INTERVENTIONS

Interpretive and Process Issues

Consultants need to consider the following issues during diagnosis in order to decide what steps, if any, will help clients solve problems and enhance organizational effectiveness (see also Burke, 1982, pp. 215–233; President et al., 1980):

(1) Does the organization need basic changes? When performance gaps and other signs of ineffectiveness show up in diagnoses, consultants and clients should decide whether small system adjustments or basic changes are needed and then choose feasible routes toward either form of improvement. The periodic adjustments in procedures that most organizations use to cope with surprises and environmental fluctuations are typical of small *system adjustments* that do not fundamentally alter any system elements. Retailers, for example, temporarily hire extra help during the Christmas rush, and most organizations go through troubleshooting episodes during which members drop everyday matters and devote themselves to meeting a deadline or resolving a crisis. In like manner, managers may adjust rules and standard operating procedures slightly to cope with problems without making any fundamental changes.

In contrast, *basic changes* such as structural reorganizations (e.g., eliminating or creating positions), processual changes (e.g., increasing participation in decision making), and technological changes (e.g., computerizing record-keeping) substantially alter practices within one or more system elements and often have consequences that are felt at many organizational levels and within many systems elements. Such changes often reflect revised goals, strategies, and plans and usually require difficult decisions about reallocating funds and other resources.

Basic changes are needed when current ways of shifting routines and procedures to cope with problems have become insufficient or are likely to become outmoded in the near future. Troubleshooting procedures and other system adjustments are inadequate if an organization has fallen into a state of permanent crisis, lurching from one troubleshooting episode to another, or if the short-term solutions to crises create long-lasting havoc in the organization (Sayles, 1979, pp. 160–162). Moreover, basic changes are probably needed if symptoms of ineffectiveness such as quality problems, operating inefficiencies, and low morale persist despite many efforts to use "quick and easy" techniques to deal with these problems.

(2) Is there readiness for change? Members of an organization and external stakeholders often realize that "something must be done" to change an organization when they are faced with mounting signs of ineffectiveness—such as declining sales, poor quality, eroding budget support, labor unrest, internal conflict, or failures to exploit opportunities—or when they adopt new goals and strategies that call for

changes like growth, diversification, and innovation. Such shifts in priorities can occur as a result of changes in management or in response to the example of other organizations that pioneer a new technique, like robotics, or create new opportunities (e.g., by creating a new market). Diagnostic feedback that shows clients and other members that organizational problems are more acute or more widespread than they had thought may also increase readiness for change *if* the recipients of the feedback are not threatened by the prospect of change.

(3) How will members and external stakeholders react to proposed interventions? In considering possible steps to improve effectiveness, consultants need to consider whether clients, other members, and external stakeholders are likely to cooperate with an intervention or resist it. In particular, during diagnosis consultants should try to determine whether key decision makers and other powerful groups (see Chapter 4) are likely to support particular interventions and provide the backing and resources needed to implement them successfully. They should also examine the extent to which possible interventions are likely to encounter resistance because they threaten people's power, prestige, job security, or other interests. Typical sources of resistance include

—community groups that oppose institutional expansion into residential neighborhoods
—regulatory bodies that require evidence that new programs or products meet environmental, equal opportunity, or safety standards
—managers who are skeptical about the efficacy of an unfamiliar intervention, like the introduction of flexible working hours, and worried about its costs
—unions and employees who fight proposals for redefining job responsibilities, consolidating jobs or units, or rolling back wages
—people whose prestige or power depends on current procedures or arrangements
—managers who fear that sensitivity training or other process interventions will pry into their personal lives and feelings.

If diagnosis suggests that a particular form of intervention may encounter serious resistance by clients, members, or outside stakeholders, then consultants should try to find other steps toward improvement that are less threatening and better fit the expressed needs and concerns of these groups, rather than trying to expose and confront resistance (Harrison, 1970). They might, for example, suggest that management consider retraining and relocating employees whose jobs would be eliminated by merging two divisions, rather than firing them.

(4) Does the organization have the capacity to implement the changes? Even if there is no active resistance to a proposed intervention, the client organization may not have the capacity to make these changes. To assess the capacity to make particular change, practitioners can check whether each system element can be expected to make the contributions required for the change to be made successfully. To make this assessment consultants can ask themselves questions such as these:

—Does the organization have the resources—people, funds, talent, knowledge, etc.—and technology needed to make the change or can it
  obtain them?
—Can current structural and technical arrangements be adapted to
  accommodate and facilitate the change?
—Will dominant behavior patterns, processes, beliefs, and values (culture)
  support the new kinds of behavior that the change will introduce?
—Will the environment provide the necessary support, permission, and
  resources to make the change feasible?

In assessing capacity, practitioners make judgments about the probable fit between current practices and proposed changes (see Chapter 4 "Diagnosing System Fits"). For example, when Sears Roebuck decided to offer a wide range of financial services such as insurance, personal loans, and automatic teller machines, observers (e.g., Business Week, 1981b) questioned whether its managers, who were steeped in the culture of mass-market retailing, could learn to adapt to the business style of the insurance and financial services industries. In addition, the question was raised whether the divergent retailing and financial services operations could successfully be integrated within a single organizational structure.

(5) Will the proposed changes achieve the desired results without having undesirable consequences? Before recommending changes, practitioners should make a final accounting of the probable benefits and risks of each possible intervention. By considering the likely impacts of proposed changes on all system elements and on the interactions among them, consultants may check whether the change is likely to have the desired consequences without creating other, unintended consequences that would undercut its benefits. Interventions are more likely to succeed if they fit the conditions in the client organization, including:

—members' characteristics (e.g., preferences for pay versus more vacation time)
—organizational and technical conditions (e.g., equipment, division of labor)
—external constraints (e.g., consumer preferences)
—organizational culture (informal norms, values, and beliefs)

In the case of 21C Scientific Instruments (see Chapter 1), for example, the consultant sought to tap the talents of division managers and help the firm move from a paternalistic management style that rewarded loyalty to the firm toward a more performance-oriented style. To do so the consultant might have proposed increasing the authority and autonomy of division managers. But this intervention could have had very undesirable consequences: Pressures by division managers for greater efficiency and productivity and the firing or relocation of veteran employees would have created shock and hostility among remaining employees, who were accustomed to job security and limited pressure for performance. These developments could have led to low morale, labor unrest, and conflict between managers attached to the old, paternalistic style of management and those who championed expanding and streamlining operations—no matter what the costs for current employees.

Consultants should weigh the likely positive and negative effects of any interventions that might produce *lasting* improvements in effectiveness. Then they can recommend the beneficial interventions that are least likely to encounter serious resistance or have other undesirable consequences and that require the lowest levels of support and commitment from members (see Harrison, 1970). If these steps succeed, more ambitious interventions can be considered subsequently.

Methodological Issues

Assessing support and resistance to change. In examining readiness for change and the likely consequences of implementing some change, practitioners should bear in mind that people's attitudes toward a proposal are not very good predictors of how they will behave if it is actually implemented (see Fishbein & Ajzen, 1975, on the difficulty of predicting behavior from attitudes). Social pressures from peers or supervisors may make people hesitate to reveal their true feelings. Moreover, after change has occurred, members may change their attitudes as they discover that its costs and benefits differ greatly from what they anticipated. Despite these drawbacks, attitudinal data may reveal previously unnoticed hostility toward proposed changes. In addition, interviews with powerful individuals, including influential leaders who lack formal authority, may indicate whether they will support or resist an intervention.

Because of the difficulty of predicting people's actions from their attitudes, consultants seeking to assess readiness for change and its likely consequences should also examine the ways in which members reacted in the past when changes were introduced. If practitioners and clients carefully consider the specific nature of past interventions and the ways in which they were introduced, they may be able to discover the most feasible types of changes and the best procedures for introducing them.

Testing for capacity, readiness, and consequences. The complexity of organizational relations and the indeterminacy of future behavior make it very difficult to anticipate peoples' reactions to change and the consequences of particular interventions. As a result, consultants and managers sometimes take a more experimental approach to implementation. They may, for instance, implement a change in stages, beginning with some preliminary activity (such as an off-site meeting with top managers to plan changes) in order to learn from members' reaction to each stage how they may react to subsequent stages. By developing contingency plans for responding to possible developments at each stage, consultants can prepare to recommend appropriate steps to implementation.

Another variation on this approach is to introduce an intervention as an experiment in one or more units within an organization. After a period of running-in and an assessment of the consequences, the innovation can be modified in light of this experience and then diffused to other parts of the organization. Managers often take this approach when introducing costly technological changes or introducing structural changes, such as job enrichment, in which routine jobs are made more complex and challenging. Unfortunately, managers in both the public and private sectors sometimes agree to introduce such a pilot program in order to show that they are forward looking, although, in fact, they have little intention of extending the program to the rest of the organization. An additional drawback to experimental programs is that the enthusiasm created by the newness and uniqueness of the program may be lost when the change is introduced widely and becomes well established.

EXERCISES

practical methods)

1. Effectiveness Criteria

Conduct an open, semistructured interview with one of the people in charge of an organization (or unit) to which you have access. First ask the person to describe an example of successful operations in the organization. Then ask in general what the objectives are toward which the organization should strive and how they know whether they are achieving them. Based on these responses and any other data you have (e.g., impressions from the previous exercise),

(1) specify the effectiveness criteria to which the respondent referred;
(2) explain whether these criteria reflect considerations of output, system state, or adaptation;
(3) suggest additional effectiveness criteria that would fit the expressed priorities and needs of those in charge of the organization;
(4) note criteria that would reflect the interests of other internal and outside stakeholders.

2. Resistance to Change

Talk with a manager or organizational authority who can describe the individuals and groups within the organization and those outside of it that have a stake in the decisions made by its top management. Then ask the manager to describe how these stakeholders would react to a particular change—some step that the manager thinks might help solve a problem or enhance effectiveness. Organize your data in a chart with a column for the stakeholders likely to support this change or cooperate with it and a column for those likely to resist it. In parentheses rank each group as strong, moderate, or weak in terms of its impact on the organization. Write a summary describing your interview, the current balance of forces supporting the change and opposing it, and the kinds of steps toward improvement that seem feasible in light of the forces shown in your table.

3. General Orientation Interviews

Plan a General Orientation Interview (see Appendix A) that concentrates on the specific unit (e.g., department) in which the person being interviewed works. Note in advance which questions are inappropriate and will be skipped (e.g., Section V) and which will need rewording to make them more applicable. Do not spend more than an hour on this first interview, even if you cannot cover all questions. Write a report in which you summarize the problems you encountered in conducting the interview (e.g., keeping the respondent on track, time pressures, skipping questions concerning areas with which the respondent was unfamiliar). Explain how you would handle the next interview. After getting feedback on your report from your instructor, conduct two more interviews with members of the same or similar units and summarize the findings to all three interviews in terms of the headings provided in Appendix A (e.g., "The Person and His or Her Job. . .").

3

Assessing Performance-Related Behavior and the Quality of Work Life

A model is provided to guide the diagnosis of factors affecting individual and group performance and the quality of work life. Techniques for gathering, analyzing, and feeding back data are also examined. Special attention is given to standardized questionnaires and to techniques for observing group processes. Broader issues of method, interpretation, and process are also considered.

"The pace and quality of work in the department are lackluster."

"We are losing our top staff people, but the less promising ones stay on."

"Our weekly program-review meetings have deteriorated to the point where we argue repeatedly about the same issues and never get anywhere."

"How can we make the clerical work less boring and more appealing?"

These statements illustrate typical problems that potential clients —who are usually managers but may also include employee representatives—might present to consultants. As the presented problems involve individual and group-level issues, consultants might reasonably begin the diagnosis at these levels. Depending on the findings, the redefined problem that emerged during the diagnosis might remain at the individual or group levels, or it might include divisional or even organizationwide features.

A MODEL FOR DIAGNOSING INDIVIDUAL AND GROUP BEHAVIOR

To analyze individual and group-level phenomena, practitioners need a guiding model that shows the important factors to examine and points to the relationships among them. The model shown in

Figure 2, which builds on the open-system model (Figure 1), specifies the individual and group-level factors that a broad diagnosis would encompass.[1] More focused diagnostic studies would consider only a subset of factors that were found to be important during scouting and were closely related to client concerns. The model in Figure 2 assumes that group and organizational contexts greatly affect individual behavior and that group behavior and processes are likewise influenced by the larger organizational context. Hence, the components are shown at three levels—the total organization, the group, and the individual. Lower-level phenomena (such as individual attitudes and beliefs) can also have significant effects on higher-level ones—such as group actions and norms—as is shown in Figure 2 by the arrows that are directed upward and by the dotted feedback loops. For simplicity the model does not distinguish between division and organization-level phenomena, but this distinction may be important if divisions differ substantially from one another. All of the components in Figure 2 are surrounded by broken lines to show their openness to environmental influences like these:

—Prevailing norms and attitudes in the environment affect employees' assumptions about the fairness of job requirements (e.g., travel) and personnel policies (e.g., paid personal leave days).
—The state of labor markets affects the ease with which discontented employees can leave the organization.
—External groups, such as unions and regulatory agencies, affect technologies and administrative procedures (e.g., by requiring the advertisement of job openings).

Let us look briefly at each of the major components of the model.

Outputs

Group performance. Clients often turn to consultants for help with performance-related problems such as poor quality of goods and services produced, low productivity, high costs, interruptions and delays in work flows, and the failure of groups to act aggressively (e.g., poor sales performance) or creatively (e.g., outmoded marketing

---

1. Figure 2 and the following discussion draw in part on Lawler et al. (1983, pp. 20–25) but expand that discussion considerably. Readers who are unfamiliar with the field of organizational behavior will probably want to consult a recent text in the field (e.g., Gordon, 1983) and the references cited in this chapter before conducting a diagnosis.

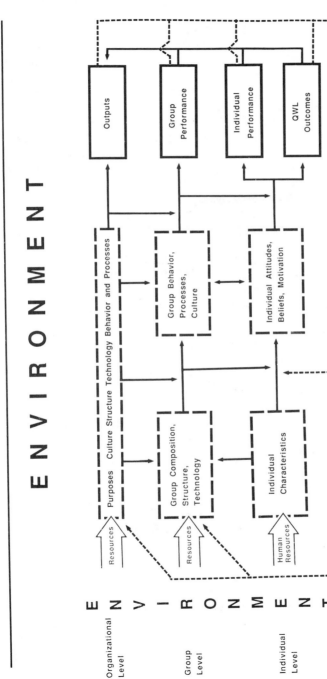

NOTE: Solid lines show main lines of influence; dotted lines show feeback loops.

Figure 2: A Model for Diagnosing Individual and Group Behavior

campaigns). To assess group functioning in terms of outputs, consultants need to define the goods or services produced by the group. In management groups these outputs often consist of solutions to problems (e.g. how to increase market share), plans, tactics, and procedures for coordinating the work of other units.

Individual performance-related behavior. This category includes the degree and quality of members' efforts, their degree of initiative, cooperation with other employees, levels of absenteeism, lateness, and commitment to the job—as opposed to attempts to leave the organization or move within it in ways that do not fit accepted career lines. The important aspects of performance will depend on the group's tasks, goals, and standards. In a surveyor's team within a city agency, for example, accuracy and reliability may be more highly valued than the speed with which the work is done.

Quality of work life (QWL) outcomes. Quality of working life refers to the degree to which the work in an organization contributes to the material and psychological well-being of its members. Diagnostic studies often assess QWL in terms of employees' levels of satisfaction with the following conditions:

—job security
—fairness and adequacy of pay
—working conditions
—interpersonal relations
—meaningfulness and challenge of work

It is also possible to obtain descriptions of QWL conditions from employees or to have independent observers rate QWL conditions. QWL studies can also examine objective and subjective indicators of physical and mental health, including the amount of stress experienced at work (e.g., Kets de Vries, 1979).

For many years consultants and researchers assumed that improving QWL would inevitably heighten employee motivation and would thereby enhance job performance and productivity. Today it is recognized that enhancing employee motivation and QWL can enhance performance under some conditions but not others (e.g., Walton, 1975). Pressures to increase productivity, for example, can reduce job safety or security, and improvements in working conditions may raise costs without showing up in "bottom line" improvements in productivity or revenues. Still, improving QWL can contribute directly to reducing turnover and absenteeism and in the long run may help create a well-trained, loyal work force that is more willing and able to adapt to change. Moreover, QWL outcomes are increasingly accepted as desirable ends in their own right. Academics and unions have been among the leaders in the QWL movement (e.g., Davis & Cherns, 1975), but some business leaders have also endorsed this trend (e.g., Business Week, 1981a).

Factors Affecting Performance and QWL

Individual characteristics. Table 3 summarizes the individual-level factors that research suggests can affect performance and QWL. Because a wide range of conditions may influence the impacts of these factors, practitioners should investigate their effects in the client organization, rather than assuming that these effects are identical to those observed in other organizations. The traits and characteristics listed in the first part of the table can all have a direct bearing on the motivation of employees to perform a task and their ability to do so. These characteristics become particularly important for organizational diagnosis when they are shared by sizable groups of employees. Suppose, for example, that the sales department of an insurance company was having difficulty attracting top college graduates even though the firm offered marginally higher commissions than its competitors. Taking into account the needs that probably characterize college graduates who are considering a career in insurance, a consultant might suggest that the department try offering recruits a chance to learn about the entire insurance business rather than just using monetary incentives to attract good candidates.

Sometimes practitioners can trace changes in employees' motivations, in their perceptions about rewards, and in group processes and behavior to shifting work force characteristics. The rise in the educational level of blue-collar employees, for example, has led to greater demands by factory workers for interesting, challenging work. Despite the importance of individual and work force characteristics like these, practitioners should be cautioned that members of an organization sometimes overestimate the importance of personal traits. They may assume, for example, that all the problems of a failing program or department could be solved, if only the "right person" could be found to run it or the right staff members were chosen. When a unit's problems seem likely to persist even if the "ideal" manager is found, then group and organizational causes should be considered, rather than personal ones

Individual attitudes, beliefs, and motivations. The second part of Table 3 lists attitudes and orientations that can affect performance and that reflect QWL. Motivation and satisfactions with rewards have repeatedly been shown to affect *job commitment* which often shows up in attendance and low turnover. Job satisfaction is also

TABLE 3
Key Individual Factors

Individual Characteristics

Physical and mental state—health, abilities, job-related traits (e.g., pleasant voice for switchboard operator).

Social background and traits—sex, age, ethnic, and regional background.

Training and education—formal education, technical training, work experience.

Individual needs—importance of various types of rewards, work conditions (e.g., job security versus high pay—see Hackman & Oldham, 1980; Salancik & Pfeffer, 1977).*

Individual Attitudes, Beliefs, Motivation

Motivation—to work well, to remain in the job.

Rewards experienced

—extrinsic: pay, benefits, promotion possibilities, peer approval, social status, nonmonetary compensation (e.g., flexible hours, opportunities for training), physical conditions, location, security.

—intrinsic: personal growth, learning, interest, feeling of accomplishment (Lawler, 1977).

Job felt to be intrinsically rewarding—job is meaningful; employee is responsible for important results, gets feedback on work, and sees its results (Hackman & Oldham, 1980).

Expectations

—link between job performance and valued rewards (e.g., If you run project well, will get promotion—see Lawler, 1977).

—consequences of personal effort, initiative, innovation (e.g., What happens to people who find new ways of doing things?).

—ability to get things done (Kanter 1977).

Equity—feeling that efforts are fairly rewarded (Goodman, 1977).

Trust—ability to rely on, believe peers, managers (Schein, 1969).

Specific attitudes—satisfaction with current procedures (e.g., grievance procedures); attitudes, evaluations of group and specific projects (e.g., customer relations campaign—Nadler, et al., 1976); attitudes toward proposed changes (e.g., early retirement proposal).

---

*References are to chapters in this book and useful sources.

associated with other aspects of performance, although the causal relations between these variables are complex. By examining employee's *expectations*, consultants may discover additional explanations for suboptimal performance. If, for example, employees in a busy city hotel are convinced that nothing can be done to make disgruntled guests more satisfied with the service, they are unlikely to improve the situation. In addition, if employees expect their efforts to improve performance to go unrewarded or to result in rewards that are not important to them (e.g., citation for service in the chain's newsletter), they will remain unmotivated to act.

Diagnoses can also benefit from the assessment of attitudes and beliefs that are directly related to questions being debated within an organization. Members may be asked, for example, how they feel about specific proposals and policies such as the proposed introduction of a new personnel policy (but see Chapter 2, "Assessing . . . resistance to change"). Repeated attitude surveys can also provide feedback on particular programs or groups. This information can then contribute to the assessment of progress toward a stated goal and can help managers spot problems before they become critical (e.g., Nadler et al., 1976).

Group composition, structure, and technology Table 4 lists and illustrates some of the major group-level factors referred to in Figure 2. As the table indicates, group behavior can be shaped by the proportions and composition of groups as well as the characteristics of their members. When women or members of an ethnic group are in the minority in management, for example, they may feel pressures to overachieve or to minimize their visibility (Kanter, 1977). Divergences in social background, work experience, and professional training can also lead to conflicts about how work should be conducted and about values and goals. Such conflicts are very common in interdisciplinary teams in the human services and in management teams that draw their members from divergent functional specializations, such as marketing and production.

The behavior of group members is also shaped by the structural and technological factors listed in Table 4. By examining them carefully consultants can sometimes find sources of ineffective behavior and discover ways to change this behavior (see Chapter 4). For example, the controls used to monitor performance and the standards for evaluating it can sometimes encourage behavior that management considers undesirable while discouraging other, desired forms of behavior. In most universities, for instance, faculty are encouraged to devote themselves more to research than to teaching

TABLE 4
Key Group Factors

Group Composition, Structure, and Technology

Social and Occupational Composition—Mix of members' social and personal characteristics (e.g., Americans versus locals in overseas office); proportions of minorities; divergence of professional training and work experience (e.g., veteran managers versus new MBAs).

Structure—nature, extent of rules and work procedures (e.g., reliance on judgment, intuition versus rules, past precedents); flexibility, clarity of task assignments, responsibilities, accountability (Chapter 4); degree of autonomy of members (How much say do they have over work procedures and assignments?) (Chapter 4); types of controls (e.g., reports, direct supervision, computer monitoring of output; evaluation by outsiders; see also, Van De Ven & Ferry, 1980, pp. 155–187); frequency, comprehensiveness of controls (Are all important processes and outcomes monitored or only some?); coordination mechanisms (e.g., meetings, supervision, committees, teams—see Chapter 4).

Technology—impact of work procedures and physical arrangements on group processes (e.g., noise prevents conversation, layout inhibits group work; see also Pasmore & Sherwood, 1978); types of work-flow interdependencies (Chapter 4); motivational potential of job (e.g., repetition, challenge; see also Hackman & Oldham, 1980).

Group Behavior, Processes, and Culture

Relationships among Group Members—cohesiveness (feelings of attachment to group; similarity of views, behavior).

Processes:

—Rewarding: types of behavior rewarded (e.g., conformity versus individual initiative), frequency, consistency, processes of delivering rewards;

—Communication: direction of information flows (e.g., downward, horizontally), openness and honesty (e.g., Do members share problems and issues or try to manipulate one another and keep themselves "looking good"?)

—Cooperation and conflict—sources, extent, nature; conflict management (collaboration in search of solution satisfying all parties, bargaining, forcing of solution by supervisor); impacts of conflict and conflict management (Robbins, 1978);

—Decision making (methods, participation),

—Problem solving (methods, confrontation versus avoidance).

Supervisory Behavior—Supportiveness (encourages learning, provides help, resources); participativeness (sharing of information and decision making); degree of emphasis on group tasks, objectives (stresses achievement of goals, common purposes); levels and nature of performance expectations (e.g., effort, quality expected); communication and conflict management styles (see Processes).

Culture—Group identity (Do language, shared rituals affirm identity? e.g., talk of "we versus them," marking of significant group events); degree of consensus, clarity about goals, objectives; trust, confidence in peers, managers; expectations about work and rewards (e.g., views on getting ahead, risk taking, cooperation); views on problems, challenges (nature of problems, realism of views); compatibility of group norms with managerial expectations (Chapter 4).

---

because their publications are monitored and evaluated carefully, whereas their teaching performance receives little attention.

The work technology can affect the degree to which jobs are motivating and the kinds of contacts members have with one another (e.g., by influencing how work is coordinated—see Chapter 4, "Fits between work flow . . . "). Many of the structural characteristics listed in the table are discussed in Chapter 4, where research is reviewed showing that people with advanced training in their professions and others who seek challenging jobs prefer to work in units that grant them more autonomy and assign tasks and responsibilities more flexibly.

Group behavior, processes, and culture. Many of the factors in the second part of Table 4 have been treated as keys to organizational effectiveness (see Chapter 2) by organization development consultants (e.g., Beckhard, 1969; Schein, 1969) and applied researchers who draw on the human relations school of organizational behavior (e.g., Likert, 1967; McGregor, 1960). These practitioners argue that the motivations and work efforts of individuals and groups improve when work relations are cooperative and cohesive, communication is honest and multidirectional, group norms support productivity, and decision making is participative. The group supervisor can encourage the development of such a team spirit by sharing information with group members (e.g., by explaining the logic behind new production targets), encouraging participation in decisions directly affecting members, supporting individual effort and learning, facilitating and directing work, and setting high standards for the group. Moving groups toward this ideal is not a panacea for all organizational problems, nor do such groups always achieve higher levels of outputs. However, members of groups like these are usually more satisfied with work, enjoy a higher QWL, and are more committed to the job and the work group (Strauss, 1977). Moreover, groups having these characteristics are often better able to handle tasks involving non-routine problems and calling for creativity and innovation (see Chapter 4, "Organic versus mechanistic structures").

Participative work groups can also enhance productivity and QWL in routine production and service tasks (Strauss, 1982). The *quality circle* movement (e.g., Ouchi, 1981, pp. 261–268), in which workers are given opportunities to make decisions about how to organize and improve their work, is the most recent attempt to use participative methods to improve performance. These participative programs can succeed only if workers and management cooperate, if job security is not threatened, and if employees gain more influence over working conditions and work-related decisions. Otherwise, employees will quickly become cynical about the intentions of management and will stop trying to contribute to decision making (Kanter, 1977).

Organizational factors. There are many links between organization-level factors and those at the group and individual levels that can profitably be explored during diagnosis (see Figure 2 and Chapter 4). First, standards and objectives set by top management (e.g., "Improve market share by 5% during the next quarter") can define the targets that lower-level managers use to evaluate group performance (e.g., "Sell 1000 more units in Tulsa by November"). Moreover, by defining the mission, strategies, and goals of the organization top management can focus individual and group efforts around shared objectives and create expectations about the kinds of behavior that will be rewarded (e.g., "We will go for clients who want full services, not cut-rate deals"). Second as was suggested by the example of faculty evaluation in universities, procedures for monitoring and controlling operations can directly affect group norms (e.g., "Don't spend too much time preparing classes or meeting students"), working styles ("Avoid hanging around the department—stay home and write!"), and output objectives (e.g., "Publish research papers").

Third, such aspects of the organizational culture as widely shared beliefs about the way work gets done, how change occurs, and who has influence also shape individual and group behavior (Argyris &

Schon, 1978; Davis, 1984). Fourth, organizational technology and structure shape coordination and control within groups, the division of labor within and between groups, and the nature of individual-level tasks. If, for example, the members of a law firm are all given personal computers, their needs for secretarial and other supporting services may change radically. They may begin to type memos and make small revisions of contract drafts on their own, thus reducing the need for dictation and routine typing services and changing their working relations with secretaries.

DIAGNOSTIC METHODS AND PROCEDURES

The section that follows examines the design and administration of a diagnosis of individual and group performance and QWL. It also notes some general issues that arise in most diagnoses, no matter what questions or organizational levels are emphasized.

Study Design

Deciding what to study. As suggested above, consultants usually select the topics for study in response to their clients' initial presentations of problems and in keeping with the preliminary diagnosis made during scouting. For instance, the complaint about the argument-ridden, unproductive meetings cited at the beginning of the chapter might lead a consultant to explore the background to the arguments that are plaguing the meetings. Preliminary conversations with participants about their work might reveal major disagreements about program goals and members' responsibilities, along with a lack of mechanisms for working out such difficulties. In keeping with these findings the consultant might decide to examine these group processes and structures more closely.

The choice of diagnostic topics also reflects the effectiveness criteria to be used in assessing individual and group behavior (see Chapter 2). In addition to the output criteria reviewed above, many of the system state criteria listed in Table 2 and developed in Table 4 can also be used as standards for evaluating work groups. Rancorous conflict, for example, is often taken as a sign of group ineffectiveness. The adaptation and resource position criteria in Table 2 can also be applied to small groups if the group's environment is defined as including other units within the larger organization along with salient features of the organization's environment.

Having chosen a particular focus for diagnosis, the practitioner must define carefully the specific factors to be studied and decide on the best way to obtain data on them. To start, practitioners can gather Basic Organizational Information and conduct a limited number of General Orientation Interviews (see Appendix A). Then additional data-gathering steps can be designed as needed. If, for example, the consultant wanted to examine methods for resolving conflicts and solving group problems, he or she could interview group members, paying particular attention to the kinds of issues that create conflicts and the ways they and their supervisors deal with these conflicts. These data might then be supplemented with observations of group meetings. Whether a broad or a narrow focus seems best, practitioners should choose data-gathering methods that are most likely to yield useful, valid results and that will contribute to a positive relationship to clients and other members of the organization (see Chapter 1). Practitioners should avoid relying on some familiar "off-the-shelf" technique like a standard attitude survey when these techniques are inappropriate to the diagnostic questions or will detract from the client-consultant relationship.

Sampling. The data should be as representative as possible of the individuals, groups, and situations under study. For example, to find out about the characteristic ways in which conflicts are handled, the practitioner should try to be sure that the instances of conflict management reported in interviews are typical or representative, as well as ensuring that a cross section of group members are interviewed. To reach large numbers of people, self-administered questionnaires can be distributed to samples of members selected through probability sampling (see Selltiz et al., 1981). Probability samples can also be used to gather secondary data, such as absenteeism rates, from large data sets. Probability sampling is rarely used to choose subjects for interviewing because of the high cost of conducting a large number of interviews. When small groups are to be interviewed or given questionnaires, all members may be included or a cross section of individuals can be selected who are likely to hold different perspectives and points of view.

Sampling issues also arise when observational techniques are used. Because large amounts of time and trained observers are needed, consultants usually prefer to observe important meetings, training sessions, or crucial work activities in which members interact intensively and many aspects of group relations can be seen at the same time. It is best to choose settings for observation that are as central to group operations as possible because behavior can vary greatly from one context (e.g., headquarters) to another (e.g., field operations). Practitioners should also be aware that a unit may operate differently when it convenes as a whole than when its members work alone or in subgroups.

In designing samples, practitioners should take into account the attitudes of group members toward the study and uses to which the data will be put, as well as strictly methodological considerations. If, for example, all members of a large division will receive feedback from a questionnaire about their departments' operations, it may be better to include everyone in the survey. By doing so consultants may increase interest in the questionnaire study and enhance the believability of the feedback.

Administering the study. The procedures used to gather, store, and analyze the data should also be chosen so that they promote a sound consulting relationship, as well as providing valid diagnostic data.[2] Practitioners should make it clear to members of a client organization that they will store and process the data in a professional fashion and maintain the confidentiality of participants. Moreover, they should explain that only group-level results will be reported, so as to preserve the anonymity of individual members.

Measurement and Data-Gathering Techniques

A combination of data-gathering techniques (see Chapter 1) should usually be used in the diagnosis of performance-related behavior and QWL. The discussion that follows emphasizes the use of questionnaires because of their popularity and appropriateness to the individual and group levels of analysis. It also illustrates the use of observational techniques that are particularly well suited to the study of group processes.

Secondary analysis. In many organizations data on the social or personal characteristics of work group members can be extracted from personnel files using standard procedures for content analysis (see Selltiz et al., 1981). Most organizations also have records of group outputs like sales, productivity, production quality (e.g., percentage of

2. For excellent discussions of the methods and procedures of conducting diagnostic surveys see Nadler (1977) and Bowditch & Buono (1982).

products serviced under warranty), and services delivered (e.g., number of outpatient visits to a hospital clinic). Organizational publications and records may also provide information on processes, structures, technologies, and purposes, but this information will be hard to code and quantify. These documentary data almost always need to be supplemented with information on actual practices, as opposed to managerial descriptions and declarations (see Chapter 4).

Practitioners who conduct secondary analyses of organizational documents or records need to be aware that these sources reflect the perspectives of the people who gathered the information and the particular reasons for which it was originally gathered. Employee evaluations that were originally used in decisions about raises, for example, may reflect the pressures supervisors felt to present their subordinates in a favorable light. In contrast, negative comments about these employees by more senior managers may reflect their desire to avoid granting raises automatically. Both views are worth examining in order to understand the many ways in which people interpret employee behavior and the factors shaping their interpretations, but neither can be accepted as unbiased.

Interviews. Much diagnostic information about the factors discussed earlier in the chapter can be obtained through General Orientation Interviews (Appendix A) and through interviews that focus more explicitly on individual and group factors. Department heads may provide basic information on their departments and work groups within them, but they are likely to be reluctant to report candidly on actual processes and behavior that may reflect badly upon their performance as managers. In such cases, interviews will be needed with additional department members.

By conducting detailed interviews with members from different backgrounds and locations within a unit and by listening carefully to their accounts of important issues, investigators can become aware of members' distinctive perspectives and viewpoints. For example, department heads may characterize their organization as dealing honestly and directly with employee grievances, whereas subordinates complain that their grievances are ignored or minimized by management. When such divergences seem to seriously reduce effectiveness, practitioners may decide to report them as feedback in order to stimulate efforts to improve communication between ranks. In other instances consultants may simply take note of divergent viewpoints, so as to avoid giving undue weight to one particular interpretation when formulating their own descriptions and analyses.

Interviews and questionnaire studies are often subject to bias because respondents seek to present themselves in a favorable light or withhold information, such as negative descriptions of supervisors, that they fear may ultimately be used against them. Practitioners can help overcome these concerns by gradually building relationships of trust with group members. Sometimes practitioners are able to develop such relationships with individuals who are highly knowledgeable about organizational affairs but somewhat detached from them, and are therefore willing to provide a great deal of valuable information.[3] Assistants to high-level managers, for example, may have a very comprehensive view of their organization and be more comfortable in describing it than the top managers themselves. When such well-placed individuals grow to trust consultants, they may provide useful information about sensitive subjects, such as the degree of influence of managers who are officially of equal authority or staff members' past reactions to risk-taking behavior (see Chapter 6 on ethical issues that arise in gathering and using such sensitive information).

Self-administered questionnaires. Self-administered questionnaires provide the least expensive way of eliciting the attitudes, beliefs, and opinions of large numbers of individuals. Aggregations of individual responses can also provide a substitute for behavioral measures of group-level phenomena. Although questionnaires typically use fixed-choice answers, a few open-ended questions can also be included to give respondents an opportunity to express themselves. Responses to such open-ended questions are often informative but hard to code. Questionnaires composed of items drawn from standardized organizational surveys (see below and Appendix B) can be prepared and administered rapidly because there is less need to develop and pretest the instrument. By including standard measures consultants may also be able to compare the responses obtained in the client organization with results from other organizations in which the same instrument was used.

Standardized instruments. One of the most useful standardized instruments is the Michigan Organizational Assessment Questionnaire—MOAQ (Cammann et al., 1983), which is part of a battery of instruments in the Michigan Quality of Work Program (Seashore et al., 1983). MOAQ is particularly well suited to the assessment of

---

3. Such individuals are called informants in academic research. I have avoided using the term here because of its negative connotations.

individual-level attitudes and beliefs. Practitioners may select one or more of its seven modules or choose appropriate questions from within modules. MOAQ's Module One covers the following important attitudes and psychological states:

—internal work motivation (satisfaction from doing the job well)
—intention to leave the organization or the job
—perceived ability to switch jobs
—satisfaction with the job and with the amount, fairness, and administration of pay
—the quality of the job (challenge, meaning, responsibility)
—identification with work and the organization
—perception that pay is based on performance
—self-report of the effort the respondent makes at work

The other modules in MOAQ expand the coverage of the factors measured in Module One and treat the following additional areas:

—respondent's personal background (including time in job and organization)
—adequacy of training and skills for present job
—job characteristics (hours, classification)
—importance of various types of rewards (pay, recognition, interest, freedom at work)
—extent to which various rewards are felt to be tied to performance
—determinants of pay (tenure, job responsibility, experience, performance by individual, group, entire organization)
—role: clarity (know what is expected), overload (too much work), conflict (can't satisfy everyone)
—supervisor's behavior (participativeness, support, work facilitation, planning, control, goal setting, production orientation, fairness, race and sex bias)
—group characteristics (homogeneity of skills, backgrounds; cohesion—i.e., mutual attraction)
—group processes (goal clarity, involvement in decision making, opinions listened to, fragmentation—bickering, lack of mutual respect, etc.)

MOAQ could contribute significantly to a comprehensive diagnosis if additional behavioral data were obtained on individual or group outputs and if more data were gathered on group processes, structures, technology, and external relations. The Organization Assessment Instrument—OAI (Van de Ven & Ferry, 1980)—provides many scales in these areas, as well as items that overlap with MOAQ.

An additional feature of OAI is that it contains separate questionnaires for supervisors and group members, so that comparisons can be made of their attitudes and reports. Other instruments within OAI assess divisional (interdepartmental) and organization-level phenomena (see Chapter 4).

Here is a list of useful scales in OAI, organized in terms of the categories used in Figure 2:

Group Composition, Structure, and Technology
—occupational specialization
—interchangeability of roles
—heterogeneity of members' skills
—concentration of authority in the hands of supervisors, group members, employee representatives, and outside authorities
—extent of automation
—standardization and specification of performance standards
—work flow: dependence of members on one another, on supervisor, on other groups
—interdependencies: segmented (members work independently), sequential, reciprocal, or team relations

Group Behavior, Processes, and Culture
—pressures for conformity to group norms
—communication (frequency and nature)
—conflict (within groups and with other units)
—conflict resolution methods
—strictness of control

Group Performance
—perceived unit performance (output quantity and quality, attainment of goals and targets, innovativeness efficiency, morale, reputation for excellence)

To obtain data on group-level phenomena from questionnaires like MOAQ and OAI, the responses from members of a particular work group or administrative unit are averaged to create group scores. For these averages to be meaningful, the questionnaires must specify clearly what work groups and which supervisors are referred to, and the investigators must make sure that all members of a work group refer to the same group in their responses. Otherwise the data cannot be used in the diagnosis of specific groups or to provide feedback to group managers and members.

Advantages and drawbacks of standardized questionnaires. MOAQ and OAI provide diagnostic tools that are extensively documented and validated and reflect current research. Unlike earlier instruments (e.g., Blake & Mouton, 1964; Taylor & Bowers, 1972), which were based on models that advocated a single administrative style, these new assessment packages reflect the widely accepted view that there is no one best way to organize groups or organizations. Instead, the optimal combination of system traits is assumed to depend on many variables including the environment, tasks, technology, personnel, history, and size of the organization.

Despite their obvious appeal, standardized diagnostic instruments also have serious weaknesses and drawbacks. First, they may give practitioners a false sense of confidence that all the factors of relevance to a particular client organization have been covered adequately. Second, because standard questions are necessarily abstract, they may not be fully applicable to a particular organization or situation. For example, a typical questionnaire item asks respondents to indicate their degree of agreement with the statement, "My supervisor encourages subordinates to participate in making important decisions" (Cammann et al., 1983, p. 108). But the responses to this general statement may mask the fact that the supervisor encourages participation in decisions in one area, such as work scheduling, while making decisions alone in other areas, such as budgeting. To obtain data on such situational variations, investigators must first determine the situations across which there may be broad variations and then write specific questions about these situations (e.g., Moch et al., 1983a, pp. 199–200).

Third, as in any questionnaire, even apparently simple questions may contain concepts or phrases that may be understood in different ways. For instance, when reacting to the statement, "I get to do a number of different things on my job" (Cammann et al., 1983, p. 94), one person may see diversity in physical actions (e.g., snipping versus scraping) or minor changes in the tools needed for the job, whereas another would consider all of those operations as "doing the same thing." Fourth, questionnaires are especially vulnerable to biases stemming from the respondent's desire to give socially acceptable answers or avoid sensitive issues. There may also be tendencies to give consistent responses (Salancik & Pfeffer, 1977). Some instruments include questions designed to detect or minimize biases, whereas others (e.g., Taylor & Bowers, 1972) may heighten bias by phrasing all questions in a single direction.

Observations. Observation can help consultants get a first-hand feel for the kinds of behavior and processes that occur within an organization and develop interpretations of situations that depend less on members attitudes and viewpoints than do data from questionnaires and interviews. People are often not very good observers of the actions occurring within their groups and often cannot describe group norms, beliefs, and informal behavior patterns or are reluctant to do so. Because observation is time consuming and requires keen observational skills, it is often reserved for the analysis of top management groups, whose decisions and solutions to problems are critical to the organization as a whole.

Observational techniques. Observations may be structured in terms of a general accounting scheme, such as the *Questions about Group Meetings,* below (see also Perkins et al., 1981) or in terms of predefined categories for coding observed behavior (see Weick, 1985, for examples). Experienced practitioners may also conduct unstructured observations so as to remain open to unanticipated phenomena.

Unless a highly structured coding scheme is used, observers record the behavior of the participants. Here are some examples:

"Chairperson shouts for order."
"Workers consult each other over how to get the machine going again."
"Nurses are quiet, do not participate in the discussion of the case."

Notations on observed behavior like these provide the data on which subsequent inferences about group functioning are based. For example, repeated observations of workers helping each other handle snags in operations may lead consultants to conclude that relationships between workers are cooperative and facilitate independence from supervisors and technicians. Including such concrete descriptions of behavior will also make feedback more useful to group members. If observations are guided by a list of topics, observers can summarize their findings for each topic and then add illustrative descriptions from the original notes.

Before beginning their observations of a particular setting, investigators often try to learn as much as possible through interviews or informal conversations about the backgrounds of the people to be observed, their roles, the nature of the task facing the group, and the ways that this task or similar ones have been handled in the past. If note taking during the observations will disturb group members, then observers should record their notes as soon as possible after the conclusion of the observation. With practice it is possible to develop the ability to recall entire conversations or discussions and to record them after completing the observation. Things that the observer did not understand can be clarified through repeated observations or through discussions with participants. Additional observations of the group under differing circumstances and repeated observations of similar events will help the observer distinguish between recurring and one-time phenomena. Once a clear picture has emerged, the results can be compared to those obtained from other data sources and can be prepared for analysis and feedback.

A guide to diagnosing meeting behavior. To illustrate observational techniques, let us consider how practitioners might observe group meetings. Meetings make an ideal focus for observations. Managers and salaried professionals spend much of their time in meetings, and meeting outcomes form an important part of managerial outputs. Moreover, participants often find meetings to be frustrating and unproductive. Hence, they may be interested in having consultants diagnose meeting behavior and helping them improve group effectiveness.

Researchers and consultants with experience in sensitivity training and organization development have created a variety of schemes for observing and diagnosing group functioning that can be applied to the observation of meetings (e.g., Benne & Sheats, 1948; Schein, 1969). These observational frames usually reflect the assumption mentioned above that groups work better when there is an open sharing of information and feelings, deemphasis on status and power differences and participatory decision making. As research (Alderfer, 1977; Porras & Berg, 1978; Strauss, 1976) has shown that no single set of group features always contributes to group effectiveness, the diagnostic questions below do not presuppose a single form of optimal group functioning. Instead, they ask about important group processes while allowing practitioners to draw their own conclusions about the importance and impact of each factor. Because the questions are only a guide to observations, they do not provide instructions about what particular behaviors to note or how to make inferences from them. Thus, to answer each of these diagnostic questions, observers will have to consult their notes on the *behavior observed* during the meeting (e.g., shouting between two members), decide how much they can *generalize* from these observations (e.g., members often shout at one another), and make appropriate *inferences* from the observations (e.g., shouting shows that members take differences of opinion personally). Users are encouraged to select among the questions, to modify them, and to apply them so as to fit the particular features of the group being observed and incorporate relevant effectiveness criteria. Besides guiding observations, these questions can provide a framework for feedback and could also be used by groups wishing to engage in self-diagnosis.

Questions about Group Meetings—For Observation or Self-Diagnosis

(1) *Goals, targets, and procedures*—Are the goals of the meeting or the problems to be dealt with stated in advance? Are clear guidelines given for the time and resources to be devoted toward reaching these ends? Do the participants understand and accept the goals and purposes of the meeting and of the group, or do people seem to have different, hidden agendas for the meeting?

(2) *Participation*—Do participants other than the leader share in developing the goals and guidelines for the meeting? Do most people participate, or do a few talk most of the time? How much airing of divergent opinions occurs? Do participants have the time and ability to examine the information they are given? Are they prepared for the discussion?

(3) *The flow of information and ideas*—Are there opportunities for the clarification and development of the ideas and proposals presented? Are ideas and proposals adequately summarized so that participants can keep track of their progress? How much does the chairperson guide and control the discussion? Does the group move easily from one issue to another, or must these shifts be forced on them by the leader or by a few participants?

(4) *Problem solving*—Do the participants define clearly the problems facing them and search for alternative solutions before deciding? Are long-term consequences of actions considered as well as short-term ones? Is more than one alternative considered, and are dissenting opinions considered by others, or is there a tendency for "groupthink"—where everyone backs one solution without seriously discussing others? Do participants draw on past experiences and learn from them? Do they consider new ideas and solutions to problems, as well as familiar, time-tested ones?

(5) *Decision making*—What kinds of procedures are used to decide on the various proposals raised—ignoring the proposal, acceptance or rejection by top authorities, decision by a minority of powerful participants, voting, consensus? Do participants seem to accept these methods? Do these methods seem to produce the best decisions? Do important issues go undecided?

(6) *Conflict*—What important conflicts arise during the meeting? How are they handled—by someone forcing a solution, by one party back-

ing down, by bargaining, or by collaboration in finding a mutually satisfying solution? What are the impacts of these conflict-resolution methods (e.g., members seem angry, alienated, anxious to work together)? Do conflicts stimulate thinking and problem solving or disrupt the meeting?

(7) *Interpersonal relations and feelings*—How cohesive is the group? Do differences among members interfere with their working together? Are there opportunities for enhancing group solidarity? What kinds of verbal and nonverbal behavior provide cues to participants' feelings (e.g., exclamations, tone of voice, posture)? Do members seem to trust one another? Do they listen to one another or interrupt and ignore others? Do they discuss differences of opinion in terms of common standards and values, or do they treat them as personal conflicts? Do they find the meetings satisfying or frustrating?

(8) *Outcomes*—What are the major outcomes of the meeting—solutions, decisions, proposals, ideas, and so on? Are their implications for action spelled out clearly—including responsibilities for executing them, the time allotted for doing so, and the forms of follow-up and evaluation? How satisfied with the outcomes of the meeting are its participants, leaders, and others who are affected by the group's work? How well do the outcomes meet other relevant effectiveness criteria (e.g., innovativeness, adaptiveness)?

To decide how important each of the listed items is to group functioning and to decide whether a particular feature, such as participation in decision making, is critical to group effectiveness, practitioners will have to define clearly what effectiveness criteria they want to apply and will need to trace the impacts of the feature on effectiveness. Consider, for example, the question of whether participants in the meeting shared in developing goals and guidelines for action. If consultants regard the satisfactions and feelings of group members as important indicators of effectiveness, then participation in goal setting may be seen as a condition that is likely to facilitate effectiveness. But the impact of this condition can depend on the nature and context of the group. Group members who are highly educated and accustomed to having their professional opinions taken seriously by others are likely to resent having goals and procedures imposed upon them. In contrast, in organizations with more authoritarian traditions, such as military organizations, members accept having goals and procedures set for them, and their satisfactions may depend more on their group's outputs than on their participation in goal setting.

Analysis

The same logical and statistical procedures that are used in nonapplied research can be used to analyze diagnostic data (e.g., Lofland, 1971; Schatzman & Strauss, 1973; Selltiz et al., 1981). Once summarized, nonstatistical data can be analyzed with the help of diagrams like Figure 2. The main findings about each of the categories shown there could be recorded on an enlarged version of the figure. The arrows between the boxes in the figure could then be labeled to describe important system interactions. If, for example, an assembly-line technology seemed to be producing boredom and alienation among workers, this relationship could be shown on the figure. Beneath the figure supporting evidence of the relationship could be recorded—such as the observation that workers who were transferred to other less routine operations at equal pay showed higher motivation and less boredom.

If the study included standard, quantifiable measures on which data exists for other organizations, comparisons can be made between the findings for the client organization and these baseline data. More frequently, statistical or qualitative comparisons can be made between all similar units (e.g., work teams) within the organization on all of the effectiveness measures and on variables that are assumed to add to effectiveness. Then, groups that are unusually high or low on the measures can be isolated for further study, or the data can be prepared for feedback to group members. Alternatively, if previous investigations suggested that certain units are particularly outstanding or problematic in some important feature, such as innovativeness, consultants may concentrate on examining the characteristics of these units.

Before undertaking extended multivariate analyses of questionnaire data, practitioners should decide how heavily their diagnosis will rely on these analyses. Alternatively, they could use other methods to gather additional information or provide members of the client group with the major single or bivariate distributions and encourage them to try to account for the findings in terms of their own understandings of the organization. Whatever approach is chosen, the data should be presented in a form that is appealing and easy to understand. Reports and trade literature that are circulating within a client organization will usually provide indications of appropriate formats for presenting data.

Feedback

Procedures. There are wide variations in the possible procedures for providing feedback from diagnostic studies (see Nadler, 1977). Sometimes practitioners only give feedback to the client or clients who called for the study. More frequently, where feedback is viewed as a means of encouraging group problem solving, consultants present their results to all the participants in the study or to everyone who is affected by its findings. The supervisors and members of an organizational unit can be given relevant feedback at the same time or separately. The major danger in providing feedback simultaneously to supervisors and subordinates is that supervisors often experience conflicts between being made a target of criticism and being expected to lead the discussion about the planning of appropriate action. An alternative design involves providing feedback to task forces or other temporary groups that cut across departmental and hierarchical lines. These groups are assigned responsibility for planning the organization's response to the findings.

Sometimes the feedback is restricted to a single oral or written presentation of findings and recommendations. In contrast, organization-development consultants usually try to collaborate with members of the client organization in interpreting the findings and deciding how to deal with them (see Burke, 1982, p. 162, and Chapter 1, "Participation in Diagnosisa ..."). First, the consultant presents a summary of the data and a preliminary analysis. A discussion usually follows in which the findings are clarified. Finally, the practitioner and the group members discuss the interpretation of the data and their implications for action.

Feedback characteristics. Whatever form feedback takes, people are more likely to accept and act upon it when the feedback has the following features (Block, 1981; Huse & Cummings, 1985, pp. 78–79; see also Chapter 6):

(1) Relevant and understandable to members
(2) Descriptive, rather than evaluative
(3) Clear and specific—referring to concrete behavior and situations, illustrating generalizations, and providing comparisons between groups
(4) Given shortly after data gathering
(5) Believable—providing information about the validity of the data
(6) Sensitive to members' feelings and motivations—rather than provoking anger, defensiveness, or feelings of helplessness

(7) Limited, rather than overwhelming
(8) Practical and feasible—pointing to issues that members can do something about
(9) Open-ended—leaving room for members to make their own interpretations and decide how to act

Practitioners can improve their feedback by adopting procedures that correspond more closely to these standards, even if it is impossible to conform to them in full.

EXERCISES

1. Using Questionnaires to Diagnose Group Processes

Choose two work groups or units on which background information is available. These groups should perform similar tasks and have similar types of employees. Try to locate one group reputed to have positive features (e.g., high quality of work life or positive supervisor-subordinate relations), and another that seems to be weak in the same areas. Develop a questionnaire on key aspects of group process with around 10 questions drawn from one or more of the standardized questionnaires discussed in this chapter and in Appendix B. Distribute the questionnaire to members of both groups after you have explained that the data will only be used for an exercise and will not be distributed to anyone outside the groups. Prepare a summary of the average responses to each question for the groups and compare your results to the previous information you had on the groups. If the results differ from what you expected, try to account for these differences. Explain how you would give feedback to the supervisors and members of both groups in order to facilitate constructive discussion and problem solving. If requested, prepare a separate summary of the findings for each new group.

2. Observing Meetings

Use the *Questions about Group Meetings* as a guide to observing at least two meetings of the same group. Write a report covering the following topics:

(1) Background on the groups and the meetings (type of meetings, purpose, circumstances—e.g., routine weekly meeting, emergency session, etc.—participants, organizational context, etc.)
(2) Summary of observations of group processes (organized in terms of the topics listed in the *Questions about Group Meetings* or a consolidated set of topics)
(3) Criteria for evaluating group effectiveness
(4) Sources of effectiveness and ineffectiveness
(5) Possible ways of improving effectiveness
(6) Ways to provide feedback to participants

4

Examining System Fits and Power Relations within Divisions and Organizations

The open system model is used as a guide to assessing the fits between such elements as structure, environment, technology, and goals. Emphasis is placed on aspects of the organization design that managers can influence. Fits between actual behavior and official objectives and practices are also discussed. The final part of the chapter treats ways to assess the distribution and uses of power—one of the most critical aspects of actual behavior.

As noted in the preceding chapter, conditions at the divisional and organizational levels can contribute to group and individual problems such as low levels of satisfaction, poor task performance, high turnover, and tense interpersonal relations. When most groups within a division or an entire organization suffer from such problems, their sources are likely to lie in broader, higher-level conditions, rather than being caused mainly by group-level factors, such as the behavior of particular supervisors or the structure of particular work groups. In addition, divisional or organizationwide forces may contribute to other kinds of problems involving several departments or groups, including,

—conflicts between units
—tasks being neglected or "falling between the cracks"
—lack of innovation
—failure to cope with changing market or technical conditions
—communication delays and failures
—inability to carry out complex projects

This chapter shows how to diagnose the causes of such divisional and organizational problems by examining the fits between system elements or between their subcomponents. The terms *fit, congruence,* or *alignment* refer to the extent to which the behavioral or organizational requirements and the constraints in one part of a system are compatible with those in other parts (Beer, 1980; Kotter, 1978; Nadler & Tushman, 1980a, 1980b).[1]

DIAGNOSING SYSTEM FITS

Introduction

Here is a case (Beckhard, 1975, p. 52) that illustrates the potential impacts of fits between system elements at the division level:

> The head of a major corporate division was frustrated by the lack of motivation of his subordinates to work with him on planning for the future of the business as a whole and their lack of attention to developing the managerial potential of their own subordinates. Repeated exhortations about these matters produced few results, although the division managers agreed that change was desirable. The barrier to change was that these managers were held directly accountable for short-term profits in their division. There were no meaningful rewards for engaging in planning or management development and no punishments for not doing so, but had the managers failed to show a profit, they would have been fired on the spot.

This case shows the impact of poor fit between the decision's objectives (purposes) and its reward mechanisms—a component of its structure. The division's objectives included planning and management development, but its reward and control procedures discouraged managers from contributing to their subordinates and instead led them to strive exclusively for more tangible, short-term results. Figure 3 provides a schematic summary of the steps required to diagnose fits. The first step in the figure, the choice of fits, is treated in the section that follows immediately. The second and third steps are addressed in the sections "Ways to Assess Fit," "Diagnosing Organization Design," and "Actual Practices." The fourth step is discussed in the section "Assessing the Impacts of Fits."

1. It is also possible to examine fits between different system levels, for example, individual-group, individual-organization, group-organization fits (see Nadler & Tushman, 1980a).

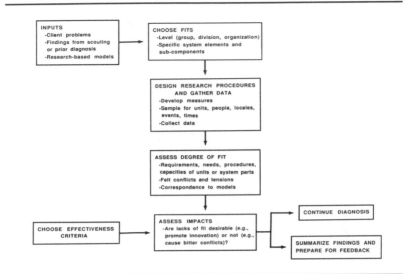

Figure 3: A Process for Diagnosing System Fits

The Choice of Fits

A checklist of important fits. One way to choose fits for diagnosis is to start with a checklist, like the one shown in Table 5 of fits that research and consulting practice have shown to be especially important. A comprehensive diagnostic study could examine each of these fits in at least a preliminary fashion. Because the divisions of large, complex organizations will differ from one another in all or most of the system elements (e.g., environment, technology, structure), it is best to begin by examining fits within divisions. If necessary, fits within the total organization can be considered subsequently.

Starting with client problems. A more focused and practical approach is to examine those fits that are more directly related to the problems that clients present or that showed up during scouting. For example, the practitioner who encounters complaints about tasks being neglected or handled poorly can deal with these complaints and clarify the links between structure, decision making, and communication through *responsibility charting*, a procedure that has been used in many large corporations (Galbraith, 1977, p. 171). First, during interviews or workshops group members are asked to list key

note: open system model p. 24

cf. OFB project

TABLE 5
Questions about Fits

Focal Area	Does focal area fit with . . .
Human Resources	*Structure, Technology, Processes:* Do employees' skills and training fit their job requirements? (Chapter 3)* Are the best people attracted and retained by the rewards and advancement opportunities offered? (Chapter 3) Are professionals and others seeking autonomy and challenge assigned to less structured and less closely controlled jobs? (Chapters 3 & 4; Lorsch & Morse, 1974)
Purposes	*Resources:* Can the organization's strategies and programs be supported by available resources? (Chapters 2 & 5; Andrews, 1971; Nadler & Tushman, 1980a) *Environment:* Do the division's strategies, tactics, and objectives help it gain and maintain a favorable position in its environment? (Chapter 5; Andrews, 1971; Porter, 1980) *Behavior, Processes, Culture:* Does management express its purposes in ways that create a sense of mission and identity among members? (Pfeffer, 1981a) Are efforts to change the division compatible with current norms, behavior, and assumptions? (Chapter 2; Argyris & Schon, 1978; Davis, 1984) *Technology, Behavior, Processes:* Do managerial plans and objectives contribute to work, or are they too inflexible to handle unforeseen developments? (McCaskey, 1979; Newman & Warren, 1977; Quinn, 1980)

Technology   *Structure:*

                      Are those people who must work together closely
                      grouped in units or otherwise linked structurally?
                      (Chapter 4; Beer, 1980, pp. 159–168; Khandwalla,
                      1977)

                      Are the procedures for coordinating work and
                      information flows appropriate to the tasks and
                      the technology? Are tasks that are poorly under-
                      stood or require creativity and innovation
                      handled by organic structures? (Chapter 4;
                      Galbraith, 1977; Tushman & Nadler, 1978)

                      Structure, Behavior:

                      Are there tasks and functions that no one is
                      doing adequately and others on which people or
                      units overlap needlessly? (Chapter 4)

Structure   *Behavior, Processes, Culture:*

                      Do members regard official rules and procedures
                      as fair and sensible? (Chapter 3)

                      Do reward and control mechanisms encourage
                      behavior and group norms that are compatible
                      with managerial objectives? (Chapter 4; Lawler &
                      Rhode, 1976)

                      Technology, Environment:

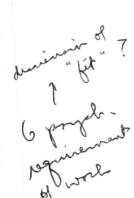

                      Are the structures of the divisions (or their sub-
                      units) differentiated enough to allow them to
                      handle the special problems created by their par-
                      ticular environments, technologies, and tasks?
                      Are the coordinating mechanisms adequate for
                      the level of differentiation? (Chapter 4;
                      Galbraith, 1977; Lawrence & Lorsch, 1969)

                      Technology, Processes:

                      Does the physical and geographic layout of the
                      division contribute to the flow of work and infor-
                      mation? (Steele, 1973)

Official Purposes,   *Actual Behavior, Processes, Culture:*
Structures,
Processes   Are managerial objectives and procedures
                      supported by actual norms and behavior?
                      (Chapter 4; Nadler & Tushman, 1980a)

Actual Behavior, Processes:

Are group actions and decisions blocked by bitter conflicts or power struggles? (Chapter 4)

Does undesirable competition between units result from departmental specialization or from rewards and controls encouraging competition? (Chapter 4; Pondy, 1967; Walton & Dutton, 1969)

Do people and units have enough power and resources to accomplish their tasks adequately? (Chapter 4; Kanter, 1979)

---

*References are to chapters of this book and to other sources in which the question is explored more fully.

tasks or decision areas. In a project group these might include budgeting, scheduling, allocating personnel, and changing design specifications of the product. Second, each member is asked to list the positions that might be involved in these areas (e.g., project director, general manager, laboratory manager) and to indicate who is assigned *responsibilty* for performing tasks and who else is supposed to *approve* the tasks performed, *be consulted*, and *be informed* about it. The data usually reveal ambiguities relating to one or more task areas. These data can be used as feedback to stimulate efforts to redefine responsibilities and clarify relationships, and they can lead clients and consultants to examine fundamental organizational features, such as the degree of delegation of authority, communication patterns, and the division of labor. For example, discussion of approval procedures for work scheduling may reveal that many minor changes are needed and that scheduling would operate more smoothly if middle-level managers received the authority to make such minor changes and to inform the project head afterwards. By starting with client concerns and then branching out in this fashion, consultants may find ways of dealing with pressing problems while also uncovering conditions that can have a wider impact on organizational effectiveness.

Fits involving design tools. Consultants to management often concentrate their diagnoses on fits involving *design tools*, organizational arrangements like job responsibilities that can most readily be redesigned by their clients (Beer, 1980). As the case of the corporate division cited above suggests, the procedures used in rewarding, monitoring, and evaluating performance are among the most powerful design tools. In that case the division head was able to build incentives for planning and management development into the reward system by recalculating bonus pay to reflect contributions in these areas.

Here are some other design tools to consider (Beer, 1980, p. 27; Mintzberg, 1979):

—the structural grouping of positions and units
—job designs
—personnel policies (i.e., recruitment, selection, training, advancement, compensation, labor relations)
—management-information systems
—mechanisms for coordinating units or positions
—performance-control procedures
—accounting and budgeting systems
—geographic location and physical layout

Design tools can structure the options available to members and create pressures to act in a particular fashion. Such administrative measures may ultimately shape the organizational culture by establishing official rules of the game according to which members must play if they wish to remain and advance in the organization. These impacts show up, for example, in the effects of task definitions, rewards, and control procedures on interdepartmental conflict (Pondy, 1967; Walton & Dutton, 1969). When departments are evaluated solely on the basis of how well they have achieved their objectives, their members lack incentives for interdepartmental cooperation. Instead, they are encouraged to compete with other departments for scarce resources and do everything in their power to "look good" at evaluation time. Competition and conflict between groups will be further heightened by rewards that are tied to outperforming other departments. In contrast, interdepartmental cooperation can be enhanced by evaluating departments on their contributions to attaining divisional or organizationwide objectives that require cooperation.

The greater the authority and autonomy of clients, the more readily they can make changes in these design factors. Collective bargaining agreements, government regulations, and internal opposition may severely restrict the options available to both public and private sector managers.

Ways to Assess Fits

One way to assess fits is to examine the compatibility of the requirements, needs, or procedures of different units or system parts. The fits between units are weak if the work of one unit, such as the medical staff of a hospital outpatient clinic, is disrupted because of inadequate inputs from another unit, such as the x-ray department. Incompatibility between units and system parts often appears in divergent or conflicting messages about the kinds of behavior required. In a newspaper bureau, for example, the official job responsibilities of reporters included suggesting topics for stories, but the reporters learned from their experiences in staff meetings that it did not pay to challenge the editor's leadership in this area.

A second way to assess fit is to investigate whether participants *feel* subject to conflicting expectations or pressures and to check whether these conflicts are the result of lacks of fit. In the case of the corporate division described above, for example, a sales manager might have complained during an interview, "My boss wants me to work on management development, but if I do, I'll be in hot water when he goes over my quarterly sales results!" The practitioner would then check whether other managers made similar comments and whether rewards were indeed closely tied to quarterly performance, while ignoring management development activities.

A third possibility is to see whether system elements or components fit together in ways that research-based models suggest they should (e.g., Miles & Snow, 1978; Mintzberg, 1979; Nightingale & Tolouse, 1977). The following section describes models of organization design that can help practitioners assess the fits between the structures of organizations and divisions and other system elements. Other useful models for diagnosing fits are referred to in the references to Table 5.

Diagnosing Organization Design

Fits between work-flow and coordination mechanisms. One useful model specifies the types of coordination procedures required by the technology (Galbraith, 1977; Thompson, 1967; Tichy, 1983; Tushman & Nadler, 1978). According to this model, work technologies create three different kinds of *interdependencies* in the work flow:

Pooled interdependencies—where units can work independently of each other (e.g., crews in a home construction firm)

Sequential interdependencies—where work must flow from one unit to another in a clearly defined sequence (e.g., assembly line)

Reciprocal interdependencies—where units must adjust to each other (e.g., sales and design groups tailor product or service to customer needs)

When the technology creates pooled interdependencies, operations can be coordinated by rules, standard operating procedures (e.g., "Discard parts that exceed standard by .003mm"), and supervision from above. When work must flow sequentially, rules and procedures must be supplemented by more detailed planning of the relationships between units, closer monitoring of unit outputs, and more supervision from above. But these familiar coordination mechanisms do not fit the requirements of technologies that create reciprocal interdependencies between units. Coordination mechanisms that build in *lateral relations* between units best fit these needs for two-way communication and mutual adjustment. These mechanisms include teams, committees, and flexible, integrative roles such as product managers (see "Differentiation and integration," below).

To examine fits between work flow interdependencies and coordination mechanisms, practitioners can observe operations or interview members about work flows between units. Interunit coordination is problematic if members view these coordination procedures as clumsy or inadequate, or if interunit contacts are characterized by frequent interruptions, misunderstandings, surprises, and high levels of conflict. In such cases members may not be using current coordinating mechanisms adequately, or these mechanisms may be inappropriate to the types of interdependencies.

Organic versus mechanistic systems. Sometimes findings from diagnoses at lower levels or client requests (e.g., Chapter 1, "Introduction," Case 1) can lead consultants to assess the design of an entire organization or that of a complex, highly autonomous division. Table 6 summarizes a useful model for assessing fits between the administrative system (structure, processes, and culture) of a division or organization and its environment, technology, and personnel (Burns & Stalker, 1961; Lawrence & Lorsch, 1969; Tichy, 1983; Tushman & Nadler, 1978). This model can also be applied to smaller units like departments.

[handwritten margin notes at top:] part of people - issue for INC — moving to more organic model ?

TABLE 6
Conditions Affecting the Fit of Mechanistic and Organic Systems

[handwritten note:] cf. Work Redesign STS / Participation Democracy

Description*	Mechanistic	Organic
Roles, Responsibilities	Specialized, clearly defined.	Diffuse, flexible, change through use.
Coordination and Control	Supervision, rules, standard procedures, detailed plans; frequent evaluation based on meeting objectives, standards.	Consultation among all having related tasks; flexible plans, diffuse, changing goals; evaluation of results over longer time frame.
Communication	Top-down emphasis: top management has key outside contacts.	Multidirectional: multilevel contacts with outsiders.
Supervision and Leadership	Nonparticipative, one-on-one: loyalty to superiors stressed: position and experience grant authority.	Participative, team styles: emphasis on task, team, organization; expertise & knowledge grant authority.
Sources of Knowledge	Local, internal.	External, cosmopolitan: professional orientation.

Fit best when		
Technology is . . .	Routine (well understood, standardized.	Nonroutine (not well understood; or designed for each problem).
Task environment is . . .	Predictable (simple, changing predictably).	Unpredictable (complex, changing rapidly).
Personnel expect . . .	High level of structure and routine; control from above.	High levels of role flexibility, challenging work.

Effectiveness criteria stress . . .	Efficiency; standard, predictable operations and outputs; ease of control from top.	Creativity, innovativeness, adaptiveness, quality of work life, development of human resources.

*See Burns & Stalker (1961), Tichy (1983, p. 276)

Organic systems provide greater information-processing capacity, encourage creativity and innovativeness, and facilitate rapid, flexible responses to change. In addition, they provide more interesting and challenging work environments than *mechanistic systems*. On the other hand, they are more costly and harder to administer. Hence, when conditions are predictable, the rules, standard operating procedures, and top-down supervision in mechanistic systems often yield more efficient and productive results than do organic arrangements. From this standpoint mechanistic arrangements are well suited to the provision of routine services in government (e.g., postal service) and the private sector (e.g., homeowners' insurance), as well as to many routine manufacturing operations (e.g., manufacturing toys). In contrast, the organic administrative style can help divisions or entire firms adapt to uncertainties stemming from poorly understood and changing technological conditions (e.g., in developing microelectronic products, cancer research), and from unpredictable environmental conditions—such as markets subject to sudden changes of taste and unstable financial conditions.

The administrative system also needs to fit the prevailing technology. If the technical tasks are well understood and the available technology makes it possible to break the work down into routine operations (e.g., assembly-line manufacturing, processing of applicants for food stamps), then mechanistic forms of coordination and control can effectively guide production or treatment processes and will usually be less costly (Perrow, 1970). In contrast, when technical tasks are poorly understood or resist standardization (e.g., design of new product. development of advertising campaign), organic arrangements are needed to allow for innovativeness, creativity, and flexibility.

Finally, administrative patterns need to fit the background and expectations of the work force (Lorsch & Morse, 1974). Organic systems will better fit the work style of employees who have been professionally trained to regulate their own work and to adjust to the needs and expectations of peers. Organic systems will also provide higher quality of working life for nonprofessional employees who seek greater autonomy and more challenging work (see Chapter 3). Unfortunately, when the work can be done using routine procedures, the introduction of more organic forms of administration may require expensive reorganizations and technological changes and may not raise outputs or cut operating costs.

To use the mechanistic-organic systems model in diagnosis, practitioners need to assess how organic or mechanistic a division's current administrative system is and how well the current system fits the conditions and effectiveness criteria listed in Table 6. Employee expectations can be measured directly (see Chapter 3 and Van de Ven & Ferry, 1980, p. 392). Chapter 5 provides details on assessing environmental conditions.

Standardized measures can also be used to assess many of the administrative features summarized in Table 6. Separate indices can be created for each of the dimensions shown in the upper half of the table, or a single combined index can be constructed. One advantage of examining each dimension separately is that low levels of fit may be found between these administrative dimensions. For example, a division head may try to encounter managers to work together on innovative projects but may inadvertently block team work by retaining a one-on-one style of supervision.

Taken as a whole, systems may be considered too mechanistic if they face very unpredictable environments and nonroutine tasks. In particular, a division may need a more organic system if it is unable to cope with the following three types of challenges:

(1) Adapt to change and respond rapidly and decisively to threats and opportunities
(2) Handle nonroutine tasks in innovative and creative ways
(3) Meet employee expectations for creative, challenging work

On the other hand, unless staff development or quality of working life is very important, divisions that use organic arrangements to handle predictable external conditions and routine tasks are probably failing to take advantage of efficiencies that could be obtained by introducing more mechanistic procedures. If a preliminary application of the model suggests that change is needed in either direction, practitioners can focus more closely on those design tools that clients can most readily change.

Divisionalization. A key question in the diagnosis of the structure of total organizations and divisions concerns the ways that units are grouped together. When consultants examine an organization's current form of divisionalization, they should investigate whether people and units that must work together intensively are located in the same administrative units or in close contact with one another. In addition they should consider whether the structure keeps costs to a minimum by avoiding unnecessary duplication of positions and underuse of resources, and whether it provides sufficient adaptiveness to variations in markets and other environmental conditions (e.g., degree of governmental regulation of products or production processes). As a rule, organizations that are divisionalized along *functional* lines (e.g., marketing, engineering, production) are less able to respond to divergencies in markets and other environmental conditions than those divisionalized in terms of *products and services* (e.g., life, home, and commercial insurance divisions), or in terms of *markets or geographical areas* (Mintzberg, 1979). However, there are many variations within types and many opportunities for combining them.

Differentiation and integration. The more the tasks, technology, and environments of divisions or other major subunits vary from one another, the more the divisional structures will have to be *differentiated* (Lawrence & Lorsch, 1969). For example, in a clothing firm with a division catering to the fashion trade (unpredictable environment) and one supplying uniforms to hospitals and other institutions (more stable environment), the fashion division would need to be more organic than the one supplying uniforms. The need for differentiation also stems from many other types of divergences in tasks, environments, and work force, such as legal conditions, levels of training of the work force, and the size of production runs, that are not summarized in the mechanistic-organic model. To assess whether an organization is sufficiently differentiated, practitioners need to decide whether each division is allowed to adapt sufficiently to its own objectives, technology, environment, and personnel. There is too much differentiation if there are unjustifiable divergences in administrative practices or other system features.

Once organizations become differentiated internally, they face serious problems of *integration* (coordination) across divisions (Lawrence & Lorsch, 1969). If an organization is highly differentiated, the mechanistic forms of coordination and control listed in Table 6 are not likely to provide sufficient levels of integration. To accommodate great divergence between divisions, top management can grant them greater autonomy and monitor divisional *results* (as opposed to monitoring operations), or management can create more *lateral linkages* between units and divisions that must work together (Galbraith, 1977; Mintzberg, 1979; Tichy, 1983). The list that follows ranks popular forms of lateral integration from the least to most complex:

(1) Direct contact between units
(2) Integrator and liason roles (e.g., coordinator of hospital geriatric services)
(3) Task forces and committees that temporarily unite members of several units
(4) Projects groups and teams that make these links more permanent
(5) Matrix structures with dual (functional and project) authority lines

In a matrix structure people retain their ties to a functional specialization, like computer services or sales, while serving in semipermanent product or market groups (e.g., "Talking Typewriter Project"). Matrix structures and other complex lateral integrating mechanisms can help organizations coordinate highly differentiated operations and cope with unpredictable environments and non-routine technologies. On the other hand, they are costly and hard to administer (Davis & Lawrence, 1977). Consultants should therefore weigh carefully the possibilities for using simpler lateral coordination mechanisms or increasing divisional autonomy before considering elaborate, risky reorganizations along matrix lines.

Actual Practices Versus Official Mandates

As in other forms of diagnosis, to examine many of the system fits listed in Table 5 practitioners need to distinguish between actual observable patterns of behavior and official descriptions of organizational life.[2] Official descriptions can provide useful insights into management's image of the organization's desired state, but they cannot serve as data on organizational behavior and practice.

2. The terms "actual" behavior and behavior "in practice" are preferable to the popular term "informal behavior." Formalization refers to the specification or programming of behavior and procedures in advance, often in writing (Hall, 1982, pp. 95–113). Thus, directives, goals, and structures can be official and authoritative without being formalized.

Examining actual practices. As noted in previous chapters, actual practices can diverge greatly from official descriptions of these practices and from official purposes and procedures. Managers, for example, may report that they frequently consult with their subordinates before reaching important decisions, but the subordinates' own reports and other sources of data on decision making may not confirm this idealized picture. What happens, for instance, when subordinates have bad news for their supervisors or hold different opinions from them (Argyris & Schon, 1978)? Actual features of other key processes (see Chapters 2 & 3)—including controlling and rewarding, supervision, and conflict management—should also be carefully examined.

Here is a listing of actual practices that practitioners may find diverge substantially from officially mandated ones:

(1) Operative goals and priorities as shown by decisions about resource allocation (e.g., budgeting, staffing)
(2) Informal structures (e.g., cliques, working ties that cut across departmental lines, end runs around immediate superiors to higher authorities; grapevines that bypass official communication channels)
(3) Role definitions and group functions in practice (e.g., actual division of labor, definitions of tasks, responsibilities, etc.)
(4) Informal leaders, influence patterns, and power relations (see below)
(5) Actual work procedures (e.g., cutting corners on safety, quality checks, reporting, record keeping; improvising solutions and procedures)
(6) Everyday beliefs (culture)—about payoffs (or penalties) for hard work and initiative; the tasks and conditions facing the organizations (e.g., "We're about to get bought out. Quit while you can!"); the kinds of information that can be taken seriously (e.g., "The forecasts from sales are always too optimistic.")

Collecting data on actual practices. Because actual organizational practices often run counter to official mandates, it is usually necessary to gather data on them through direct observations, intensive interviewing, or the analysis of organizational records. If respondents are especially cooperative and candid, data on informal social and working relationships can be obtained from sociometric questionnaires, in which respondents name people or positions with whom they work closely or have frequent contact (Moch et al., 1983b; Tichy et al., 1980). The patterns of one-way and mutual choice between respondents can then be analyzed to provide maps of relationships. Alternatively, questions about group leadership and work relations can be incorporated into open interviews.

Open or semistructured interviews should obtain explicit descriptions of how the respondents act in a range of work situations, rather than generalizations or expressions of attitudes, because explicit behavioral reports are somewhat less subject to bias than generalizations or attitudes. For instance, to obtain data about the actual division of labor within a project group, practitioners could ask several members to describe what each member of the group did during the design phase of a project and then draw the appropriate conclusion after examining all of these data. This procedure is more likely to yield valid results than asking members to generalize about whether "responsibilities are clear" in the group or asking attitudinal questions (e.g., "Are task assignments flexible enough to allow for unforeseen circumstances?").

Useful techniques for studying organizational cultures and practices include asking individual respondents or groups of members to describe the history of the organization or unit (Leach, 1979) or requesting accounts of organizational successes and failures (Argyris & Schon, 1978, pp. 32–48). In analyzing such accounts, close attention should be paid to assumptions and behavior that members take for granted (see Chapter 6, "Helping clients develop the capacity for self-examination").

Another fruitful strategy is to gather data from organizational records and from interviews concerning the entire process by which an idea, service, or product moves through the organization. In a study of hospital coordination mechanisms, for example, practitioners might trace the entire course of treatment of representative hospital patients, from reception to release. In a study of decision making and relationships in a product design unit they might follow a new product from its earliest design stages until it goes into routine production.

An advantage of direct observations and the analysis of existing data is that much information may be obtained *unobtrusively* (Webb et al., 1966), without interfering with people's behavior or influencing it. For example, by observing attendance at meetings or by checking records, practitioners may discover that a project that is officially assigned high priority is being neglected by senior staff members. The meaning of organizational phenomena may also be evident in the jargon and local vocabulary used by members. Nonverbal behavior such as physical gestures, dress patterns, physical arrangements, and office decor can also provide meaningful information (Goffman, 1959; Steele, 1973), provided that the observer is familiar with the context in which this behavior occurs and checks interpretations against other data sources. Although such observational data can be very informative, their reliability is often low, and they are usually hard to quantify.

Assessing the Impacts of Fits

As Figure 3 suggests, consultants should assess the impacts of system fits directly, rather than assuming, as some authors do (e.g., Beer, 1980, Nadler & Tushman, 1980) that high levels of fit or system integration are always preferable. Instead, any particular pattern and level of fit can be assumed to have both costs and benefits that can only be identified and weighed in terms of specific effectiveness criteria (see Chapter 2). For example, gaps between official rules and actual behavior, such as the hoarding of supplies by units on a military base, may cause wastage and raise costs but may also contribute to unit solidarity and morale. In some instances employees may even produce higher quality work by violating official procedures. For instance, Blau (1955, pp. 91–116) reports how group solidarity and work quality were strengthened when employees in a federal agency consulted peers about problems, rather than turning to their supervisors as instructed. As the following discussion on power shows, there are also many instances where unofficial relationships and processes contribute directly to task performance. Hence, practitioners should try to assess the impacts of actual practices directly with clear effectiveness criteria in mind rather than assuming in advance that they are either positive or negative.

The implications of fits between design variables, technologies, and environments also need to be carefully assessed. Consider, for example, the following case:

> Central Acadamy is a small, religiously affiliated private school. It has enjoyed growth in its student body for several decades, is generously supported by a group of donors, and has developed structures, processes, technologies, and an organizational culture grounded in religious teachings that seem to fit well with one another. Conflicts are rare, administration is trouble free, and school-community relations are placid.

In terms of the school's resource position and its internal system states, the fit between system elements is highly effective. On the other hand, the administration and faculty lack new ideas about how to run the school and what programs to develop. Thus, the school may have become incapable of meeting new challenges and opportunities. Like many other organizations, when judged in terms of innovativeness and adaptive capacity, its fits are too high, rather than too low (see Katz & Kahn, 1980, p. 174).

System incongruities and lacks of fits are often necessary for organizational growth and change. Lacks of fit often characterize organizations in which certain parts of the organization or system elements—such as the technology, goals, or human resources—are changing more rapidly than others. In cases like these, the resulting tensions may reflect and even foster creativity, innovation, and adaptation to external change (Burns, 1961: Robbins, 1978). If these states are desired, it would be unwise to try to reverse the technological changes or otherwise force elements into alignment.

Practitioners should also bear in mind that many organizations operate successfully with fairly high levels of structural incongruity and inconsistency. Some "high tech" firms, for example, tolerate overlaps between units, ambiguous definitions of unit goals and assignments, and high levels of infighting and politicking in order to sustain and encourage creativity and initiative (e.g., Kidder, 1981). From one point of view the gaps between official policy and actual practice in educational and service organizations also have positive consequences, as they help their members ward off outside interference (Meyer & Rowan, 1977). In addition, in most types of organizations there seem to be a range of ways in which basic organizational problems may be handled and much room for variation within the recurring organizational types—such as the organic and mechanistic types—observed by consultants and researchers (Van de Ven & Drazin, 1985).

For all of these reasons, consultants should assess system fits and lacks of fit in terms of explicit effectiveness criteria. Then they can decide whether a particular lack of fit is detrimental and what steps, if any, should be taken to improve fits. Consider, for example, the case of the fit between the division's objectives and its reward mechanisms described at the beginning of the chapter: If adaptability to external change was used as the key effectiveness criterion, the consultant and client might legitimately have concluded that managerial behavior should be evaluated over a longer time frame and more emphasis given to planning and management development. In contrast, if satisfying stockholders was used as a key measure of effectiveness, then there might be no choice but to continue linking rewards to short-term results. Management development would continue to be a low priority, whereas responsibility for planning might be assigned to staff specialists, who would not be held responsible for the division's short-term profits.

POWER RELATIONS AND PROCESSES

Power relations and influence processes are among the most important types of actual behavior to examine in diagnosis. Even if an understanding of "political" processes and power distribution does not lead directly to proposals for organizational improvement, it can greatly help consultants manage the consulting process. The following typical "war story" (Quinn, 1977, p. 23) illustrates the potential impact of power on efforts to introduce organizational change:

> In a major textile fibers company there were constant fights between strong managers in the divisions of marketing, production, and research and development. Yet when the creation of product-management teams was proposed in order to "coordinate the very things that caused the friction," the feuding managers formed a powerful coalition to resist the innovation.

The terms *power* and *influence* are used interchangeably in this book to refer to the ability to get people to do things that they might otherwise not do and to the capacity to get things done (Kanter, 1977; Mintzberg, 1983, p. 5). Political actions—attempts to achieve desired outcomes—often aim at influencing budgeting decisions and other forms of resource allocation, at shaping goals and programs, promoting or resisting personnel changes, and at determining the resolution of conflicts and crises (Burns, 1961; Pfeffer, 1981b; Zald & Berger, 1978).

If they understand an organization's power structure and politics, consultants may be able to work in ways that are in keeping with these political realities without compromising the consulting relationship. If they ignore these realities, they are likely to encounter resistance to their diagnoses and may recommend interventions that will have negative consequences or cannot be implemented. In the case cited above, for example, the proposed product management teams would have drawn their members from each of the three functional divisions. But this scheme could only work if the division managers were willing to surrender some of their autonomy. Innovations such as quality circles for production or clerical workers also cannot be implemented successfully unless supervisors and managers are willing to give real power to the members of quality circles. Furthermore, where substantial power differences and fundamental conflicts of interest prevail, many popular organization development techniques—including process consultation (see Chapter 1), Open Systems Planning (see Chapter 5), and team building (Burke, 1982, pp. 258–290; Huse & Cummings, 1985, pp. 113–125)—cannot be used, because they require high levels of trust and interpersonal openness (Huff, 1980; Strauss, 1976; Tushman, 1977).

Diagnosing the Distribution and Uses of Power

Outcomes of influence processes. One problem facing consultants is assessment of the consequences of peoples' efforts to use power to influence others and to attain particular ends. Rather than assuming that any attempt to shape or manipulate others is by definition undesirable, consultants need to acknowledge the essentially political nature of nearly all organizations and look directly at the impacts of influence processes. For example, members may use their power to oppose change, as in the case described above, or they may use it to press for change (Burns, 1961). In many organizations proposals for new products and other innovations only get accepted when powerful managers work hard to convince decision makers to provide the resources needed to develop a new idea and then fight to overcome opposition to its implementation (Kanter, 1983). In some cases such champions of new concepts have even violated official directives and procedures by diverting resources to new product development.

Practitioners can only evaluate such political efforts from the viewpoint of particular actors within the organization and in terms of clear effectiveness criteria. Consider, for example, a situation in which workers marshaled the support of local politicians in order to delay the closing of an unprofitable plant while proposals for keeping the plant going could be reviewed by joint labor-management committees. Consultants to top management who accept their client's concern for profitability would regard the workers as threatening organizational effectiveness. In contrast, a consultant to the workers would probably view their actions favorably (e.g., Alinsky, 1971; Chesler et al., 1978), as might a consultant to management who placed greater stress on job security, plant morale, and the standing of the firm in the community.

Influence tactics. It is important to assess the effects of the tactics people use to influence others, as well as evaluating the outcomes of these efforts. People who have formal authority or control over valued resources may try to influence others and accomplish things by changing the flow of material and social rewards and sanctions to others. Other influence tactics include appealing to logic and common standards, and manipulating people by providing them with selective information about a situation or by creating indirect pressures to act in a particular fashion (Porter et al., 1981). To assess the impacts of such influence tactics and other uses of power, practitioners need to consider issues like these:

—How do those who are subject to a particular influence tactic react to it?
—Does the use of this tactic increase tensions or conflicts between groups?
—Does reliance on personal loyalties or the striking of political deals undercut the organizations's stress on performance or professional excellence?
—Do the methods used to resolve conflicts produce solutions that last and that are regarded as fair?

The power to act. People and groups need power in order to accomplish their tasks and contribute to organizational objectives, as well as to oppose them. A critical question for diagnosis is whether particular groups have sufficient resources and influence to accomplish their tasks. First-line supervisors, for example, often cannot do their jobs adequately because they cannot control or influence the lines of supply to their units, lack vital organizational information, and cannot advance within the organization (Kanter, 1979). Because of their lack of power, the supervisors become resistant to managerial initiatives, administer programs mechanistically, and achieve low productivity. Middle managers also need to acquire power to do their jobs well (e.g., Izraeli, 1975), and staff specialists, like psychologists and planners, often lack both the formal authority and the informal standing needed to get their ideas implemented. Consultants need to be on the lookout for situations like these where group and divisional effectiveness can be enhanced by giving people more control of needed resources and easier access to key decision makers.

Power distribution. Consultants may also approach the question of whether units have enough power by examining the overall power distribution in a division or organization. When power is highly *centralized*, control over important resources and decisions is concentrated in the higher ranks of the organization. Here is a list of possible consequences of shifting toward a more decentralized distribution of authority and power (Carlisle, 1974; Child, 1977; Kanter, 1983; Khandwalla, 1977):

Positive Consequences of Decentralization

Reduced burden on top management to make decisions and process information

Cost savings from reduction in number of levels in the administrative hierarchy

Improved information flow and decision quality

Enhanced ability of middle managers to solve problems on their own

Improved morale

More innovation

Better management development

Negative Consequences

Reduction in top management's ability to forge a unifying strategy for the organization and to shift directions rapidly in response to changes or opportunities

Increased costs for training, compensation, capital equipment, and plant

Duplication of positions

Creation of local power centers

Heightened interunit conflict

To diagnose the distribution of power, practitioners should assess the degree to which the organization is currently decentralized and weigh the probable costs and benefits of changing the current power distribution in the light of explicit effectiveness criteria. Decentralization is more likely to be preferred when high priority is placed on the ability of subunits to respond rapidly and appropriately to local and specialized problems. The need to do so is most likely to arise in very large organizations; those that are geographically dispersed; organizations facing rapidly changing, very complex, or highly competitive environments; and organizations dealing with nonroutine tasks.

INVESTIGATING POWER RELATIONS AND PROCESSES

Indicators of power and influence.[3] Gathering trustworthy information on power relations and processes is a challenge to organizational
consultants. First, they need to decide which individuals and groups
have acted or might act in ways that could influence the consulting
process or the aspects of the organization being studied. In addition
to high-ranking managers, there may be interest groups that form
along the lines of departments, occupations, ranks, and social
characteristics (e.g., sex, ethnic background). Naturally, the actors
concerned with one issue, such as the redesign of jobs, may be
different than those concerned with another, such as budget allocations. Once key issues and actors have been identified, it is useful to
make a chart listing the key actors for each issue, their position on the
issue, and their relative power (Pfeffer, 1981 pp. 37–43).

Then practitioners can try to learn how much power various actors
have and how they use that power. To do so directly would necessitate
following the treatment of specific issues in different parts of the
organization and examining political struggles directly. Because this
kind of information is rarely available, it is usually necessary to look
for overt manifestations of power (Kanter, 1977). Table 7 takes this
approach in providing questions on the current state of power
relations and suggesting techniques for gathering relevant information. If most of the answers to these questions point to the same
groups or individuals, it is very likely that they are indeed the most
powerful actors. On the other hand, if some actors appear to be
powerful according to one set of criteria (e.g., status symbols) but not
according to another (e.g, access to decision-making bodies), investigators will need to obtain additional information in order to determine whether some of the indicators of power are invalid, or whether
there are several distinct power bases and no single group of powerful
actors.

Data collection techniques. The sensitivity and subtlety of political
processes make them hard to measure with questionnaires. Still,
some authors have developed questionnaires for identifying powerful groups or individuals, describing prevalent influence tactics, and
measuring power distribution (Moch et al., 1983a; Price, 1972;
Tannenbaum, 1968; and see the discussions of MOAQ and OAI in

3. This section draws substantially on Pfeffer's (1981b, pp. 35–65) discussion of
   assessing power.

Chapter 3). As Table 7 suggests, a wide range of qualitative and largely unobtrusive techniques can be used as alternatives or supplements to questionnaires.

Some of the strategies and methods listed in Table 7 can also provide data on the uses of power and on its distribution. If practitioners can observe the meetings of major decision-making forums, for example, they may obtain invaluable data on how members resolve differences and conflicts and the degree to which top executives share power with subordinates. Unfortunately, many influence processes occur outside of such formal gatherings and are hard to observe.

TABLE 7
Finding Out Who Is Powerful

Focal Area and Guiding Questions	Research Strategies and Methods
Resources: What kinds of resources are most important to members—funds, equipment, personnel, information, knowledge, and so on. Which groups & individuals get disproportionate shares?	Observe (&/or interview on) key resources and distribution, status symbols; look for disproportionate budget allocations.
Who controls distribution?	Examine organization charts, job descriptions; interview.
Centrality: What technical and administrative processes are vital to everyday operations? What processes are critical to organizational success? Who influences & participates in them?	Interview unit heads; study organization charts, job descriptions; observe operations; analyze reports from interviews and workshops on crises, failures, successes.
Who handles contacts with powerful external groups?	Interview; examine organization charts, job descriptions; survey (i.e., with questionnaires) individuals, unit heads about contacts.
Who is regarded as irreplaceable?	Interview knowledgeable members; survey members of relevant units.

Participation and Influence in Decision Making: Who participates in key (formal and informal) decision-making forums? Who has access to top decision makers?	Examine organization charts, job descriptions, reports on membership in forums; observe participation; interview on access, participation.
Whose views dominated major decisions? Who came out on top in power struggles and conflicts?	Analyze decisions reported in documents, press, interviews, workshops.
Whom do members turn to for help in sponsoring a new idea?	Interview; analyze successes, failures reported in interviews, workshops.
Reputation: Which units and individuals are especially powerful?	Survey members for ranking of influentials; interview; observe attention, deference given to individuals.
Which units do members who want to get ahead join? With whom do they try to develop relationships?	Interview; examine executives' prior positions to find units that are avenues to the top.

To gather data on influence processes, consultants often have to rely on interviews or on discussions during meetings or workshops. In workshops or interviews consultants may ask members to provide detailed accounts of organizational successes, the resolution of past organizational problems and crises, and accounts of the treatment of new ideas or proposals. In providing these accounts, members may, of course, justify and improve upon their own behavior and that of others to whom they are loyal, and they may exaggerate the failings of those they hold in low esteem. Still, when conducted and analyzed with sensitivity to these possibilities, interviews and group discussions can provide insight into members' perceptions of political processes, key political actors, and the kinds of influence tactics in use within the organization. To develop an understanding of power relations and processes that is independent of the perceptions of particular members, practitioners will have to carefully cross-check members' reports with one another and with other kinds of information.

EXERCISES

1. Rewards

Interview the head and at least one subordinate in a department or division. Use a list of guiding, open-ended questions about rewards and their relationships to other features of the unit. In addition to writing questions on your own, you may want to use the following items listed in Appendix A: I-1 & 2; II-1; III-1, 2 & 3; IV-2; VI-1, 2, 5 & 6; VII-1, 2, 3, 6, 7, 8 & 9; VIII-1, 2 & 3; IX-1, 3; XI-1, 2 & 3. Cover the following issues in your interviews and discuss each of them in your report:

(1) What rewards and sanctions (punishments) are widely used?

(2) What kinds of behavior are subject to rewards and sanctions? (be specific)

(3) What types of actions are encouraged and discouraged? Consider hard work versus taking it easy, personal loyalty to supervisors and peers, risk taking, exercising initiative, generating new ideas, cooperation with others in or outside the unit.

(4) Are the same rewards offered to everyone, or can people receive the types of rewards that are more appealing to them? (e.g., one person may want a bonus, whereas the next wants a chance to earn a degree while working.)

(5) How do each of the following influence the current system of rewards—peers, supervisor, higher level management, labor agreements?

(6) If you have sufficient information, assess the fits between the current reward system and the other system elements (see Table 5).

2. Assessing Fits

In this exercise you may draw on your prior knowledge of an organization or gather Basic Organizational Information (see Chapter 2) and then conduct several General Orientation Interviews (Appendix A) before beginning the exercise. Then take a large sheet of newsprint and make a matrix in which all eight of the system elements are listed as rows and columns. Subdivide the resources category further into three categories: people (human resources), knowledge and information, and material resources. If you constructed the matrix correctly, it should be 10 by 10 with 45 cells above the diagonal. Then for each cell ask the following: How well does the row entry (e.g., human resources) fit with the column entry (e.g., knowledge and informational resources)? To make these queries more concrete look at the questions about fit listed in Table 5. Where no question appears in the table, suggest your own. For example, Do the employees (*human resources*) have the *knowledge* needed to perform their tasks or can they readily obtain it? Then make notes on the degree of fit between each pair in your matrix. Be explicit about the criteria you are using for assessing fit. Once you have completed the matrix, note the two cases of poor fit that seem to be most harmful to effectiveness. Be clear about your effectiveness criteria. Write a report on these two relationships in which you explain the nature of the lack of fit, its impacts, and make suggestions for improving the fits.

3. Power to Act

Use at least two of the approaches listed in Table 7 to determine which people have the most power within some subunit of an organization, such as a branch, a division, or a department. Interview two of them about a major problem or challenge facing their unit. Find out during the interview or by some other method whether they have the resources needed to deal with the problem. If not, specify what resources they would need in order to take action and what could be done to help them attain these resources or solve the problem some other way.

5

Org. Strategy

Diagnosing Environmental Relations

The first part of the chapter shows how to examine the demands and pressures placed on an organization by its environment and how to assess its responses to external conditions. Techniques for conducting intensive interviews are discussed along with other methods for gathering and analyzing data. A discussion follows of Open System Planning, a technique that gives clients most of the responsibility for diagnosing their organization's external relations and for planning appropriate actions.

"High Court to Rule on Job Leaves for Pregnant Workers"
"Citizens' Groups Vow to Defeat Nuclear Dump Proposal"
"IBM Will Enter the Lap-Sized Computer Market"
"$11.7 Billion in Federal Budget Cuts Loom"
"Massive Damage Claims by Former Asbestos Workers"
"Suburbs without Kids! Demand for Family Homes Slumps, Condo Construction Booms"

News items like these remind us daily of the kinds of developments in government, business, technology, and social institutions that can create problems for an organization or pose new opportunities. These external developments can shape the flow of resources to an organization, affect demand for its products and services, and make an impact directly or indirectly on its internal system elements. Naturally, such developments have divergent implications for organizations and stakeholders with divergent interests. State hotel operators, for example, support efforts to block the location of a nuclear dump in the state, whereas members of government agencies and firms developing nuclear power in the region fear that such opposition could lead to industry setbacks. Damage suits against asbestos manufacturers create nightmares for managers in industries where production processes pose health risks. But these corporate liability suits probably encourage workers who face health risks daily, and the growth of such suits opens new markets for the services of legal firms.

This chapter expands the discussion of diagnosing environmental relations begun in Chapters 2 and 4 by providing techniques for diagnosing the responses of a client organization to external conditions and for assessing the organization's strategies for achieving a favorable environmental position. The diagnostic approaches discussed here are usually applied to entire organizations or semi-autonomous divisions but can also be applied to less autonomous units. The less the automony of a focal unit, the more its environment includes other units within the larger organization (e.g., top management) as well as forces beyond that organization's boundary.

GUIDELINES FOR DIAGNOSIS

Diagnosis of an organization's responses to external demands and of its overall relationship to its environment can contribute to managerial decision making or provide a basis for interventions aimed at improving organizational adaptation (see Lauffer, 1977, pp. 47–54 and "Open Systems Planning" below). The key issues in this type of diagnosis are listed here as a set of guidelines for consultants.

(1) *Identify the key conditions in the task environment of the client organization (or unit)—relevant technical and scientific conditions, labor pools, the behavior of competitors, and so on. Describe the external organizations with which the organization interacts—suppliers of resources, consumers of goods and services, supervisory and regulatory groups, unions, competitors, community and political groups having a stake in the organization's actions, and nonmanaging owners (e.g., stockholders).*

The key environmental conditions affecting a manufacturer of microcomputers, for example, include the market for its products, the state of competition within the field, the state of computer technology, and the pool of available talent from which the firm recruits. The external constituencies that have a stake in an organization's affairs and try to influence its operations may include community groups, like those opposing the nuclear dump location, as well as national public interest groups concerned with issues like health, minority employment, and women's issues. Public agencies and service organizations are especially subject to pressures and constraints from external regulatory and certifying bodies (Meyer & Rowen, 1977).

(2) *Describe the nature of the demands and pressures placed on the client organization by the external conditions and organizations and the impacts of these forces.*

Each external group or condition can be thought of as pressing the organization to act in some particular fashion. A city council may be pressing its Youth Services Division to cut back on staff, while community groups are demanding fuller services and greater involvement in decision making. In analyzing external demands, practitioners should describe the degree to which they:

—threaten the flow of needed resources
—disrupt or alter internal operations
—shape receptiveness to organizational outputs

Acquiescence to a demand for community involvement in decision making, for example, would probably require changes in administrative processes and would disrupt current routines. In contrast, external developments may offer *opportunities* for

—expansion or diversification of services or sales
—acquisition of new forms of knowledge or technology
—improvement of political standing and influence over the environment
—recruitment of personnel

Besides examining the specific content of external forces, consultants should also evaluate the degree of *predictability* of important environmental developments. As suggested in Chapter 4, mechanistic administrative procedures can more readily handle predictable environmental developments than rapidly changing, unpredictable ones. One way of assessing environmental predictability is to examine whether the services, work materials, or resources delivered to the environment and received from it during the past year have changed significantly or have remained stable. If they have changed, how well could members of the organization anticipate these changes? Other indications of predictability include the frequency of interruptions, exceptions, and problems associated with obtaining resources such as inputs and delivering goods and services such as outputs (Van de Ven & Ferry, 1980, pp. 141–158).

(3) *Assess the degree to which the client organization depends on the organizations in its task environment.*

The ability of outside groups to influence an organization depends on their authority over that organization's affairs and their control over resources on which the organization is dependent (Pfeffer & Salancik, 1978). In examining external dependencies, consultants should not overlook a client organization's need for public support and approval. These can be as important a resource as cash, personnel, or legal authorization. If decision makers in the client organization can ignore unwanted external demands and continue with "business as usual" without losing public support, they will probably do so.

(4) *Describe how the organization responds to environmental demands and opportunities. Then describe any demands that it places upon its environment as it tries to manage its external relations.*

Practitioners should consider both the concrete actions taken in response to external demands and the implications of these actions for organization-environment relations. For example, the Director of Youth Services could have responded to the demand for greater community participation in decision making by informing the citizens' group that their request was being considered. This response might have reduced external pressure and delayed or avoided the need for a decisive response.

In the short run, organizations can respond to external pressures by using reactive *coping tactics* or they may proactively *intervene* in the environment in order to reduce pressures or shape demands at their source (see Child, 1972; Galbraith, 1977; Miles, 1980; Pfeffer & Salancik, 1978). Here is a list of common *coping tactics* to examine:

—ignoring or evading external demands or pressures
—acceding to those portions of demands that least threaten organizational routines
—adjusting work procedures or flows to take account of changes in the availability of resources or the demand for services
—limiting the impact of pressure groups by assigning responsibility for dealing with them to functions or units (e.g., customer relations) that are isolated from the rest of the organization and have limited impact on it
—monitoring external developments to reduce surprises and disruptions and to facilitate planning

The heads of a junior college, for example, have a variety of options for coping with changes in computer technology and growing student demand for appropriate computer training. They can monitor these developments further by appointing a committee to study the problem, add an introductory course on computers, or incorporate computer skills into existing courses.

In contrast, common ways that organizations may *intervene* in their environments include:

—lobbying and maneuvering for political support
—using economic power to influence external groups (e.g., boycotts, pricing below market to drive out small firms)
—advertising to shape demand or attitudes
—cooperating with other organizations to share resources, reduce competition, and shape other environmental conditions
—creating structural ties with other organizations (contracts, mergers, purchases) that increase control over the environment

(5) *Assess the effectiveness of the organization's coping responses and its interventions in the environment.*

Consultants and their clients should evaluate responses and interventions in terms of agreed-upon effectiveness criteria. In the case of the college, for example, no extra funds were available for computer training, so its costs would have to be balanced by increased revenues. Therefore, adding a course in computers that could attract additional students as well as serving current students was a more effective response from an economic standpoint. Course enrollment fees could generate additional revenues, whereas the purchase of computer equipment for use in existing courses would add expenses without generating revenues.

The Adaptation and Resource Position criteria listed in Table 2 are often used to evaluate organization-environment relations. These criteria emphasize the quality and quantity of resources obtained and the ability of the organization to adapt to external change (see also Chapter 4, "Diagnosing System Fits"). In addition, effectiveness can be defined in terms of the organization's position within its industry and markets and its ability to create favorable external conditions in which to operate.

Consultants may also evaluate the effectiveness of tactics for managing environmental relations in terms of their impact on internal processes. For example, if an organization uses tactics that limit external interference in the work flow, then routines can more readily be established and less expensive and complex forms of coordination can be used (see Chapter 4, "Diagnosing Organization Design").

[handwritten notes in top margin: "29. as assess. current 6t-13 ng. What change / demands for future - are there any opp.? Anticipate"]

If external forces create chronic problems and crises, or disruptions periodically reach major proportions, then current responses may be judged to be inadequate. Other signs of ineffective tactics include severe internal tensions and conflicts that result from external pressures, or short-term responses to the environment that create additional organizational problems (see Chapter 2, "Assessing the Feasibility of Change. . . ").

(6) *Identify trends in the general environment that are already affecting the organization or are likely to affect it in the future.*

Changes in the general environment (see Chapter 2), like the legal, social, and political developments illustrated in the news items above, can make current responses outmoded and can present an organization with new problems and opportunities. Many influential developments originate in the general environment and are only felt later in the immediate, task environment. The demand for college courses in computers, for example, reflects changes in the computer industry that have led to the widespread acceptance of computers in the workplace and at home. Some developments in the general environment in areas such as demographics, consumer tastes, life styles, governmental policies, and business cycles may not yet be directly impinging on a client organization, but may be expected to do so in the near future. The declining proportion of suburban families with young children, for example, will eventually show up in declining demand for services to children—such as elementary school education and pediatric medicine—and a growth of demand for adult-oriented services. Practitioners can sometimes help members of an organization anticipate and deal with such important developments. Even though no one can predict external developments with complete certainty, it is usually better to develop plans for dealing with emerging trends than to undergo crises subsequently or miss crucial opportunities.

(7) *Identify alternative responses to the environment that could enhance current or future effectiveness.*

Consultants and clients should first consider whether tactics for coping and environmental intervention might be improved. For instance, a manufacturing firm that is plagued by fluctuations in the price and availability of key raw materials might consider purchasing commodity futures. National parks that suffer from overcrowding during peak season can require campground reservations and restrict access to overcrowded sites in order to spread usage over a wider area.

If effectiveness cannot be achieved by improving coping and external interventions, two types of long-run alternatives can be considered. First, the client organization might *reorganize* by redefining its strategies and goals or by making basic changes in its structure, processes, technology, resource acquisitions and allocations, or even in its culture (see Chapter 4 on possible ways to reorganize). Reorganizations require a significant investment of time and money, and they often have unintended impacts on organizational components that were not direct targets for change. The introduction of new forms of automation in manufacturing, for example, may increase the importance of those functions charged with monitoring and controlling the automated operations and thereby lead to conflicts between this new interest group and older occupational groups. Hence, in considering the possibility of reorganization, consultants need to pay attention to the organization's readiness and capacity for change and should help clients weigh the potential benefits of reorganizations against their potential costs and any likely negative consequences (Chapter 2). A useful way to assess likely consequences is to examine the ways in which reorganizations will affect fits between system elements (see Chapter 4).

A second way that an organization can handle external problems and improve its environmental standing is to *change one or more of its environmental domains*—by entering into a new field or by changing products, services, or markets (e.g., IBM's entry into the lap-sized computer market). The key issue in evaluating such a possibility is whether the shift will strengthen or weaken the organization's *strategic position* (Andrews, 1971; Porter, 1980)—its ability to obtain resources and dispose of outputs on favorable terms. Strategic advantage often derives from the ability to provide a product or service that is superior in price, quality, or terms of delivery than those offered by the competition—or in being their sole supplier. To obtain such an advantage over potential competitors, organizations need to exploit their *distinctive capacities* to the fullest. In the case of the lap-sized computer market, for example, IBM's advantage may stem from its reputation and from the compatibility of the new, portable machines with the personal computer (PC) and other IBM computers. In assessing the possible effects of entering a new domain, consultants will have to rely on estimates by members of the organization or on studies by market researchers or other experts.

It is possible to analyze the strategic position of nonprofit organizations, as well as of businesses. If, for instance, the directors of a new art museum seek to attract donations and public support in a city that already has a well-established art museum, they should try to develop areas of distinctive competence for the new museum. They could, for example, develop collections in areas where the veteran museum has few holdings or provide unique educational services to the public. Although many nonprofit organizations can shift environmental domains, others may be unable to do so because of their charter, public pressures, or their commitments to a particular organizational identity and mission.

DIAGNOSTIC METHODS

Data Gathering

Interviewing. Information about environmental relations is often gathered primarily through interviews with top management and other officials with responsibility for handling external relations (e.g., sales, public relations, customer services, fund-raising) or for monitoring external developments (e.g., long-range planning). The first six entries in the guidelines above give the main issues to cover in an interview on external relations. To prepare questions in advance, a schedule could be created using questions like those shown in sections IV and V of the General Orientation Interview in Appendix A.

Constructing an interview guide. Alternatively, investigators with experience in semistructured interviewing could construct an interview guide (Schatzman & Strauss, 1973). The guide lists all the topics to be investigated and then allows the interviewer to frame each question to reflect the distinctive circumstances of the client organization and take into account previous answers. Interview guides ensure coverage of major topics while allowing flexibility, but they provide for less reproducible results and require more interviewer skill than do more structured schedules. A guide designed to cover the aspects of external relations discussed above might contain the following major headings:

(1) Key conditions—main markets, fields in which organization operates
(2) Key outside organizations

(3) Main units, people handling contacts with outside
(4) Demands, pressures from outside; problems, difficulties, opportunities encountered in dealing with environment
(5) Indications of impacts of external forces on dynamics (growth, contraction, adjustments, etc.); effects on internal states (conflict, cohesion, etc.); impacts on resource flows (money, human resources, etc.); organization's level of adaptation to external forces
(6) Responses (coping/intervention) to external problems, demands, and opportunities
(7) External trends that are affecting or may affect organization

Then each major heading in the guide would be broken down into subheadings to cover particular issues. For example, item 6 might be broken down as follows:

(6) Responses to external problems, demands, opportunities
(6a) Specific actions—describe in detail what was done, by whom
(6b) Impact of these responses on external actor (Sample question: "How did x react to the steps you took?")
(6c) Other actions (Interviewer: look for interventions to change external forces versus reactions to pressures—e.g., "Did your group ever make any other attempts to moderate these pressures, deflect these criticisms, anticipate such developments, etc.?")
(6d) Internal impacts (Interviewer: probe for felt effects of tactics, whether they produced desired results, how successful they seem to respondent, and meaning of success for him or her.)
(6e) Changes in tactics and impacts—were similar problems handled in same way in past? (Probe for shifts in tactics, stance toward environment, variations in impacts.)

Naturally, when practitioners conduct interviews with a guide like this, they are prepared for the possibility that the person's answers will range across the topics listed in the guide. During the interview the responses are recorded in the order given. Afterward, to facilitate analysis they can be organized according to the topics in the guide.

Standardized questionnaires. Standardized questionnaires can be used to gather data on external relations if reliable, structured measures are needed to facilitate comparisons between units. To assess the degree to which members of a unit view their environment as unpredictable, heads of units and several subordinates may be asked directly about the nature of external forces, the extent to which they have changed in recent years, their predictability, and the difficulties they pose for conducting the work at hand. (See Lawrence

& Lorsch, 1969, pp. 247–250, for open and closed questions appropriate to manufacturing firms, and Van de Ven & Ferry, 1980, pp.
241–258, for items applicable to both profit-oriented and nonprofit
organizations.) Measures can also be developed of other variables,
such as members' perceptions of environmental competitiveness and
munificence, environmental demands and opportunities, the tactics
used to deal with the environment, and the perceived impacts of these
tactics.

Other data sources. Valuable information about external relations
can also be obtained from the popular press and business-oriented
publications, from information sources like Standard and Poors, and
from organizational documents. Sometimes it is also feasible to
interview members of key external constituencies, such as the head of
an environmental defense group that opposes the expansion of a
client's physical plant. Outside experts on topics like the state of an
industry or technology may also be consulted. Additional data may
come from market studies that were conducted prior to the diagnostic
study. Moreover, if issues of marketing are especially critical to the
diagnosis, consultants may suggest that clients conduct further
market studies before deciding to move into new domains or change
their products or services.

Analysis and Feedback

Data analysis and interpretation. The organization design models
presented in Chapter 4 can provide guides to analyzing the fits
between external conditions and a client organization's structure,
technology, and processes. In particular, practitioners can assess
whether coordination mechanisms are appropriate to the degree of
environmental predictability. Units that face very unpredictable
environments (e.g., customer preferences influenced by sudden
changes in fads and fashions) and those facing poorly understood
conditions (e.g., scientific knowledge about mental illness) will
usually need to make more use of complex, lateral coordination
mechanisms and organic administrative systems.

Another approach to analyzing data on environmental relations
is to examine the extent to which a focal unit uses each of the tactics
listed in number 4 of the guidelines above and to consider the
impacts of commonly used tactics like advertising or seasonal adjustments of the work force. In this way consultants may uncover ways
that current tactics could be made more effective and may discover

neglected possibilities for managing external relations. An additional procedure for mapping external contacts is described in Exercise 1 at the end of this chapter.

Except in very small organizations, each unit in a client organization will deal with a different *subenvironment* consisting of those sectors of the environment most relevant to the unit's operations. In a manufacturing firm, for example, the subenvironment of sales includes customers, the competition, and the pool of potential sales employees. In contrast, production managers will deal with the production technology, the availability of raw materials, suppliers, distributors, unions, and the labor pool of production workers. During analysis of environmental relations in complex organizations, practitioners should construct profiles of the main features of the *subenvironments* of such major units. These profiles should note the following features:

—predictability
—complexity (number of relevant external organizations and degree of difference between them)
—competitiveness
—degree of economic or political threat to unit and the organization as whole
—distinctive problems and challenges posed
—appropriate coping and intervention tactics

Units will have to be organized differently to respond to variations in their subenvironments. The greater the differences between subenvironments, the greater will be the need for differentiation and for complex forms of integration within the organization as a whole.

To make characterizations of the environments faced by an entire organization or division—for example, to determine how threatening or supportive the environment is—practitioners will often have to create a composite picture drawn from the reports of people who are knowledgeable about particular subenvironments. Information on organizationwide impacts of responses to the environment can be synthesized in the same fashion. In addition, to decide which responses to the environment work best, practitioners may be able to compare past responses to current ones, or to contrast the approaches of units facing similar conditions.

Preparations for feedback. Once the consultant has obtained an integrated view of the organization's environment, its current environmental responses, the impact of these responses, the possible ways of improving environmental relations, the findings can be prepared for feedback. Feedback can focus directly on the effectiveness of current relations and ways to enhance effectiveness or it can present findings on the state of the environment and external relations as stimuli for self-analysis and decision making. One important issue to consider in preparing feedback is the extent to which members are correctly reading external conditions and have an accurate picture of their organization's's relationship to the environment. If members are misreading environmental conditions and relations, then judicious feedback of data can help members discover the gap between their perceptions and actual conditions and motivate them to look for ways to improve their monitoring and interpretation of external forces.

Drawbacks of a consultant-centered diagnosis of external relations. Although the approach to data gathering and analysis described here is feasible, it has several drawbacks. First, because the burden for gathering and analyzing the data rests heavily on the consultants, they may be encouraged to draw most of the conclusions about the effectiveness of current responses and available alternatives, without involving organizational decision makers in this interpretive process. If the diagnostic conclusions and recommendations are presented in a finalized fashion, clients and other members are unlikely to identify with them or view them as practical and appropriate (see Chapter 3, "Feedback characteristics"). Skillful consultants can partly overcome this limitation by meeting periodically with clients to discuss their findings and interpret them and by proposing that clients draw the conclusions from the findings.

A second drawback of the consultant-centered approach is that it is time consuming and costly, as only highly skilled interviewers and analysts can gather and interpret the necessary information. Third, there is a risk that the feedback will not seem valid to clients because the data and interpretations do not reflect the clients' own experiences and points of view. Fourth, a consultant-centered analysis of external relations may founder on divergences in members' interests and goals. Feedback from diagnoses of external relations is especially vulnerable to conflicts and ambiguities of this sort, because the diagnosis of external relations usually raises questions about the appropriateness of current strategies and about the fits between an organization's purposes and its responses to the environment. Unless clients can agree on goals and strategies, they are likely to disagree on the implications of the diagnosis and find it impossible to implement its recommendations.

OPEN SYSTEMS PLANNING

Where get more on this?

Open Systems Planning (OSP) is a client-centered, diagnostic intervention that may help consultants overcome the limitations of a consultant-centered diagnosis of external relations (Beckhard & Harris, 1977, pp. 58–69; Burke, 1982, pp. 65–70; Fry, 1982; Jayaram, 1976.) In OSP, consultants conduct a series of workshops with members of an organization or subunit who have responsibility and authority to engage in planning and to make decisions affecting the organization's strategic relations to its environment. The workshop participants diagnose their organization's current situation and decide what steps to take to deal with external challenges. The consultant facilitates and guides the discussion, records and summarizes it, and gives feedback without dictating the content of the diagnosis and the planning. Groups whose members are familiar with the background and approach of OSP could also use it without the aid of an external consultant. Here is a summary of the main steps in OSP, phrased as a set of instructions to participants:[1]

(1) *Analyze current environmental conditions*—Create a map showing the external conditions, groups, and organizations in the task environment, and the demands, problems, and opportunities created by these forces.

(2) *Analyze current responses to the environment*—Describe the ways in which the organization is currently handling these environmental demands and conditions. All important transactions with the task environment should be considered.

(3) *Analyze actual priorities and purposes*—Define current goals, values, and priorities by examining current responses to the environment and the organization's internal features (structure, processes, culture, etc.). If possible, reach agreement on the organization's current guiding mission.

(4) *Predict trends and conditions*—Predict likely changes in external conditions over the next two to five years. Assess the future of the

---

1. This summary, which synthesizes and slightly adapts Jayaram's (1976) approach, also draws on Burke (1982, p. 66) and Plovnick et al. (1982, pp. 69–70). The main advantages of Jayaram's approach over that of Beckhard and Harris (1977, pp. 58–69) is that it allows the definitions of purposes and priorities to emerge from the discussions of the current and ideal states, and only requires the achievement of working agreements about operating priorities. This approach to defining goals and priorities seems more realistic than expecting participants to agree in advance on the organization's core mission (see Fry, 1982).

organization if it maintains its current responses to the environment.

(5) *Define an ideal future*—Create scenarios for an ideal future state. These scenarios can envision changes in the organizational purposes and priorities, in external conditions, and in responses to the environment.

(6) *Compare current and ideal states*—In light of projected trends (step 4), define gaps between current and ideal future states in purposes, external conditions, and organizational responses. These gaps may be thought of as differences between where the organization seems to be going and where you want it to be.

(7) *Establish priorities*—Assign priorities to the gaps between ideal and current conditions. Define areas of working agreement and identify disagreements about values, priorities, and purposes.

(8) *Plan appropriate actions*—Plan ways of moving toward agreed-upon future states by narrowing the most important gaps identified in stages 6 and 7. Plan immediate actions and those that will be undertaken after six months and two years. Consider actions for resolving disagreements. Create a schedule for following up on actions and updating plans.

OSP requires participants to use constructive problem-solving techniques to discover and deal with differences in their priorities and objectives. As Jayaram notes, this approach can only work well where members trust and cooperate with one another. If participants can reach a working consensus on ideal future states, they may be able to use OSP successfully to assess the organization's current strategic stance toward its environment and to plan changes in this stance (see Beckhard & Harris, 1977, for examples). An additional requirement for the effective use of OSP is that participants must have the power to put their plans into action (see Chapter 4). Otherwise, the whole process will become an exercise in frustration that may ultimately alienate and embitter participants. To conduct OSP, consultants need to be highly skilled in working with groups in training-type situations, as well as having diagnostic skills.

EXERCISES

1. **External Contacts**
    Based on information gathered in previous exercises or on your own involvement in an organization, choose a unit within an organization that has substantial external contacts (both within and beyond the organization's boundaries). Interview the head of the unit using

parts IV and V of the General Orientation Interview in Appendix A. Make a chart showing the focal unit at the center and all the other units and groups around it. Then color code the chart to show the external groups or units on which the focal unit is most dependent for resources or services, the ones with which contact is most frequent, and any outside units that have authority over the focal unit. Describe the routines and procedures linking the focal unit to two of the most important external units and indicate how these procedures could be improved or how relations with these important units could be improved through other means. (For additional, related exercises see Lauffer, 1977, pp. 50–51; 1982, pp. 30–42.)

2. **Diagnosing External Relations**

Construct a detailed interview guide that reflects the issues raised in the Guidelines for Diagnosis given above. Using this guide, interview the head of a unit or small organization. Organize the responses to the interview and your conclusions about it in terms of the categories given in the guidelines.

6

Challenges and
Dilemmas of Diagnosis

Practitioners of diagnosis may seek ways to solve specific problems, or they may aim higher—at discovering enduring ways to improve organizational effectiveness or at promoting organizational learning. This chapter examines ways in which practitioners can manage the consulting practice to promote such higher-level goals and to make their work as useful as possible to clients. Then it examines ways of dealing with some of the recurring ethical and professional dilemmas that arise during organizational diagnosis.

The preceding chapters focused on diagnostic processes, interpretations, and methods. The examination of each of these facets of diagnosis raised somewhat different issues for the practitioner. *Process* issues concern the relationships that develop between consultants and clients. *Interpretive* issues include the definition of diagnostic problems and the interpretation of findings. *Methodological* issues relate to the techniques for gathering, summarizing, and analyzing data. Chapter 1 introduced all three kinds of concerns. Chapters 2 through 5 presented diagnostic models that can guide interpretation, methods for applying them, and related process issues.

Despite their usefulness, the models discussed in this book and others like them cannot serve as step-by-step guides to diagnosis. Nor can they be used like equations into which bits of data can be inserted in order to produce a completed assessment. No such recipes for diagnosis or for action planning exist, and none is likely to be discovered. Instead, these interpretive models can serve as accounting schemes and guides to help both experienced and would-be practitioners sort out what is going on within an organization. A further limitation of these models is their selective emphasis on particular organizational phenomena. Some focus mainly on one level of analysis (individual, small groups and units, or the total organization), and all stress certain organizational features more than others. Only by combining these partial views and shifting back and forth between them can practitioners deal with the multifaceted nature of modern organizations.

Anyone who undertakes a diagnosis thus faces many choices as to which models and methods to use and how to manage the consulting process. In most cases each available alternative has some advantages and some drawbacks. Frequently the emerging relationship between clients and practitioners and practical considerations, such as the accessibility of data, have a decisive influence on the choices among alternatives. Although we have referred throughout the book to these choices and have suggested issues to consider in making them, would-be practitioners will need firsthand experience in diagnosis and consulting processes, along with further training in organizational analysis and research methods, to develop the ability to make these judgments themselves (see Appendix C).

This chapter seeks to place these immediate choices within the context of the larger challenges and dilemmas facing practitioners of diagnosis. The first part of the chapter discusses five possible goals for diagnosis and some of the requirements for attaining these goals. The second part deals with ethical and professional dilemmas that often confront practitioners.

A successful diagnosis can sometimes contribute directly to organizational improvement or provide the foundations for a program of organization development. Still, even successful studies may make only modest contributions and may serve the needs of powerful clients more than those of other members of the client organization. Even to achieve these limited ends, practitioners must be as attentive to considerations of consulting process as they are to methods of collecting and analyzing data and to models of organizational functioning.

CHALLENGES OF DIAGNOSIS

Diagnostic Goals

The goals toward which consultants and clients may aspire when planning a diagnosis form a hierarchy.[1] Higher-level goals envision more significant and durable impacts on the organization than lower-level ones. Achieving higher-level goals also requires the consultant to be more skilled in managing the consulting process and requires stronger client commitments. Consultants and clients often

1. This section applies and adapts Turner's (1982) discussion of consulting goals.

begin their relationship by defining lower-level goals and gradually adopt a higher-level goal as the consulting relationship evolves. The following discussion presents these goals in ascending order.

(1) Provide specific information or evaluation. The most modest goals involve providing specific information to clients (e.g., public satisfaction with automatic teller machines) or evaluating operations according to clearly defined standards (e.g., determining whether day care programs enable mothers to go to work). Strictly speaking, gathering and reporting such specific information are not forms of diagnosis, as defined in this book. This informational goal is noted here because discussions between clients and consultants about such fact-finding studies often lead to the negotiation of diagnostic goals. Before agreeing to gather specific information, practitioners should try to clarify what clients will do with the information and why they need it. Sometimes clients ask for very specific data on the assumption that the data will help them resolve more general problems or improve organizational functioning. In these cases the practitioner may suggest that a higher-level, diagnostic goal would more accurately reflect the clients' needs.

(2) Solve a specific problem. Clients often seek help in handling specific problems, such as turnover or public dissatisfaction with an organization's services. Sometimes clients' descriptions of problems pin the blame on specific people or groups. In attempting to understand and discover possible solutions to the problems presented by clients, practitioners may discover more general states of which the presented problems are symptomatic. Thus, practitioners should examine ways in which the problems have been handled in the past, groups and relationships that are linked to the problems, and the clients' ability to implement steps that might help solve their problems. In exploring these issues consultants and clients may redefine presented problems in terms of broader problems or challenges, or they may redefine the goal of the relationship as a general assessment of organizational effectiveness.

(3) Assess organizational effectiveness. In this book, we have treated the assessment of effectiveness and the discovery of routes to its improvement as the central goals of diagnosis. Some diagnostic studies assess current effectiveness but leave the discovery of routes to improvement up to the clients. Even studies of this type may contain some implications for action in the very selection of the factors that are examined and reported upon. Whether or not the report on the study includes recommendations, it must use clearly defined criteria of organizational effectiveness (see Chapter 2).

(4) Recommend ways to improve effectiveness. Clients who request assessments of effectiveness typically also want to receive recommendations for improving effectiveness. The search for ways to improve operations requires consultants and their clients to identify the causes of effectiveness and ineffectiveness and to find ways in which clients can intervene (with or without the help of practitioners) to improve current functioning. Most interventions concentrate on changing one or more of the major system elements, such as structures, strategies (purposes), people (human resources), or processes (see Chapter 1, "Organization development interventions"; Chapter 2, "The System . . ."). As they consider routes to improvement, consultants should bear in mind that there may be several alternative ways of intervening to produce a particular result.

The choice of which interventions to recommend and the clients choice of which, if any, to implement will depend on the following considerations (see Chapter 2, "Assessing the Feasibility of Change. . ."):

(1) Diagnostic findings about problems and workable solutions
(2) Available resources—including the skills of consultants and members who are to be involved in the implementation
(3) Anticipated costs
(4) Likely effects—possible benefits versus possible negative consequences
(5) Members openness to various interventions
(6) Support for the interventions by members responsible for implementation and powerful members of the organization

Consultants and clients must therefore weigh the potential costs and benefits of any intervention carefully before planning to implement them. Consider, for example, the use of workshops and training sessions to teach people the concepts and interpersonal skills necessary for teamwork in committees and project groups. These interventions require substantial investments of time but may have very limited or temporary impacts, unless they are accompanied by changes in organizational structures and processes (Katz and Kahn, 1978). On the other hand, structural reorganizations—such as the restructuring of coordination procedures or the redesign of reward patterns—are also expensive and often have unintended consequences. Structural changes are likely to be resisted if they do not fit the prevailing beliefs and norms within the organizational culture and if they conflict with the ways in which people are accustomed to working with one another.

(5) Contribute to organizational learning. In the long run organizational effectiveness—no matter how it is defined—depends on the ability of members to adjust to future states and solve problems that have not yet arisen. Consultants seek to promote organizational learning in order to contribute to the capacity of client organizations to deal with challenges and problems that lie in the unforeseen future (Argyris and Schon, 1978; Hedberg, 1981; Turner, 1982). *Organizational learning* refers to changes in the body of interpretations and accepted responses that guide members in their treatment of problems and challenges. It involves two separate processes—learning by individual members of an organization, and the incorporation of new understandings and directives for action into the organization. Past understandings and responses to problems are embedded in many aspects of the organizational structure, including:

—rules and standard operating procedures
—assignments of jobs and responsibilities
—control procedures
—reward systems

Past interpretations and accepted categories for analyzing problems are also stored in the organizational culture in such forms as

—symbols, terminology, jargon, and stereotypes
—myths and stories about past successes and failures
—widely accepted beliefs about the organization and its environment

Suppose, for example that consultants help an international corporation develop ways to monitor and analyze potentially threatening political events in developing countries as a guide to making investment decisions. The firm can only be said to have *learned* to use this new approach when procedures for conducting political analysis have become an established and influential part of its planning and decision making. When the concepts and images from these new analyses start to pepper the lunch conversations and the more formal deliberations of top executives, the new approach is starting to penetrate the organizational culture.

Organizational learning is needed when environmental and technological conditions are changing substantially and the existing repertoire of responses is becoming incomplete or inadequate (see Chapters 4 and 5). Even if external and technological conditions remain stable, learning is needed to improve the ways in which the organization deals with them. Organizational learning can lead to *small adjustments* within the bounds of current routines or to *significant reorganizations* of the ways members think about their organization and its environment. In contrast to modest adjustments, learning that results in basic changes in structures, processes, technologies, and other system elements requires the *unlearning* of previous responses and the introduction of new behavior patterns. Unfortunately, many structural, interpersonal, and psychological forces resist such basic learning. Even rarer and more difficult to accomplish are fundamental revisions of the underlying theories or models that members use to interpret their organization and its environment. Major crises or imposed reorganizations are usually prerequisites to such radical transformations of an organization's culture.

Making Diagnosis Useful:
The Role of Process

Successful management of the consulting process is necessary for the achievement of even the lower-level, more modest diagnostic goals and becomes all the more complex and critical as diagnostic goals become more ambitious. Here are some of the main features of the consulting process that affect the ability to attain diagnostic goals.

Providing useful feedback. Although feedback is important for all levels of diagnosis, it is especially critical for studies that include recommendations for improving effectiveness or that seek to promote organizational learning. A primary requirement for feedback is that it be valid and relevant to the recipients (Argyris, 1970). No matter what their goals, practitioners should exercise care to provide valid, accurate feedback. The validity of feedback on the organization's current state can be checked by independent investigations by members or practitioners, and by generating predictions from the feedback. In addition to being valid, feedback must be intelligible and meaningful to recipients. Recipients may ignore or reject feedback that is too technical or too distant from their everyday concerns and experiences.

To make feedback useful practitioners need to pay close attention to its motivational implications (Block, 1981; Nadler, 1977). For example, feedback that explicitly compares the performance of units can help motivate action by showing that some people have overcome obstacles facing the client group and have achieved greater effectiveness. This approach reduces the tendency for recipients of the feedback to feel that nothing can be done and may point the way toward workable solutions. Similarly, feedback that points toward attainable ends is more motivating than feedback that sets goals too far beyond the current state or suggests that members must totally transform themselves or their organization (see Chapter 3, "Feedback," for other characteristics of feedback that enhance motivation).

Fostering commitment and ownership of findings and recommendations. As consultants pursue higher-level diagnostic goals, they need to invest increasing efforts in insuring that clients become committed to feedback and to proposals for intervention. The best way to foster commitment of this sort seems to be to involve those members who will have to implement recommendations as fully as possible in all stages of the diagnosis (see Chapter 1, "Participation in Diagnosis. . . ."). Sometimes practitioners encourage involvement of this sort by asking that a liaison group be formed within the client organization which will take an active part in the study. Encouraging members to engage in self-diagnosis is another approach to enhancing commitment to diagnostic findings and interpretations. Even if they cannot participate actively in the diagnosis itself, members who will have to act on its findings should be encouraged to decide themselves what to do about the results, rather than having recommendations pressed upon them by the consultant or by their supervisors (Argyris, 1970). Although these more client-centered approaches to diagnosis can lead to findings and engender commitment to them, these approaches are not suitable for every diagnostic study. Practitioners must be careful to use a consulting style that will fit the culture and expectations of the client organization and that reflects their own training and disposition.

Most diagnoses threaten the interests of at least some members of the focal organization, but practitioners can heighten members' responsiveness to the study by moderating such personal threats whenever possible. In particular, they can make it clear to all participants that they will not make recommendations concerning the placement or retention of individuals and will not report any findings about specific people. Although this approach can increase trust and cooperation, it often cannot be applied to heads of units, who are closely identified with the unit's operations and are held responsible for them by management.

Identifying feasible solutions and interventions. Close contact with knowledgeable and influential members of the client organization can substantially increase consultants' ability to develop workable recommendations for change and can heighten internal support for the diagnosis and its findings. Hence, if consultants work with a liaison group, they should be sure that the group includes influential members of the organization and is not entirely composed of members of advisory units (such as personnel and planning), who may lack influence and inside information. Unless practitioners become aware of the political realities of the client organization early in the diagnostic engagement and actively deal with these realities, they are likely to find that their feedback and recommendations are dismissed by decision makers as irrelevant or unworkable (see Chapters 2 and 4). Even if practitioners do try to take account of political realities, resistance to change may be overwhelming.

Helping clients develop the capacity for self-examination and problem solving. To promote organizational learning consultants must help members view themselves and their organization objectively and develop the capacity for self-examination. To promote learning diagnosis needs to surface hidden assumptions and approaches to problem solving, negative information, conflicts, dilemmas, and basic approaches and routines that are built into the organization's structure and culture. One way consultants can help members surface their hidden interpretations is to give them a limited amount of descriptive feedback, encourage them to analyze these data, and then help them see what assumptions they made as they were analyzing the data.

In addition, to promote problem solving and testing of assumptions by members, consultants can encourage members to develop models or hypotheses about the way their organization is operating, to test them against reality, and to reformulate them accordingly (Schon, 1983). Consider, for example, the division head who received feedback that linked a lack of planning among division managers to a reward system that stressed short-term performance (see Chapter 4). The division head could have been encouraged to test the hypotheses that the reward system was causing the neglect of planning by looking at managerial behavior in units in which planning and longer-term results *were* rewarded. To encourage this kind of problem solving, consultants need to take on a *facilitative*, reflective role, rather than that of the *expert*, who supplies clients with completed solutions to their problems. Diagnostic interventions like Open Systems Planning (Chapter 5) seek to develop this kind of self-understanding and to foster new forms of problem solving. Interventions that promote periodic self-study and evaluation are another way of encouraging organizational learning (e.g., Nadler et al., 1976; Torbert, 1981; Wildavsky, 1972).

In summary, adequate diagnosis is a necessary, but not a sufficient condition for promoting effectiveness and organizational learning. In addition, members of the client organization must deal constructively with the diagnostic feedback, plan appropriate actions, and implement them successfully. Developing these critical links between diagnosis and action is central to organizational consulting but lies beyond the practice of diagnosis itself.

ETHICAL AND PROFESSIONAL DILEMMAS

As the preceding discussion suggest, the role of the practitioner of organizational diagnosis contains many ambiguities and internal tensions (Mirvis and Seashore, 1980). Moreover, there are many possible conflicts between practitioners and members of the client organization. These conflicts and ambiguities can create serious ethical and professional dilemmas for both in-house and external practitioners of diagnosis. Whether or not they are aware of it, as they carry out their work and negotiate their relationships with members of a client organization, consultants are opting for particular resolutions of these dilemmas. The following discussion raises some of these issues in order to help readers better understand diagnosis and prepare to confront these dilemmas in their own work.[2]

Who Benefits?

The sponsors and beneficiaries of diagnosis. No matter how cooperative the relationships between groups within a client organization, some groups and individuals will benefit from a diagnostic study more than others, and some may actually suffer in consequence of it. People who sense that they stand to gain will applaud and support the decision to conduct a diagnosis, whereas those who expect to lose from it will understandably oppose the study. Diagnostic findings may also support certain value positions at the expense of others. For instance, behavioral science practitioners often recommend increas-

---

2. The following discussion of professional dilemmas draws on Walton and Warwick (1973). See also Bowen (1977) and O'Conner (1977).

ing members' participation in decision making. But this proposal may clash with the values of those who currently hold positions of authority.

Thus, consultants need to consider whether they can legitimately promote certain interests and values at the expense of others. This issue is illustrated by questions like these:

—Are consultants responsible for weighing the conflicting interests and values within an entire organization, or is this solely the job of management?

—Should consultants be willing to have their findings feed into internal political struggles?

—Are consultants supposed to promote the narrow interests of the client who originally sponsored the study, or should they try to help "the whole organization"; some broad stratum within it, such as top management; or all the members of the group whose problems were initially presented?

An additional dilemma arises when consultants discover that they cannot identify personally with the goals or the behavior of their clients or other members of the client organization. External consultants can, of course, decline assignments when the client has prejudged the results of the study and plans to use it to justify getting rid of someone or to make some other change. Similarly, external consultants may decline to accept assignments when the organization's mission, goals, culture, or practices directly clash with their own personal values. But what are internal consultants to do about such dilemmas, and what should consultants do when they realize during a study that their findings will encourage behavior that they cannot condone personally or professionally?

Power and politics. Closely related to these issues are those concerned with the role of diagnosis in organizational politics. The mere process of providing people with additional information and understanding of parts of their organization may increase their power. Moreover, a study's recommendations may directly or indirectly enhance the influence and resources of some members or units, at the expense of others. There may also be hidden power implications in the ways in which clients and practitioners define problems and selectively focus on some organizational levels or features (e.g., motivational problems among workers versus structures and managerial styles that affect motivation). At the very least, practitioners should be aware of the power implications of their behavior and should not allow abstract terms like organizational health, system needs, and effectiveness to mask the power trade-offs that are inevitable by-products of diagnosis and intervention.

Top managers are usually the dominant clients for diagnostic studies. Practitioners should ask themselves whether—from the standpoint of their own values and from the standpoint of organizational functioning—they want their work to further enhance the power of those who are already powerful. Some authors (e.g., Alinsky, 1971; Chesler et al., 1978) have responded to the inequalities of power distribution by advocating the use of behavioral science knowledge to assist less powerful groups, such as tenants' unions and block associations in slums. But these change agents do not usually gain sufficient access to the organizations they want to influence to be able to conduct diagnostic studies.

To reduce unforeseen political consequences of their work, practitioners can contract with clients on how diagnostic data will be used. In general it is best if clients do not use diagnostic data to evaluate individual members. Consultants can also try to avoid assignments where the client seems to want to use the study for political purposes—for instance, to diffuse criticism by showing higher-level managers or subordinates that "the issues are being studied." Consultants may also seek to moderate the effects of power struggles by encouraging members to deal with feedback in a spirit of trust and by emphasizing common, nondivisive interests. But consultants can never be certain that some of the recipients of feedback will not react defensively or vindictively to feedback or try to use the findings to enhance their own power at the expense of others.

Implications for individual members. Practitioners also need to confront questions about the privacy and well-being of individual participants in a diagnosis. When employees are told to cooperate with a study even though its findings may be harmful to them, practitioners cannot honestly describe participation as voluntary or as benifiting all members equally. An additional problem involves preserving the privacy and confidentiality of participants.

Naturally, every effort should be made to ensure that none of the data or findings are used in such a way that the opinions or actions of individuals become known. Even if appropriate precautions are taken, the data may still have negative implications for the heads of units, and clients may demand that data relevant to specific individuals be shown to them. Although it is legitimate to refuse to provide such data if the initial agreement ruled out its use, consultants have very little control over what members do with the reported findings. The head of a unit who receives negative feeback from his or her subordinates may punish them for their honesty.

Although there is no way to avoid the ethical dilemmas posed by such possibilities, practitioners can moderate them somewhat by not misrepresenting the purposes and sponsorship of the study and by avoiding manipulative forms of questions and measurement, such as projective tests, that make it difficult for participants in a study to figure out what the investigator really wants to know. Consultants should understand and may even sympathize with participants who are reluctant to expose themselves to criticism or threats to their jobs. On the other hand, consultants should weigh such sympathies with reluctant participants against the responsibility to provide clients with valid and useful diagnostic findings.

Some solutions. Underlying many of the issues discussed so far is the possibility of conflict between clients' interests and those of other members of the organization. Consultants have worked out a variety of solutions to this critical dilemma, ranging from client-oriented to member-oriented.[3] At one extreme lies the Machiavellian view that practitioners of diagnosis, like other types of consultants, owe their loyalties entirely to their clients, who sponsored the diagnosis, judge its outcomes, and are often responsible for paying for it. From this point of view, consultants are absolutely obligated to gather the data and provide the interpretations needed to further their clients' needs. Aside from the serious ethical limitations inherent in this position, it is often unworkable. In practice, it is often very hard to determine who is the client to whom the consultant owes this total loyalty. Is it the person who authorized payment for the study, the individuals who first asked for it, those who approved and sponsored it, or those who will receive the feedback and act on it? In many cases these are quite different people, with divergent needs and interests.

Diametrically opposed to the Machiavellian position is the view that has dominated much of the organization development literature: Consultants are obligated to strive for the improvement of the

3. As the Machiavellian and organization development views described here are ideal types, authors who hold these views are not identified. The former approach dominates much of the writing by instructors in business schools and by management consultants, who often think of consultants as aides to top executives. The organization development view dominated much of the applied work of psychologists and specialists in organizational behavior until the late 1970s and is still prevalent today.

organization as a whole, not to enhance the position of individuals within it. From this vantage point the goals of diagnosis and intervention are the ultimate improvement of organizational properties such as health, effectiveness, cohesion, and so on. This comforting approach solves the dilemmas of power and politics by denying that they exist. Its advocates overlook the realities of differences of interest and talk of abstract organizational needs and states, without recognizing that organizations are composed of individuals and groups who often do not agree on what is good for the system.

Between these two extremes are several approaches that seek to cope more realistically and directly with the essentially political character of organizations. One approach is to seek broad sponsorship and supervision for a diagnosis, so that the members of the organization take on the responsibility for negotiating and resolving many of the power implications of the study. In the Michigan Quality of Work Life project, for example, consultants work with a committee composed of representatives of management and labor (Mirvis & Seashore, 1980). This committee is responsible for reviewing problems and change opportunities and for initiating actions and solutions.

Bowen (1977) has offered a way of relieving consultants of power dilemmas and other conflicts that turns on the definition of the goals of the consultation. Following Argyris (1970) he suggests that the main obligation of consultants is to provide clients with valid information and to allow them the freedom to decide whether or not to take action. This approach has the virtue of discouraging consultants from trying to impose their values on the client organization and encouraging them to accept the fact that power and responsibility for acting on diagnostic findings lies with the members of the organization and not with the consultant. On the other hand, Bowen does not sufficiently specify what constitutes valid information or who the real clients are. His approach may thereby encourage consultants to underestimate the impacts of their own behavior on the organization and to blame clients for failure to enact recommendations.

A less elegant but more realistic solution acknowledges that consultants are responsible to one or more clients and that they must work out a way of handling members' conflicting expectations about their work.[4] Once the priorities of the study and the clients' effectiveness criteria have been clarified (see Chapter 2), practitioners can

---

4. Thanks to my wife, Jo Ann, who helped me work out this solution.

introduce other criteria that are compatible with client goals. In addition, practitioners may try to define problems and look for solutions that avoid divisive, win-lose outcomes that can only benefit one party at the expense of another. Instead they may seek to promote gains for all or most interest groups. As they define problems and seek solutions that will benefit the broadest range of constituencies, rather than generate conflict, consultants can select appropriate effectiveness criteria within the *range* of criteria that are acceptable to powerful clients. Finally, this approach recognizes that consultants may advocate particular priorities and effectiveness criteria, but that they do not always succeed in convincing members to adopt them. Like Bowen's approach, this solution suggests that the members of the organization have the ultimate responsibility for interpreting diagnostic feedback, for deciding what actions are warranted, and for implementing any interventions.

Professional Standards and Responsibility

A somewhat separate set of dilemmas relate to consultants' needs to retain professional standards in the face of the pressures of the consulting practice. First, there is the risk that the need to maintain credibility in the eyes of clients will clash with the dictates of professional honesty. For example, practitioners sometimes find themselves forced to decide whether to risk using new and untested models and techniques or to rely on familiar diagnostic procedures that will provide quick, impressive results but do not entirely fit the diagnostic questions or promote a positive consulting relationship. In like manner, practitioners may feel that they will appear ignorant in the eyes of their clients if they admit that certain organizational problems lie outside of their specialization. But, in fact, many important issues will lie far beyond the competencies of consultants trained mainly in the social and behavioral sciences.

A related difficulty stems from the tentative and ambiguous nature of behavioral science data and findings. As researchers, practitioners are aware that using a different measurement technique or a slightly different definition of the variables might have produced different results. They also realize that issues can be framed in a variety of ways, and that there is more than one plausible interpretation of the state of an organization and the ways to improve it. Can consultants explain such ambiguities to members of the client organization, without making themselves look amateurish and unprofessional? The answer to this question depends on the ways that they define their relationships with clients.

If consultants present themselves as science-based experts who possess all the knowledge and the tools needed to find a solution to any organizational problem, they will have difficulty admitting to such ambiguities. On the other hand, they may acknowledge that both consulting and management are professions that must cope with high levels of *ambiguity and complexity* (Weick, 1979). Both managers and consultants can respond to these challenges by continually formulating, checking, and reformulating interpretations and explanations (Schon, 1983). From this vantage point, consultants should encourage clients to confront ambiguities head on by adopting an *experimental attitude*—"We seem to have a good understanding of what is causing that problem and some good ideas about what to do about them. Let's try them out to see what will happen."

Experiments of this sort can range from systematic tests of the effects of interventions, to less rigorous pilot projects, and to an experimental hypothesis-testing approach to daily affairs. This experimental attitude is illustrated by the manager who has heard about the benefits of delegating authority and decides to test out the theory by encouraging subordinates to assume greater responsibility. Then the manager examines the ways that delegation is affecting the subordinates and their relationships to the manager. In light of this assessment, the manager then adjust his or her subsequent behavior accordingly.

A second dilemma related to professionalism is that a diagnosis that is highly competent from a research standpoint may be counterproductive in terms of its ability to foster clients' receptivness to feedback and commitment to action. The very techniques of data gathering and analysis that spell competence in the eyes of researchers may make particpants in a diagnosis feel anxious and cut off from the study. More client-centered approaches avoid this danger but often have to rely on less sophisticated and less rigorous methods of data gathering and analysis (see Chapter 1).

A third dilemma centers on the evaluation of diagnostic studies. One difficulty is that objective measures of results are often unobtainable. Diagnosis is only one step in a chain of actions that must be completed if effectiveness is to be enhanced. Thus, diagnosis often cannot be evaluated in terms of direct impacts on organizational effectiveness. The task of evaluating a diagnosis is further complicated by the requirement that consultants cannot reveal privileged information about clients and their organizations. Yet evaluation by outside investigators along with criticism and review by peers are needed for objective evaluation and can greatly contribute to the improvement of diagnostic practice. Practitioners can partially compensate for these weaknesses by conducting their own evaluations. In addition, they may publish accounts of their work in which they disguise the identities of client organizations and deal with the abstract, generic significance of their research and experience (Argyris, 1970).

Criteria for evaluating a diagnosis that can be derived from the diagnostic goals discussed above include:

(1) the perceived usefulness of the diagnostic information to clients and other members
(2) the extent to which the diagnosis helped clients and members solve specific problems
(3) the contribution of the diagnosis to members' assessment of their organization's effectiveness
(4) the perceived usefulness of recommendations for improving effectiveness
(5) the degree of use of the diagnostic feedback in decision making and action planning

A fourth dilemma involves conflicts between personal or professional interests and those of clients. University-based consultants, for instance, may be tempted to exploit client organizations as research sites. Similarly, consultants may undertake studies that will pay well, even though it is clear that the client organization is unlikely to use the diagnostic feedback constructively. In both instances, the same kinds of standards that apply to other consulting professions seem to be appropriate here: Practitioners should be encouraged to publish reports of their experiences and findings, and no one would have them take vows of poverty before entering the profession. But they cannot legitimately pursue personal gain in ways that harm their clients or generate unjustified, hidden costs.

CONCLUSION

This chapter has sought to convey some of the crucial challenges and dilemmas facing practitioners of organizational diagnosis. It has emphasized the relationships that develop during the diagnostic process between practitioners, clients, and other members of the client organization. In diagnosis, as in other forms of consultation (Turner, 1982), the ability of practitioners to contribute to organizational improvement depends heavily on the ways they handle these relationships, as well as on their methodological and interpretive expertise.

Practitioners of diagnosis must therefore engage in an elaborate balancing act. They must balance the needs and desires of their clients against those of other stakeholders in the organization and their own professional understandings of organizational effectiveness. They must also balance the requirement for valid, believable data and interpretations against the constraints placed on their time and their resources and the need to generate commitment and openness to the study's findings.

These then, are some of the challenges of diagnosis: To find out what is going on and why, while engaged in a complex and dynamic set of interpersonal relationships. To find a way of serving clients who may be ambivalent about being helped and to deal with people who may be dead set against the consultation. To sort between the constraints of the moment and professional and personal standards. To draw upon a broad range of academic and interpersonal skills in order to provide useful knowledge.

APPENDIX A

GENERAL ORIENTATION INTERVIEW

The orientation interview provides data on the important features of a department or unit and any problems it is experiencing.[1] Orientation interviews are usually conducted after the practitioner has obtained basic descriptive data (See Chapter 2, "Basic Organizational Information"). If such information is lacking or greater depth is needed on the organization or the division as a whole, the following interview can be adapted so as to apply to the total organization or some major division within it. Additional questions can then be added about the major differences within the organization. The interview is divided into labeled sections to show the main system features covered and the levels of analysis (see Chapter 2). The order and wording of the questions should be modified to fit the organization and to allow the interviewer and respondent to move comfortably from one topic to another. Moreover, interviewers should feel free to drop questions on issues that respondents have already covered in their previous answers or to modify questions in light of earlier responses. An orientation interview can last from 30 minutes to up to 2 hours. The starred items can be left for subsequent interviews or covered by other forms of data gathering if time is short or respondents seem uncomfortable with sensitive issues.

Before starting, the interviewer should explain that the purpose of the interview is to learn about what it is like to work in the unit and explain who is sponsoring the study (e.g., division management, with the approval of the union). The interviewer can then explain how the respondent was selected (at random, by recommendation, because of his or her position), and state that each person's answers are confidential and that only general summaries of the results will be revealed (see Chapters 2 and 3 on analysis and feedback).

1. This interview draws in part on Burke (1982, pp. 200–202), Levinson (1972, pp. 527–529), Nadler (1977, pp. 187–191). For additional interviewing guides see Kotter (1978, pp. 91–99) and Levinson (1972, pp. 55–65).

GENERAL ORIENTATION INTERVIEW

I. The Person and His or Her Job (Individual Level)

1. What do you do here? Please tell me about your past experience in the organization and your current job. (Probe for job title, description of work, department, or unit in which person works, previous positions in organization, time spent in them.)
2. What is it like to work here? (Probe for feelings about work and atmosphere, e.g., fun, frustrating, competitive.)

II. Work Roles, Technology, and Outputs (Individual and Group Levels)

1. What tasks does your unit (group, department, division) perform? What are the main techniques and means used to do these things?
2. What are the main outputs of this unit—products, services, ideas? What units in the organization or outside it receive these output?
3. How does your job fit into the work done here? With whom do you have to work (inside and outside the organization) to get things done? How do you communicate with them—informal discussions, meetings, telephone, written reports, computer links, and so on?
*4. What kinds of problems do you have to handle at work? When problems occur, how do you handle them? (Probe for solutions that are well known versus need to discover solutions.) Do you run into many variations and unexpected situations in your work, or is it fairly similar from day to day?
5. Are there any difficulties and barriers to getting the work done here or doing it the way you would like to?

III. Group Structures and Processes—Controls, Coordinating Mechanisms (Group and Organization Levels)

1. How is the work coordinated within the unit? (Probe for the kinds of controls used, e.g., budgets, direct supervision, quality control, periodic evaluations, MBO, etc.).
2. Are goals and objectives spelled out for your unit? If so, how? (Probe for the specification of specific targets versus general direction and for the ways in which specified.)

*3. How do you know when you have done a job well? (Probe for nature of criteria, type of feedback, and time involved in feedback.)

IV. Environment—Relations to Units within the Organization (Group and Organization Levels)

1. What other units do you have to work with to get the work done? How are contacts with other units coordinated?

2. What kinds of things does your unit need to get from other units—funds, approval for action, materials, people, information, and so on? How do you get these things?

3. Are relations to other units pretty smooth and trouble-free or do uncertainties and problems arise? (If so, please describe them.)

V. Environment—External Relations (Group and Organization Levels)

1. What kinds of contacts does your unit have with external groups or organizations? (see also Question II-2) What markets or fields (areas) does your unit work/compete in? What kinds of things do people in your unit need to know about what is going on outside the organization? (Probe for important technological conditions, if not mentioned.) How do they find out?

2. What are the main kinds of resources—people, materials, services, funds, and information—you get from these groups? On which groups are you most dependent?

3. Do you run into problems and challenges in obtaining or supplying these resources and in dealing with external groups and conditions? If so, please describe them and explain how you handle them.

VI. Structure (Group and Organization Levels)

1. How is the work in this unit organized and how does the unit fit into the whole organization? (Probe for formal structure, e.g., who is the head of the unit? To whom does the head report? Who reports to the head? If appropriate, ask respondent to draw an organization chart for the unit and to show its relationship to the rest of the organization.)

2. What are the main rules or procedures in your unit that everyone has to follow? How well do they seem to work?

3. What arrangements are there for taking care of people's health, safety, and retirement needs here?

4. Are there opportunities for obtaining additional skills or training while working here?

5. Is there a union here? If so, what is the climate of union-management relations? How involved is the union in issues other than salary and benefits? (Probe for union involvement in issues such as changes in job titles, work arrangements.)

6. What other (informal) groups are there besides the official unit? (Probe for work teams, cliques, links between and within departments, groups of employees from similar ethnic backgrounds, and so on.)

VII. Processes (Group Level)

1. How do the informal groups you mentioned affect the way the work is done here? Do they get along with one another?

*2. Do you feel a part of any of these groups? If so, if you came up with a new idea or worked especially hard, how would the other people in your group(s) react?

3. Who is your supervisor—the person who is directly responsible for your work? How closely do you work with the supervisor? What is it like to work with him or her?

4. What is it like to work with the other people in you unit? (Probe for behavior indicating quality, nature of interpersonal relations, e.g., chat a lot, versus keep to themselves; help out one another.)

5. How do people find out about what is going on in the unit and in the organization as a whole? (Probe for informal and official communication channels and their use.)

6. How are decisions made in your unit? What about the organization/division as a whole—how are the decisions made that affect your unit?

*7. How much say do you have in decisions affecting your work? To what extent does your supervisor consider your opinions or consult you when making decisions affecting you? (Probe for variations by types of decisions.)

*8. Who are the really influential people in your unit? Who really controls what goes on in the organization as a whole?

9. What do you have to do to get ahead around here? Do you get rewarded for doing your job well? (Probe for kinds of rewards—pay,

promotion, praise, feeling of doing well—and the kinds of behavior which is rewarded in the unit and the organization.)

10. When people within the unit disagree about things, how are these differences resolved? (e.g., "The boss decides alone, we discuss all the sides of the question until we have the best solution, we compromise," and so on.)

VIII. Culture and Processes
(Group and Organization Levels)

*1. If you were telling a friend what it was really like to work here, how would you describe the atmosphere at work? (Probe for norms, beliefs about the nature of the work, how it should be done, and employee's involvement in work.)

2. What aspects of work are most emphasized here—quality, costs, speed, quantity, innovation, etc.?

*3. Does it pay to take risks or stick your neck out in your unit? (Probe for support for initiative, risk taking, attitudes toward criticism.)

IX. Purposes and Culture
(Group and Organizational Levels)

*1. Can you give me an example of one of your unit's major successes or achievements? What about a failure? (Probe for criteria for deciding that something succeeded or failed.)

2. What would you say is the overall mission or purpose of your organization? (or, what does your organization say it stands for?) How does the organization pursue its mission? (Probe for differences between official and actual purposes.)

3. Do you feel that your unit is operating effectively? What do you mean by effective?

X. History of Unit/Organization
(Group and Organization Levels)

1. We have talked a lot about the way things are done today in your unit. Could you tell me something about how they got this way? How have things changed since this unit got started? (Note timing of changes.)

*2. What about the organization as a whole, how has it changed?

XI. Problems and Challenges
(Group and Organization Levels)

1. What do you see as the main challenges that will be facing your unit and your organization during the next two or three years? Do you have any suggestions for how to handle them?

2. What do you feel are the main strengths of your unit? What are the strengths of the organization as a whole? What are the main problems in the unit? What are the main problems in the organization (or division) as a whole?

3. What things seem to be most in need of change in your unit? What about the organization as a whole? (Probe for reasons for mentioning these problems.)

XII. Individual Satisfactions

*1. (If not already evident—)In general how satisfied are you with working here? What things make you feel most satisfied? What are the things with which you are least satisfied?

APPENDIX B

STANDARDIZED DIAGNOSTIC INSTRUMENTS[1]

Three Major Instruments

These instruments are long, research-based questionnaires with many subscales. Technical information (e.g., scale construction, reliability, validity) and advice on administration are contained in the published sources. Practitioners may select among these scales or choose items from within scales. Permission to reproduce or use these and other instruments should be obtained from their publishers.

Michigan Organizational Assessment Questionnaire (MOAQ). MOAQ (Cammann et al., 1983) covers a wide range of individual-level attitudes and beliefs that can be averaged to obtain group-level data (see Chapter 3). See Seashore et al. (1983) for information on other instruments in the Michigan Quality of Work Life Program. Readers may contact Dr. Cortland Cammann for more recent information on these instruments (Institute for Social Research, Ann Arbor, MI 48104).

Organizational Assessment Inventory (OAI). OAI (Van de Ven & Ferry, 1980) is a family of questionnaires that provide sophisticated, sometimes complex, measures of processes, structures, technologies, and relations to external units (see Chapter 3 and Van de Ven & Ferry, 1980, for overviews). For information on recent revisions research using OAI contact Professor Andrew Van de Ven, School of Management, University of Minnesota, Minneapolis, 55455.

Survey of Organizations. This machine-scored instrument measures the following sets of variables that Likert (1967) and his associates identified as the strongest predictors of employee satisfaction and performance:

—Organizational Climate (respondents' perceptions of organizational processes such as communication flows, decision-making processes, conflict resolution; the extent to which work facilitated, and the basis for motivation to work)

1. Information on the status of these instrument as of early 1985 was graciously provided by Professors Stanley Seashore (MOAQ), Andrew Van de Ven (OAI), J. Richard Hackman (JDS), and by Mr. David Summers (Goodmeasure).

—Supervisory Behavior (support, work facilitation, interaction facilitation, and goal emphasis)
—Peer Relationships (variables are parallel to those for supervisors)
—Group Processes (trust, communication, decision making, flexibility, etc.)

In addition, there are a range of measures of satisfaction. See Taylor and Bowers (1972) for extensive methodological documentation and Hausser et al. (1975) on using the survey in organization development projects. The major drawbacks of the instrument are its reliance on a model of organizational effectiveness that is no longer regarded as universally valid and its exclusive use of subjective, attitudinal questions, which are especially prone to response biases (see Chapter 3).
The instrument has not been revised or updated since 1972. For additional information contact Rensis Likert Associates, 3001 S. State St., Ann Arbor, MI 48104.

Brief Instruments

Here are examples of short questionnaires that can be helpful in signaling problem areas or for gathering data for self-diagnosis and problem solving:

Group Effectiveness Survey. This 25-item questionnaire (Nadler, 1977, pp. 194–198) elicits generalizations about such internal organizational features as group tasks, processes (conflict, leadership, interpersonal relations, etc.)—for example, "How much conflict is expressed in your group?" Questions also cover satisfaction and five aspects of group effectiveness. A computerized feedback form is shown, but no technical information is provided.

Organizational Diagnosis Questionnaire. Perziosi (1980) provides 35 items on respondents' evaluations of their organization with regard to 6 areas: purposes, structure, relationships, leadership, rewards, and coordinating mechanisms (see Weisbord, 1978). No technical data are provided.

Job Diagnostic Survey (JDS) and the Job Rating Form (JRF). JDS (Hackman and Oldham, 1980) focuses specifically on job characteristics that affect motivation (see Chapter 3). Questions cover:

—Job Characteristics (skill variety, task identity, task significance, feedback, autonomy)

—Psychological States (meaningfulness of work, sense of responsibility, and knowledge of the actual results; satisfaction with job and work context, and respondents' need for growth at work)

JRF is a companion measure in which supervisors describe their subordinates' jobs. These instruments, which were used extensively in research, appear in Hackman and Oldham (1980), along with instructions for their administration, national norms for each variable, and discussions of their theoretical basis and their use in programs of job redesign. A short form of JDS is also available. The authors of JDS are no longer working on the instrument.

Other instruments. Shorter instruments are often reported in academic journals (see Appendix C) and are sometimes available from consulting firms. For example, Goodmeasure Inc. (Directors: Dr. R. Kanter and B. Stein, 330 Broadway PO Box 3004 Cambridge, MA 02139) developed Power Dimensions in Your Job, an instrument that could be used in training or action planning or adapted for use in diagnosing power relations. The firm also makes available parts of Assessment of Organizational Character, an instrument for assessing features associated with innovation (Kanter, 1983).

Many other focused diagnostic instruments have been published in the *Annual: Developing Human Resources* (previously titled *Annual Handbook for Group Facilitators and Consultants*). However, the articles prior to 1984 do not provide any theoretical background for the instruments, and in no case are technical data on reliability and validity given. Most of these instruments are brief questionnaires designed to be used in workshops or training sessions where participants engage in self-diagnosis with the help of a consultant or trainer. Many are designed to provide diagnostic data for use in team building. For example, Costigan and Schmeidler (1984) give measures for diagnosing the climate of group communication and conflict resolution (e.g., extent to which the atmosphere is judgmental and authoritarian, supportive of worker participation, and encourages free and open exchange of information and constructive conflict resolution). Another useful instrument in the *Annual* is a questionnaire for measuring the feelings and conditions concerning the quality of work life (Sashkin & Lengerman, 1984.)

APPENDIX C

WHERE TO GET TRAINING AND EXPERIENCE
IN ORGANIZATIONAL DIAGNOSIS

Academic training. Social and behavioral science departments and professional schools offer many courses relating to organizations and organizational behavior that can equip students with methods and conceptual frames that are useful in diagnosis and a smaller number of courses on applied research and organization development. Concentrations in organizational behavior are often available in schools of management. Courses in statistics and quantitative research techniques are widely offered, whereas, nonquantitative research techniques, such as unstructured observation and open interviewing, are most often taught in departments of anthropology and sociology.

Workshops, seminars, and conferences. Many universities offer evening courses that are often more practically oriented than courses for credit. Workshops, seminars, and conferences are also sponsored by many of the professional and academic organizations which have sections devoted to organizational studies or applied organizational work—for example, the American Psychological Association.

Three organizations offer a wide variety of courses and workshops throughout the United States and Canada in organization development, including training in diagnosis. They provide opportunities for experiential learning of skills like giving and receiving feedback and team building:

—The National Training Laboratories (PO Box 9155 Rosslyn Sta., Arlington VA 22209) is the largest and oldest of the organizations that applied the approach of sensitivity training to organization development. NTL programs have become very diverse but still retain an emphasis on sensitivity training and experiential learning.
—University Associates Publishers and Consultants (8517 Production Ave. PO Box 26240, San Diego CA 92126) offers a broad range of workshops and training programs, publishes many materials on organization development, and holds annual conferences.
—The Organization Development Institute (11234 Walnut Ridge Rd., Chesterland OH 44026) sponsors a variety of local, national, and international conferences and publishes an *International Registry of Organization Development Professionals.*

This listing is not intended to imply approval or recommendation of any particular course or program.

Readers may also wish to inquire whether local applied behavioral science consulting firms offer any workshops or training programs in organization development and diagnosis. Names of local firms may be obtained from university professors specializing in organizational research; the listings under Management Consultants in the Yellow Pages; the list of firms in the *1983 Annual for Facilitators, Trainers, and Consultants;* and the Organization Development Institute's registry of professionals.

For further reading. Those who want to read further on their own in fields like organizational behavior, diagnosis, and organization development can begin with basic texts (e.g., Gordon, 1983; Huse & Cummings, 1985; Miles, 1980) and then consult the references to this book. Journals for keeping abreast of academic developments include:

—*Annual Review of Sociology*
—*Annual Review of Psychology*
—*Review of Organizational Behavior*
—*Administrative Science Quarterly*
—*Academy of Management Review*

Periodicals with a more applied emphasis include:

—*Organizational Dynamics*
—*Journal of Applied Behavioral Sciences*
—*Annual: Developing Human Resources*
—*Harvard Business Review*
—*Sloan Management Review*
—Business periodicals (e.g.,*Business Week, Fortune)*

REFERENCES

Abrahamsson, B. (1977). *Bureaucracy or participation: The logic of organization.* Beverly Hills, CA: Sage.

Alderfer, C. (1977). Organization development. *Annual Review of Psychology, 28,* 197–223.

Alinsky, S. (1971). *Rules for radicals.* New York: Random House/Vintage Books.

Andrews, K. (1971). *The concept of corporate strategy.* Homewood, IL: Dow-Jones, Irwin.

Argyris, C. (1970). *Intervention theory and method.* Reading, MA: Addison-Wesley.

Argyris, C. and Schon, D. (1978). *Organizational learning: A theory of action perspective:* Reading, MA: Addison-Wesley.

Austin, M. (1982). *Evaluating your agency's programs.* Beverly Hills, CA: Sage.

Beckhard, R. (1969). *Organization development: Strategies and models:* Reading, MA: Addison-Wesley.

Beckhard, R., and Harris, R. (1975). Strategies for large system change. *Sloan Management Review, 16,* 43–55.

Beckhard, R. and Harris, R. (1977). *Organizational transitions: Managing complex change.* Reading, MA: Addison-Wesley.

Beer, M. (1980). *Organizational change and development—A systems view.* Santa Monica, CA: Goodyear.

Benne, K. and Sheats, P. (1948). Functional roles of group members. *Journal of Social Issues, 2,* 42–47

Bennis, W. et al. (1976). *The planning of change.* (3rd ed.). New York: Holt, Rinehart and Winston.

Blake, R. and Mouton, J. (1964). *The managerial grid.* Houston: Gulf.

Blau, P. (1955). *Dynamics of bureaucracy.* Chicago, IL: University of Chicago Press.

Block, P. (1982). *Flawless consulting.* San Diego. CA: University Associates.

Bowditch, J., and Buono, A. (1982). *Quality of work life assessment.* Boston, MA: Auburn.

Bowen, D. (1977). Value dilemmas in organization development. *Journal of Applied Behavioral Science, 13,* 543–556.

Burke, W. W. (1982). *Organization development.* Boston, MA: Little, Brown.

Burns, T. (1961). Micropolitics: Mechanisms of institutional change. *Administrative Science Quarterly, 6,* 257–281.

Burns, T., and Stalker, G. M. (1961). *The management of innovation.* London: Tavistock.

Business Week. (1981a). The new industrial relations. May 11, 1981, 85–93.

Business Week. (1981b). The new Sears: Unable to grow in retailing, it turns to financial services. (International Edition) November 16, 110–114.

Cameron, K. (1980). Critical questions in assessing organizational effectiveness. *Organization Dynamics, 9,* 66–80.

Cammann, C. et al. (1983). Assessing the attitudes and perceptions of members. In S. Seashore et al. (Eds.), *Assessing organizational change* (pp. 71–138). New York: John Wiley.

Campbell, D. (1977). On the nature of organizational effectiveness. In P. Goodman and J. Pennings (Eds.), *New perspectives on organizational effectiveness* (pp. 13–55). San Francisco, CA: Jossey-Bass.

Cannell, C., and Kahn, R. (1968). Interviewing. In G. Lindzey and E. Aronson (Eds.), *Handbook of social psychology.* (2nd ed. pp. 526–595). Reading, MA: Addison-Wesley.

Carlisle, H. (1974). A contingency approach to decentralization. *Advanced Management Journal,* July.

Chesler, M., Crawfoot, J., and Bryant, B. (1978). Power training: An alternative path to conflict management. *California Management Review, 21,* 84–91.

Child, J. (1972). Organization structure, environment, and performance: The role of strategic choice. *Sociology, 6,* 1–22.

Child, J. (1977). *Organization: A guide to problems and practice.* New York: Harper and Row.

Costigan, J., and Schmeidler, M. (1984). Exploring supportive and defensive communication climates. In J. Pfeiffer and L. Goodstein (Eds.), *The 1984 annual: Developing human resources* (pp. 112–118), San Diego, CA: University Associates.

Davis, L., and Cherns, A. (1975). *The quality of working life.* (Vols. 1 and 2). New York: Free Press.

Davis, S. (1984). *Managing corporate culture.* Cambridge, MA: Ballinger.

Davis, S., and Lawrence, P. in collaboration with Kolondny and Beer. (1977). *Matrix.* Reading, MA: Addison-Wesley.

Fishbein, M., and Ajzen, I. (1975). *Beliefs, attitudes, intention, and behavior.* Reading, MA: Addison-Wesley.

Fottler, M. (1981). Is management really generic? *Academy of Management Review, 6,* 1–12.

Fry, R. (1982). Improving trustee, administrator, and physician collaboration through open systems planning. In M. Plovnick et al. (Eds.), *Organization development: Exercises, cases and readings* (pp. 282–292), Boston, MA: Little Brown.

Galbraith, J. (1977). *Organization design.* Reading, MA: Addison-Wesley.

Goffman, E. (1959). *The presentation of self in everyday life.* Garden City, NY: Doubleday.

Goodman, P. S. (1977). Social comparison processes. In B. Staw and G. Salancik (Eds.), *New directions in organizational behavior.* Chicago: St. Clair.

Goodman, P. S., and Pennings, J. (1980). Critical issues in assessing organizational effectiveness. In E. Lawler et al. (Eds.), *Organizational assessment* (pp. 185–215), New York: Wiley.

Gordon, J. (1983). *A diagnostic approach to organizational behavior.* Boston: Allyn and Bacon.

Hackman, R., and Oldham, G. (1980). *Work redesign.* Reading, MA: Addison-Wesley.

Hall, R. (1982). *Organizations, structure and process* (2nd ed.). Englewood Cliffs, NG: Prentice-Hall.

Harrison, R. (1970). Choosing the depth of organizational intervention. *Journal of Applied Behavioral Science, 6,* 181–202.

Hausser, C., Pecorella, P., and Wissler, A. (1975). *Survey guided development: A manual for consultants.* Ann Arbor: Institute for Social Research, University of Michigan.

Hayes, R., and Abernathy, W. (1980). Managing our way to economic decline. *Harvard Business Review, 58,* 67–77.

Hedberg, B. (1981). How organizations learn and unlearn. In P. Nystrom and W. Starbuck (Eds.), *Handbook of organizational design* (Vol. 1, pp. 1–27). New York: Oxford University Press.

Huff, A. (1980). Organizations as political systems: Implications for diagnosis, change and stability. In T. G. Cummings (Eds.), *Systems theory for organization development* (pp. 163-180). Chichester, England: John Wiley.

Huse, E., and Cummings. T. (1985). *Organization development* (3rd ed.). St. Paul, MN: West.

Izraeli, D.N. (1975). The middle manager and tactics of power expansion—A case study. *Sloan Management Review*, 16, 57-70.

Jayaram, G. K. (1976). Open systems planning. In W. G. Bennis, et al. (Eds.), *The planning of change*, (3rd ed. pp. 275-28). New York,: Holt, Rinehart and Winston.

Kanter, R. (1977). *Men and women of the corporation.* New York: Basic.

Kanter, R. (1979). Power failure in management circuits. *Harvard Business Review, 57,* 65-75.

Kanter, R. (1983). *The change masters: Innovation for productivity in the American corporation.* New York: Simon and Schuster.

Kanter, R., and Brinkerhoff, D. (1981). Organizational performance. *Annual Review of Sociology, 7,* 321-349.

Katz, D., and Kahn, R. (1978). *The social psychology of organizations* (2nd ed.). New York: John Wiley.

Katz, D., and Kahn, R. (1980). Organization as social systems. In E. Lawler et al. (Eds.), *Organizational assessment.* (pp. 162-184). New York: John Wiley.

Kets de Vries, M. (1979). Organizational stress: A call for management action. *Sloan Management Review, 21,* 3-14.

Khandwalla, P. (1977). *The design of organizations.* New York: Harcourt Brace Jovanovich.

Kidder, T. (1981). *The soul of a new machine.* Boston: Little, Brown.

Kolb, D., and Frohman, A. (1970). An organization development approach to consulting. *Sloan Management Review, 12,* 51-65.

Kotter, J. (1978). *Organizational dynamics.* Reading, MA: Addison-Wesley.

Lauffer, R. et al. (1977). *Understanding your social agency.* Beverly Hills, CA: Sage.

Lauffer, R. et al. (1982). *Assessment tools: For practitioners, managers, trainers.* Beverly Hills, CA: Sage.

Lawler, E. (1977). Reward systems. In J. Hackman & J. Suttle (Eds.), *Improving life at work: Behavioral science approaches to organizational change* (pp. 166-226). Santa Monica, CA: Goodyear.

Lawler, E. and Drexler, J. (1980). Participative research: The subject as co-researcher. In E. Lawler et al. (Eds.), *Organization assessment* (pp. 535-547). New York: John Wiley.

Lawler, E., Nadler, D., and Cammann, C. (Eds.). (1980). *Organizational assessment.* New York: John Wiley.

Lawler, E., Nadler, D., and Mirvis, P. (1983). Organizational change and the conduct of organizational research. In E. Lawler et al. (Eds.), *Assessing organizational change* (pp. 19-48). New York: John Wiley.

Lawler, E., and Rhode, J. (1976). *Information and control in organizations.* Santa Monica, CA: Goodyear.

Lawrence, P., and Lorsch, J. (1969). *Organization and environment* Homewood, IL: Irwin.

Leach, J. (1979). The organizational history: A consulting analysis and intervention tool. In G. Gore and R. Wright (Eds.), *The academic consultant connection* (pp. 62-69). Dubuque, IA: Kendall/Hunt.

Levinson, H. (1972). *Organizational diagnosis.* Cambridge, MA: Harvard University Press.

Likert. R. (1967). *The human organization.* New York: McGraw-Hill.

Lofland, J. (1971). *Analyzing social situations.* Belmont, CA: Wadsworth.

Lorsch, J., and Morse, J. (1974). *Organizations and their members: A contingency approach.* New York: Harper and Row.

McCaskey, M. (1979). A contingency approach to planning. *Academy of Management Journal, 17,* 281–291.

McGregor, D. (1960). *The human side of enterprise.* New York: McGraw-Hill.

Meyer, J., and Rowan, B. (1977). Institutionalized organizations: Formal structure as myth and ceremony. *American Journal of Sociology,* 83, *340–363.*

Miles, R. E., and Snow, C. (1978). *Organizational strategy, structure, and process.* New York: McGraw-Hill.

Miles. R. H. (1980). *Macro organizational behavior.* Santa Monica, CA: Goodyear.

Mintzberg, H. (1979). *The structuring of organizations.* Englewood Cliffs, NJ: Prentice-Hall.

Mintzberg, H. (1983). *Power in and around organizations.* Englewood Cliffs, NJ: Prentice-Hall.

Mirvis, P., and Seashore, S. (1980). Being ethical on organizational research. In E. Lawler et al. (Eds.), *Organizational assessment* (pp. 583–612). New York: John Wiley.

Moch, M., Cammann, C., and Cooke, R. (1983a). Organizational structure: Measuring the degree of influence. In S. Seashore et al. (Eds.), *Assessing organizational change* (pp. 177–202). New York: John Wiley.

Moch, M., Feather, J., and Fitzgibbons , D. (1983b). Conceptualizing and measuring the relational structure of organizations. In S. Seashore et al. (Eds.), *Assessing organizational change* (pp. 203–228). New York: John Wiley.

Nadler, D. (1977). *Feedback and organization development: Using data-based methods.* Reading, MA: Addison-Wesley.

Nadler, D., Mirvis, P., and Cammann, C. (1976). The ongoing feedback system: Experimenting with a new management tool. *Organizational Dynamics.* 4, 63–80.

Nadler, D., and Tushman, M. (1980a). A congruence model for diagnosing organizational behavior. In E. Lawler et al. (Eds.), *Organizational assessment* (pp. 261–278). New York: John Wiley.

Nadler, D., and Tushman, M. (1980b). A model for diagnosing organizational behavior. *Organizational Dynamics, 9,* 35–51.

Newman, W., and Warren, E. (1977). *The process of management.* Englewood Cliffs, NJ: Prentice-Hall.

Nightingale, O., and Toulouse, J. (1977). Toward a multi-level congruence theory of organization. *Administrative Science Quarterly, 22,* 264–280.

O'Conner, P. (1977). A critical inquiry into some assumptions and values characterizing O.D. *Academy of Management* Review. 2, 635-644.

Ouchi, W. (1981). *Theory Z.* Reading, MA: Addison-Wesley.

Pasmore, W., and Sherwood, J. (Eds.). (1978). *Socio-technical systems: A source book.* San Diego, CA: University Associates.

Pennings, J., and Goodman, P. (1977). Toward a workable framework. In P. Goodman and J. Pennings (Eds.), *New perspectives on organizational effectiveness* (pp. 164–184). San Francisco, CA: Jossey-Bass.

Perkins, D., Nadler, D., and Hanlon, M. (1981). A method for structured naturalistic observation of organizational behavior. In J. Pfeiffer and J. Jones (Eds.), *The 1981 annual handbook for group facilitators* (pp. 222–244). San Diego, CA: University Associates.

Perrow, C. (1970). *Organizational analysis: A sociological view.* Belmont, CA: Wadsworth.

Perziosi, R. (1980). Organizational diagnosis questionnaire (ODQ). In J. Pfeiffer and J. Jones (Eds.), *The 1981 annual handbook for group facilitators.* (pp. 112–120). San Diego, CA: University Associates.

Pfeffer, J. (1981a). Management as symbolic action: The creation and management of organizational paradigms. *Research in Organizational Behavior, 3,* 1–52.

Pfeffer, J. (1981b). *Power in organizations.* Marshfield, MA: Pitman.

Pfeffer, J.,and Salancik, G. (1978). *The external control of organizations.* New York: Harper & Row.

Plovnick, M., Fry, R., & Burke, W. (1982). *Organization development: Exercises, cases and readings.* Boston, MA: Little, Brown.

Pondy, L. (1967). Organizational conflict: Concepts and models *Administrative Science Quarterly, 12,* 296–320.

Porras, J., and Berg, P. (1978). The impact of organizational development. *Academy of Management Review, 3,* 249–266.

Porter, L., Allen R., and Angle, H. (1981). The politics of upward influence in organizations. *Research in Organizational Behavior, 3,* 109–150.

Porter, M. (1980). *Competitive strategy: Techniques for analyzing industries and competitors.* New York: Free Press.

President and Fellows of Harvard College. (1980). *Action planning and implementation: A manager's checklist.* No. 9-481-010. Boston: HBS Case Services.

Price, J. (1972). *Handbook of organizational measurement.* Lexington, MA: D. C. Heath.

Quinn, J. B. (1977). Strategic goals: Process and politics. *Sloan Management Review, 19,* 21–37.

Quinn, J.B. (1980). *Strategies for change: Logical incrementalism.* Homewood, IL: Irwin.

Robbins, S. P. (1978). Conflict management and conflict resolution are not synonymous terms. *California Management Review, 21,* 67–75.

Rossi, P., and Freeman, H. (1982). *Evaluation: A systematic approach* (2nd ed.). Beverly Hills, CA: Sage.

Salancik, G., and Pfeffer, J. (1977). An examination of need satisfaction models of job attitudes. *Administrative Science Quarterly, 22,* 427–456.

Sashkin, M., and Lengerman, J. (1984). Quality of work life-conditions/feelings. In J. Pfeiffer and L. Goodstein (Eds.), *The 1984 annual: Developing human resources* (pp. 131–144). San Diego, CA: University Associates.

Sayles, L. (1979). *Leadership.* New York: McGraw-Hill.

Schatzman, L., and Strauss, A. (1973). *Field methods.* Englewood Cliffs, NJ: Prentice-Hall.

Schein, E. (1969). *Process consultation: its role in organization development.* Reading, MA: Addison-Wesley.

Schon, D. (1983). *The reflective practitioner—How professionals think in action.* New York: Basic Books.

Seashore, S., Lawler, E., Mirvis, P., and Cammann, C. (Eds.). (1983). *Assessing organizational change.* New York: John Wiley.

Sellitiz, C. et al. (1981). *Research methods in social relations* (3rd ed.). New York: Holt, Rinehart and Winston.

Steele, F. (1973). *Physical settings and organization development.* Reading, MA: Addison-Wesley.

Steele, F. (1975). *Consulting for organization change.* Amherst, MA: University of Massachusetts Press.

Strauss, G. (1976). Organizational development. In R. Dubin (Ed.), *Handbook of work, organization, and society* (pp. 617–363). Santa Monica, CA: Goodyear.

Strauss, G.(1977). Managerial practices. In J. Hackman and T. Suttle (Eds.), *Improving life at work.* (pp. 297–363). Santa Monica, CA:Goodyear

Strauss, G. (1982). Worker's participation in management: An international perspective. *Research in Organizational Behavior. 4,* 173–265.

Sutherland, J. (Ed.) (1978). *Management handbook for public administrators.* New York: Van Nostrand.

Tannenbuam, A. S. (1968). *Control in organizations.* New York: McGraw-Hill.

Taylor, J., and Bowers, D. (1972). *Survey of organizations: A machine scored standardized questionnaire instrument.* Ann Arbor, MI: Institute for Social Research, University of Michigan.

Thompson, J. (1967). *Organizations in action.* New York: McGraw-Hill.

Tichy, N. (1978). Diagnosis for complex health care delivery systems: A model and case study. *Journal of Applied Behavioral Science, 14,* 305–320.

Tichy, N. (1983). *Managing strategic change: Technical, political and cultural dynamics.* New York: John Wiley.

Tichy, N., Tushman, M., and Fombrun (1980). Network analysis in organizations. In E. Lawler et al. (Eds.), *Organizational assessment* (pp. 372–398). New York: John Wiley.

Tilles, S. (1961). Understanding the consultant's role. *Harvard Business Review, 39,* 87–99.

Torbert, W. (1981). The role of self-study in improving managerial and institutional effectiveness. *Human Systems Management, 2,* 72–82.

Turner, A. (1982). Consulting is more than giving advice. *Harvard Business Review, 60,* 120–129.

Tushman, M. (1977). A political approach to organization: A review and rationale. *Academy of Management Review, 3,* 613–624.

Tushman, M., and Nadler, D. (1978). Information processing as an integrative concept in organizational design. *Academy of Management Review, 2,* 206–216.

Van de Ven, A., and Drazen, R. (1985). The concept of fit in contingency theory. *Research in Organizational Behavior, 7,* 333-365.

Van de Ven, A., and Ferry, D. (1980). *Measuring and assessing organizations.* New York: John Wiley.

Walton, R. (1975). Quality of working life: What is it? *Sloan Management Review, 15,* 11–21.

Walton, R., and Dutton, J. (1969). The management of interdepartmental conflict: A model and review. *Administrative Science Quarterly, 14,* 73–84.

Walton, R., and Warwick, D. (1973). The ethics of organization development. *Journal of Applied Behavioral Science, 9,* 681–698.

Webb. E. et al. (1966). *Unobtrusive measures: Non-reactive research in the social sciences.* Chicago, IL: Rand McNally.

Weick, K. (1979). *The social psychology of organizing* (2nd ed.) Reading, MA: Addison-Wesley.

Weick, K. (1985). Systematic observation methods. In G. Lindzey and E. Aronson (eds.). *Hardbook of Social Psychology* (3rd ed.). Vol. 2 (pp. 567-634), Reading MA: Addison-Wesley.

Weisbord, M. (1978). *Organizational diagnosis: A workbook of theory and practice.* Reading, MA: Addison-Wesley.

Wildavsky, A. (1972). The self-evaluating organization. *Public Administration Review, 32,* 509–520.

Zald, M., and Berger, M. (1978). Social movements in organizations: Coup d'etat, insurgency, and mass novements. *American Journal of Sociology, 83,* 823–861.

INDEX

ABOUT THE AUTHOR

Michael I. Harrison is a Senior Lecturer at Bar Ilan University in Ramat Gan, Israel, where he has been a faculty member since 1974. He served as Chairperson of the Department of Sociology and Anthropology there and currently heads its graduate Program in Organizational Sociology. Since 1981 he has been an Adjunct Associate Professor in the Department of Organization Studies/Human Resources Management of the School of Management, Boston College, where he has also served as a Visiting Associate Professor. During 1980–1981 he was a Visiting Scholar at the Graduate School of Business of Harvard University. He is active in the Israeli and American Sociological Associations and the Academy of Management. Originally from New York, Professor Harrison received his B.A. in sociology from Columbia College in 1966 and his Ph.D. in sociology in 1972 from the University of Michigan, where he was a National Science Foundation Fellow. From 1970 to 1974 he was a member of the Sociology Department at SUNY, Stony Brook. Professor Harrison has worked as a consultant and conducted research in businesses, service and governmental organizations, worker-managed cooperatives, and voluntary groups working for social and political change. His research on organizations, social conflicts and movements, and on social institutions in America and Israel has been published in leading academic journals and has been presented at numerous academic meetings. His current research deals with managerial planning and problem solving, mobilization processes in social conflicts, and professional unionism.